Executive Stress

by
HARRY LEVINSON

Revised and Updated

A MENTOR BOOK
NEW AMERICAN LIBRARY
TIMES MIRROR
NEW YORK AND SCARBOROUGH, ONTARIO

Library of Congress Catalog Card Number: 74-85523

Published by arrangement with Harper & Row, Publishers. The
hardcover edition was published simultaneously in Canada by
Fitzhenry & Whiteside Limited, Toronto.

MENTOR TRADEMARK REG. U.S. PAT. OFF. AND FOREIGN COUNTRIES
REGISTERED TRADEMARK—MARCA REGISTRADA
HECHO EN CHICAGO, U.S.A.

SIGNET, SIGNET CLASSICS, MENTOR, PLUME AND MERIDIAN BOOKS
are published *in the United States* by
The New American Library, Inc.,
1301 Avenue of the Americas, New York, New York 10019,
in Canada by The New American Library of Canada Limited,
81 Mack Avenue, Scarborough, 704, Ontario

FIRST PRINTING, OCTOBER, 1975

1 2 3 4 5 6 7 8 9

PRINTED IN THE UNITED STATES OF AMERICA

To My Parents:

DAVID AND GUSSIE LEVINSON

though impoverished, uneducated, and victimized by prejudice, they taught me the meaning of family and the importance of learning.

Contents

ACKNOWLEDGMENTS

I am indebted to the editors of *Nation's Business* for their permission to include in this volume "Anger," which is adapted from "Turn Anger into an Asset" (© 1964, *Nation's Business*—the Chamber of Commerce of the United States, reprinted from the May issue) and "Stress at the Bargaining Table," by permission of the publisher from *Personnel*, March-April 1965 © 1965 by the American Management Association. "Self-Doubt" is adapted from "How to Get Out of a Dead-End Job," reprinted courtesy of *Popular Science* © 1965 by Popular Science Publishing Co. Inc. "What Is Mental Health?" appeared in *Think*, 31:2 (March-April 1965). "What Work Means to a Man" appeared in *Think*, 30:1 (January-February 1964). "Problems of Promotion" appeared in *Think*, 31:1 (January-February 1965). "Problems That Walk in Your Door" appeared in *Think*, 33:1 (January-February 1967). "What an Executive Should Know about Scientists" appeared in *Think*, 31:5 (September-October 1965). "How to Retread a Bureaucrat" appeared in *Think*, 33:3 (May-June 1967). "Do You Look for Culprits —or Causes" appeared in *Think*, 31:3 (May-June 1965). "How to Undermine an Organization" appeared in *Think*, 32:4 (July-August

1966). "Where Did Loyalty Go?" appeared in *Think*, 32:1 (January-February 1966). "The High Return of Enlightened Giving" appeared in *Think*, 32:5 (September-October 1968). "Getting Along with Your Boss," appeared in *Think*, 34:2 (March-April, 1968). "After Thirty-five" is included with the permission of the editors of the *Harvard Business Review*, 47:4 (July-August 1969).

FOREWORD

"As a class," writes Dr. Harold Boverman of the University of Chicago Department of Psychiatry, " 'how to' books run the risk of implying there is a right way of doing things; there is an expert somewhere who knows the right way; this right way *can* be communicated (the most troublesome issue); and that failure to do things right may well result in consequences ranging from unpleasant, to dire, to catastrophic." The author who undertakes to write a "how to" book indeed assumes a formidable task.

As if that were not enough to give him pause, members of the helping professions know from long experience that giving advice is not the best way for them to help their clients or patients, that prescriptions rarely solve problems. "One might question the long-term value of psychological prescriptions," wrote psychologist Edward Glaser in his review of my earlier book *Emotional Health in the World of Work*. "The world is well stocked with profoundly good advice. Jesus, Lao Tse, Socrates, Shakespeare." Even housewives who follow recipes have varying degrees of success with a matter which, compared to human behavior, is relatively simple. Why then should a psychologist write yet another book directed to executives which presumes to offer advice?

Despite its limitations, the fact is that advice

and guidance can be helpful. As Dr. Karl Menninger once put it, "If a man loses his way and stops at a service station for direction, it would hardly be appropriate for the service station attendant to ask him why he got lost. He need only tell him where his route lies."

Not all problems call for clinical interpretation. Not even a significant proportion of the daily issues which confront each of us requires that we obtain deep insights into our own personalities before we can solve them. Often another conception of the nature of the problem, which enables a person to get a different perspective on it, permits him to tackle it anew with greater promise of success. Sometimes a new clue, a cue to forces which he did not previously recognize, an angle he did not previously take into consideration, opens avenues for further effort.

In my experience with executives, I have been impressed repeatedly with how a restatement of a problem, a suggestion, a discussion of some of the issues surrounding the problem, has been of help. I have been particularly gratified with letters from readers of my articles and books reporting how they have put some of my conceptions to the test of practice. That's why, despite the limitations inherent in giving advice, I have written this book.

In doing so, it is my intention to put names on issues and problems, to illuminate their dimensions, and to suggest ways of acting upon them. I offer this book not as prescription, *the* answers, nor as the only or even the right way. As every reader knows, he himself differs widely from the man who inhabits the next office. Capacities, understanding, opportunities to act vary even more. Each situation, furthermore, differs tremendously from every other one; from company to company; section to section. Therefore, this volume can be only a point of reference, a mode of obtaining one, I hope helpful, perspective, and some thoughts based on that perspective which may save trouble, avoid pain, ameliorate anguish, and even contribute to greater satisfaction.

Thus, I dare write a "how to" book, in the hope of enhancing mental health. I dare hope that the reader will treat it with benevolent skepticism— that he will look upon it as a stimulus to his thinking and as a statement of hypotheses and alternatives. If he will ponder in reading it as I have in writing it, then it will indeed have served a most useful purpose.

I am indebted to James B. O'Connell, editor of *Think*, and his former managing editor, Thomas P. Murphy, for their thoughtful stimulation and creative editing of those parts of this book which first appeared in their publication. My wife, Roberta, made many useful suggestions about the individual chapters and the work as a whole. Mrs. Jean Senecal patiently and meticulously typed and retyped these pages through their many transitions. They have my gratitude and thanks.

Preface to the Second Edition

Those aspects of management which have changed most significantly in the last decade, and especially in the last few years, have to do with the motivation of women and their roles in the business world. As a result, Chapters 4, 16, 20, and 21 have been completely rewritten.

I am indebted to Deborah A. Hudson for her collaboration in the rewriting.

Harry Levinson, Ph.D.
Cambridge, Massachusetts
May 1975

Introduction

1

OVERVIEW

"MENTAL HEALTH," according to a contemporary slogan, "is everybody's business." Indeed it is. Businessmen, plumbers, morticians, architects, even forest rangers—judging from my mail—are interested in it. Some, of course, are seeking only a commercial angle. Most are interested in bettering their own mental health, or, through their efforts, the mental health of customers, clients, and employees.

Books on mental health, or more accurately, on how to be happy though alive, sell by the millions. People pursue peace of mind as if it were something like a Fountain of Youth, to be discovered, grasped, and gripped. Scientists have tried to define it, not very successfully. A whole host of professionals—ministers, physicians, social workers, rehabilitation counselors, psychiatrists, bartenders, marriage counselors, psychologists, and a wide range of quacks—try to help people obtain it.

Businessmen, particularly executives, don't like to use the words "mental health." To them they seem to connote "pure thoughts" or "clean living" or some other state of sanitized existence. Besides, to profess an interest in mental health is almost like admitting one has a mental problem. Perish the thought!

Executives would rather talk about stress. Everyone agrees that every human being experiences stress. Furthermore, almost everyone thinks stress is something bad that results from obvious pressures: worry about business reverses, concern about a child's illness, fear about a coronary. Since most such pressure comes from outside a person, a man does not admit anything negative about himself if he is interested in preventing it. In fact, he feels pretty

3

good about preventing stress; it's so much like preventing cancer or elephantiasis.

There is much talk, too much written, and not enough known about the stress of the executive role and its impact on health. In some circles ulcers have almost become a badge of honor, the equivalent of the Purple Heart in executive combat.

Much of the talk and even more of what has been written is nonsense, particularly that which is based on questionnaire surveys rather than on intensive physical and psychological examination under controlled conditions. Nevertheless, there are aspects of the man-job relationship, particularly how a man *feels* about himself in his work role, which affect his health.

To illustrate, Dr. Herman K. Hellerstein, of Case-Western Reserve University, studied the blood pressure changes of surgeons while they were doing surgery. Dr. Hellerstein concluded that the variations in the surgeons' blood pressure while they were operating depended ". . . on something other than the requirements of work. This 'something' resides in the individual, not in the job." The Hellerstein study was not of men in an organization so it could not take organizational pressures into account, but it serves to point out the importance of how a man feels about what he is doing.

Stress, then, is not something which occurs from outside sources alone. Much of it has to do with what goes on within the person.

Another facet of the same issue is reflected in the research of biochemist George Brooks and social psychologist Ernest Mueller, of the University of Michigan. They found an excess of uric acid, and therefore a higher incidence of gout, among professors who, on psychological tests, scored significantly higher than their colleagues in drive, leadership (manipulation of people rather than things), and achievement. They differed in their attitudes toward their work from other professors who had high cholesterol levels. The hard drivers reveled in their work. The others felt tired and overburdened by their work, and that they were struggling to reach a forever unattainable goal. The researchers concluded that a tendency to gout is a tendency to the executive suite.

Some executives may question the similarity between professorial leadership and their own. Physics professor F.

Reif, of the University of California at Berkeley, has illustrated in considerable detail that professors and scientists live in a highly competitive world, too, and are subject to many of the same conflicts as executives.

But the finding that the "something" of stress resides in individuals and that highly competitive people have a greater tendency to gout should not lead us automatically to the conclusion that executive drive equals stress. Drs. Meyer Friedman and Ray E. Rosenman, of Mount Zion Hospital in San Francisco, make a finer differentiation from their research on heart disease. Those researchers have followed 3,182 healthy men in 11 California companies since 1960. From initial interviews they classified their research subjects into two types. Type A was characterized as aggressive, having excessive drive, ambition, and a sense of time urgency. According to Dr. Rosenman, this group seemed to be fighting time itself. Type B did not have these characteristics. The researchers predicted that Type A men would be more likely to have coronaries. Of those in the 39–49 age group who subsequently had coronaries, 85 percent had been predicted. Incidentally, the Type A hard driver did not usually rise to become president. Rather, the more relaxed Type B man did, drawing on the A's and B's below him.

Thus the man who is excessively competitive against his own standards (the sense of time urgency) is more likely to have physiological difficulty. He is also more likely to have other kinds of difficulties.

Summarizing observations which have been confirmed by others, Professor William E. Henry, of the University of Chicago, says that men in the 30-40 age range view their outer world primarily as "achievement-demanding." Comparing men in this age range with those of later decades, he reports, "As they look at the outer world, the first thing that occurs to them is the notion that it is a world which is going to ask of them one thing—or at least that one thing first—and that is accomplishment. They further argue that if they act acquisitively and assertively and follow the cues which that outer world provides for them, they are going to be successful." Focusing primarily on the outer world, they do not pay adequate attention to their own feelings and their intimate personal relationships. Professor Henry contends that as a result they subsequently have difficulties in their forties and fifties. In their forties, men begin to look at themselves and their relationships and to raise more questions about the ways of the world. In the fifties, they become more concerned about their more deeply personal goals and objectives. If, in their thirties, they have given too much attention to their careers at the expense of introspection and relationships, they subsequently have much difficulty. They cannot give up some of their entrenched business goals when, for their own psychological sakes, they have to re-establish those relationships in order to adapt to the aging process and prospective retirement.

There are, then, at least two kinds of people in executive ranks. Some are overdriven by deep-seated personality factors. This drivenness, in turn, compels them to compete continuously for increasing achievement and leadership. The competitive impulses of both types are fanned further by organizational and cultural expectations. Those who cannot control this psychological and physiological racing almost literally race themselves to death.

As the studies demonstrate, not all competent successful people—who must also be competitive to achieve competence and success—suffer impairment of health. However, *executives most often do not differentiate between creative and self-destructive competitiveness. They assume that if they have chosen organizational life, the inevitable product is stress and they will have to take their chances, worrying all the way and unable to do anything about it.*

It isn't, and they won't.

As a matter of fact, mental health is not something you can get and hold on to. It doesn't mean a sanitized mind or pure thoughts. And, though certain kinds of stress contribute to mental ill health, or emotional disorders, not all stress is bad. Just as some physical stress, like exercise, is good for the body, so some kinds of mental and emotional stress are good for the mind.

But there is no simple way of distinguishing good stress from bad. Nor are there simple mental exercises which can be prescribed to keep the mind in trim. That's why so many people stop reading books on mental health in the middle of the first chapter—at about here, for example.

Fortunately, mental health has to do with everyday life, and so does stress. That means that even though there are no ready prescriptions for solving life's problems, everyone can learn from what happens to him or her each day. There is therefore much that one can do about oneself.

One can learn about oneself—one's psychology. By examining one's own experiences and becoming more aware of those which trouble one, by trying alternative ways of carrying on one's daily tasks, one may simultaneously find ways of easing some of the stresses which are burdensome, and strengthening a sense of well-being.

One can learn also something about what one's work means to oneself and to others. A person can understand more clearly some of the pressures he or she experiences in the family and community. He can examine some of his own feelings in the context of specific crisis events on the job. He can review some of his own executive behavior in his relationships with those whom he must lead or follow. He can analyze some of the forces which impinge on organizations and the implications of those forces for his activity. In the process of those considerations he can examine how he might deal differently with this or that problem, with his own and others' feelings, and with the inevitable instability of the outside world which constitutes the social stratosphere he must negotiate.

This book is written to help the executive—and would-be executive—do just that. It is written for executives for two reasons: (1) they are the people with whom I work most closely and therefore know the most about; (2) as leaders, managers, supervisors of others, their behavior has an important influence on the feelings and behavior of the people with whom they work (spouses and children, too).

Since the book is intended to help the executive examine his or her own daily experiences, the chapters which follow are centered around them. The frame on which this book is constructed has two basic girders: mental health and work. Both will be elaborated in the first section. There I will talk about some conceptions and theories—how we understand man. The second section is devoted to those enduring, underlying feelings which, under undue stress, tie a person in psychological knots or make him feel as if he is undone. The third section is devoted to typical and characteristic problems of advancement, and the fourth to those of the executive role. Mental health and work are intimately related to family and community experiences. These are discussed in sections five and six. Finally I will consider the perennial task of remaining effectively adaptive.

First I will try to understand, then clarify, then suggest

alternatives. Throughout I will be talking about activities which are common to all executive work. The specific suggestions offered in each chapter are derived from research, clinical experience and professional association with hundreds of executives. However, they are suggestions and should be taken for just that. No person can tell another how to live his or her life. One can only help the other person to examine his own experiences, obtain insights, and apply principles. Each person has to use principles in ways which are congenial to his own personality, suitably modified according to his circumstances and problems.

This book, therefore, should not be used as a recipe book. Rather, it will be more useful as a lens for magnifying experience, as a mirror for reflecting it, and as a guideline for changing it—*if that's what you want to do.*

The italicized part of the sentence is the most important part because it reflects the underlying assumption of this book. It is not the job of the psychologist to prescribe right and wrong behavior. The work of the psychologist is to help people examine their feelings, the behavior which results from those feelings, and the alternative costs of acting one way versus acting another. He assumes that the better people can understand themselves and the costs of their behavior, the freer they are to make choices about what they want to do and how they want to do it. The freer they are to make conscious choices, the more rational their behavior is likely to be and the greater the possibility that they will find life gratifying.

The reader will find it helpful to talk over, chapter by chapter, some of the thoughts and notions in this book. A critical examination with someone else will help qualify those too dogmatic statements which need to be qualified, to ask what applies to him or her and how. If with a colleague or a group of colleagues, then they can help each other, thus strengthening their complementary roles. If that "someone else" happens to be a spouse, so much the better for the marital relationship.

My assumption is that, regardless of one's personality, each person can relieve some of the stresses which impinge on him or her by dealing more effectively with some of his problems. If that which costs him physiologically and psychologically is the product of cumulative stress, then to the extent to which he impedes the cumulation he is that much more healthy and less vulnerable.

Therefore the reader will find no philosophy of life here—no thesis about why man exists and how to do so ideally. What he or she will find on the subsequent pages is a series of familiar issues—held up for more careful examination—and, if he looks closely, a description of his own behavior in a range of executive contexts. These are the raw material for one's contribution to one's own mental health. My assumption is that the executive owes himself or herself that concern and that the reader wants to meet that obligation. Reading this book is an initial step toward that end.

PART ONE

Work and Mental Health

Work and mental health are closely interrelated. As the executive examines the meaning of work in the context of mental health, the implications of the discussion for executive action will also carry echoes of its relevance for him or her.

2

WHAT IS
MENTAL HEALTH?

SIGMUND FREUD said that in order to have mental health a person had to be able to love and to work. Well, what goes into being able to love and to work?

To answer this question we have to understand what motivates people, particularly their feelings. Though one likes to believe otherwise, a person's behavior is guided more by feelings than by rational thinking.

FOUR FORCES

Man's feelings come from the interaction of four major forces:

• *Love and hate.*

One constructive and the other destructive, a pair of drives form the basis for the feelings of love and hate. These drives are derived from and analogous to the biochemical forces of anabolism and catabolism, the forces toward growth and death that we see in all living matter. These feelings are always with us, and they are expressed in every thought and action. The feeling of love is derived from the constructive or growth force and the feeling of hate from the destructive or death force. When the energies of both forces are combined and directed into solving problems, a person is using them in self-interest, and on behalf of others—in supporting a family, pursuing a career, attacking social problems, building a business. The aggressive energy is tempered and guided by the constructive energy. When, however, these energies are diverted from

12

ideally useful channels, a person makes less efficient use of them and to that extent is less healthy mentally.

For example, a person may overcontrol feelings of aggression and fume with anger or hate. This produces tensions which literally wear away his body organs and result in a physical ailment called psychosomatic illness. Or a person may, instead of directing anger to problem solving, displace it onto a spouse, children, subordinates, store clerks, waiters, and other people who cannot defend themselves. This is the mechanism which lies behind scapegoating, racial prejudice, exploiting others. Or a person may turn anger on himself, in which case we see men or women who are their own worst enemies, who have painful accidents or repeatedly get themselves into trouble, or, in extreme instances, commit suicide.

This same kind of thing can happen with feelings of love. Some people can love children, pets, causes, and many other things, but they are inhibited from loving other adults of the opposite sex. When this happens these are displacements of normal heterosexual affection. Other people, because of events which occurred in the course of growing up, find it extremely difficult to have close, affectionate two-way relationships with others. Still others are so narrowly confined to themselves that they are preoccupied with their own bodies and spend inordinate amounts of time treating themselves and talking about their illnesses. These ways of mishandling love, of course, drive other people away.

All of us have the problem of dealing with these drives, even though we may be unaware of their existence.

• *The conscience.*

We are not born with a conscience; we acquire it, and we acquire much of it while we are still young children so we are unaware of having done so. It is made up of the values we are taught—like religious values, moral precepts, and proper behavior.

Each of us, too, has an ego ideal, which is part of the conscience—a vision of oneself as the person one could be if only one could achieve those aspirations parents and other respected figures held out. Our aspirations usually far exceed our achievements so we are rarely satisfied with ourselves. In addition, many aspects of our ideal image are unconscious so we may not be aware of much of what we are striving toward. The more unconscious and the more conflicted our ideal, the more difficult it is to satisfy ourselves. We don't know what we really want.

Finally, each of us has an internal policeman-judge which calls us to account if we have violated our rules and values or are not working toward achieving our ego ideals. This policing-judging function works by inducing feelings of guilt. Inasmuch as the conscience must be strong if we are to conduct ourselves reasonably without constant control by somebody else, we all have a goodly share of guilt feelings which make us feel inadequate and unworthy. The stronger the conscience, the more difficulty we have living up to it and with it and the more guilty we feel. The more guilty we feel, the more angry we become with ourselves and others. Such feelings become more acute when we fail at something or when we seem to be unneeded, reflecting the demands of the ego ideal.

All of us therefore have the problem of dealing with these feelings of inadequacy and unworthiness.

• *The need to master.*

Everyone wants to have the feeling of being in charge of oneself, of being, as time goes by, more and more in charge of the forces which affect him or her. No one likes to feel helpless, buffeted about by forces he cannot control. If a person feels he cannot do anything about these forces, he stops trying and becomes apathetic. This is what happens to people when they are unemployed for long periods, or spend their whole lives on welfare. They become dependent on someone else, and being dependent, feel childlike. Their consciences then make them feel even more worthless, and they redirect their drives to themselves, being at once angry and preoccupied with themselves. This is what we see as apathy; apparently they just do not care. Or sometimes they get angry at the world and strike back by committing a crime. Any situation in which people are discriminated against, manipulated, or demeaned produces the feeling of being a target. One of our major social problems is that so many people feel this way.

To be master of oneself and the forces that affect one, a person must continue to grow psychologically. He or she must have the feeling that he is becoming wiser as he grows older, that he is discovering new and interesting things about the world, has a more adequate perspective on what goes on in life, and enjoys close, affectionate relationships with old friends. In a word, to grow is to feel ever richer.

Man has many ways of trying to increase his mastery. For some, religion provides an important avenue; for others, science and reason; for still others, expertness in their work or profession. And, for many, the acquisition of money. Most people evolve some combination of these means of achieving mastery. Yet there are some who are afraid of growing up and who forever remain dependent and childlike. Usually these are people who have learned painfully that the price of growing up is too expensive ("Be a nice *little* boy (girl) or mother won't love you").

All of us have the wish to master ourselves and the forces which affect us.

• *The environment.*

The three internal forces—love-and-hate, the conscience, and the need to master—interact with the events which go on *outside* the person, in short, from the interaction of a person with his environment. The conscience is formed in large measure from the values the culture offers and the modes of behavior it requires. A person may or may not be able to master some aspect of the environment, depending on how his or her parents and schools teach him to cope with problems, what skills he has opportunities to develop, and what freedom he has to act on his own.

The most influential aspects of the environment are other people. We may love them, hate them, laugh at them, sympathize with them. They may love us, become angry with us, boost our self-esteem, deflate our aspirations, attack us, nurse us, amuse us, enrage us. Whatever they do, they stimulate our own feelings of love and hate, increase or decrease our feelings of adequacy, and support or thwart our wish to master.

Certain nonhuman forces have some of the same effects—a depression which may cause one to lose a job; an accident which may make it difficult to pursue a career; the loss of a loved one in a tornado or in war; a fortunate break in the stock market which eases financial pressures.

All of us must cope with the environment in which we live; from the air we breathe to the dust we become, we are a part of it and it is a part of us.

Man keeps trying to maintain his equilibrium by balancing all of these forces—all of the time. Now you know why you feel so tired even when you are not doing anything. It is easier for a person on a tightrope to balance if he or she keeps walking and has a balancing pole in his hands which gives him a medium to use his muscles. It is easier to stand erect on ice skates or to remain erect on a bicycle when one is moving, acting, doing—the same is true for maintaining psychological equilibrium. This is what mental health really is. When we say a person is mentally healthy we mean that he or she is doing a good job of maintaining an equilibrium among these four forces which give rise to feelings about oneself and others. Mental health is not a static state—it is forward motion on course, so to speak—like a ship, airplane, or even a space capsule, which is moving ahead while at the same time maintaining its balance in the face of the forces of weather, water, and gravity.

A CONCEPTION

How does one *act* to maintain mental health? There are as many prescriptions as there are people. Every prescription is based on a conception of mental health, either tacit or explicit. The conception I like best was derived from a study made by Drs. Charles Solley and Kenneth Munden for a larger project on which we were then working at The Menninger Foundation. These men asked each of fourteen senior members of the Foundation clinical staff to describe people he or she considered to be mentally healthy. They then analyzed the forty-one descriptions they were given and concluded that mentally healthy people behave consistently in five important ways:

1. *They have a wide variety of sources of gratification.*

This does not mean they chase frenetically from one activity to another, but rather that they find pleasure in many different ways and from many things. If for any reason they lose some of their sources of gratification, they have others to turn to. For example, a person who loses a good friend by death may sorrow, but if he has other good friends, he draws psychological sustenance from them and recovers. But if a person loses his only good friend, he has little else to fall back on and continues to grieve in his loneliness. A person has the same problem if his only interest is a job, or the immediate family, or a single hobby.

In a sense, the difference between having few gratifications and a range of them is the difference between existing and living. Unfortunately, many people merely exist in psychological poverty, blind to the possibilities all around them for enjoying life.

2. *They are flexible under stress.*

This means simply that they can roll with the punches. If trouble comes their way, they are not floored by it. When faced with problems, they can see alternative solutions. They are not rigidly stuck with one way of looking at things, or one solution.

A simple analogy is what happens when a person gets a blister on his or her heel from a new pair of shoes. If one can be flexible enough to shift one's weight to another part of the foot, one simultaneously eases the pain and permits healing to take place while at the same time stretching the shoe. When the foot is healed and the shoe is stretched, one can once again walk comfortably. If, however, the person persists in walking in such a way as to irritate the blister, he or she may well wind up unable to walk for awhile. So it is with emotional problems. Many people seem unable to shift their psychological weight, so to speak, and keep attacking problems in the same repetitively futile way.

Flexibility under stress is closely related to having a wide variety of sources of gratification. With more supports to fall back on, a person is less threatened by situations which produce fear and anxiety. With a wider, fuller range of experiences and relationships, one can come at problems from different perspectives.

3. *They recognize and accept their own limitations and their assets.*

Put another way, they have a reasonably accurate picture of themselves, and they like what they see. This does not mean that they are complacent about themselves but rather that they know they cannot be anyone else and that is all right with them. They do not deprecate their talents and skills nor do they try to hide their weak spots from themselves. The mere fact that they are alive makes them important; they do not feel impelled to make a case for their existence.

4. *They treat other people as individuals.*

This is a very subtle phenomenon and an important one. People who are preoccupied with themselves pay only superficial attention to other people. They are so tied up in themselves that they cannot observe the subtleties in another person's feelings nor can they really listen. As a result, they cannot really respond to other people as individuals, even though they may exchange many words with them. Mentally healthy people really care about what other people feel.

5. *They are active and productive.*

Mentally healthy people use their resources in their own behalf and in behalf of others. They do what they do because they like to do it and enjoy using their skills. They do not feel driven to produce in order to prove themselves. They are in charge of their activities; the activities are not in charge of them. When they are chosen for leadership of one sort or another, it is because they have the skills to lead in a given situation, not because they have to exercise power over others. They seek achievement for what they can *do*, not for what they can *be*, for when one tries to *be* something or someone he will never be satisfied with himself even if he achieves that desired goal.

One of the reasons so many apparently successful people are so discontented with themselves despite their achievements is that their goal in life was to *be* someone—someone bigger and better than they are. Yet no matter to what position we rise, we remain much the same inside, and if inside we are dissatisfied with ourselves we will still be dissatisfied, no matter what the achievement. This is not to gainsay the fact that many people have become exceedingly successful with such motivation, and many have made singular contributions to the world along the road to success. Rarely is such a path free of painful self-doubt—a fact quite evident in the biographies of famous (and infamous) people.

EINSTEIN'S FORMULA

One of the best examples of a person in whom these prime characteristics of mental health were evident was Albert Einstein. Though he was a shy and gentle man, sometimes even remote from others, he had close ties to a number of people, to his work, his family, his music, the sea, and other phenomena of nature. He had had to leave his native land, and though a man of peace, lend his efforts to his adopted country's defense. "He was," says his friend, Dr. Thomas Lee Bucky, "the only person I knew who had come to terms with himself and the world around him. He knew what he wanted and he wanted only this: to understand within his limits as a human being the nature of the universe and the logic and simplicity of its functioning. He knew there were answers beyond his reach. But this did not frustrate him. He was content to go as far as he could."

Einstein turned down the presidency of Israel because he knew he did not fit the job. He could teach a lad to yo-yo, another to sail a boat, and express compassion for others in simple but eloquent communications. Medals, honors, fame—these meant nothing to him. Einstein never tried to *be*; he was content to do, and let whatever he could do speak for itself.

How does one go about obtaining this grace, this condition called mental health? As a matter of fact you cannot *get* it and when you think you have it, you usually have a mess of make-believe. Mental health is had in the working-toward, in the process of pursuit.

The subsequent chapters are devoted to more specific steps in the working-through process. They take up various aspects of the executive role which have implications for mental health—beginning with the meaning of work itself.

3

WHY MEN WORK

For all of man's preoccupation with work over thousands of years, no one has yet proposed a satisfactory definition of it. To understand the paradoxical meaning of work is no simple task. It is simultaneously a curse and a blessing. Man cannot free himself from work, nor would he do so if he could. A man works when he is hungry; it is equally obvious that he still labors when he is so satiated with material goods that he cannot even use what he has. Some men's work is other men's play; some make work out of play, and some make play out of work. There are those who gird themselves relentlessly to take lives, and others who struggle desperately to save them. A few men spend their adult years trying to escape work; more escape into it. Some sing of working to pass the time away; and some, in a more anguished vein, of being oppressed by barges and bales. A man devotes nearly half of his waking hours to his job. It is said, he both works to live and lives to work.

When Professors Nancy C. Morse and Robert S. Weiss, of the University of Michigan, asked a national sample of 401 employed men whether they would continue to work if they inherited enough money to live comfortably, 80 percent said they would. The researchers were particularly impressed with the vividness of the responses. "It was almost as if they had never consciously thought what working meant to them but now that they were presented with the imaginary removal of it, they would see for themselves and verbalize to another person the feelings which had really been there implicitly all the time."

Nowhere does man do without occupation; in the West,

20

occupation is synonymous with work. With this conception, the occupational millennium which automation promises is not freedom from work, but rather freedom from being a substitute for a machine. Man will always find, and always have, work.

THE NEED FOR MONEY

Realistically, most people need to provide financially for themselves against possible emergencies as well as the realities of aging. Work, then, as a medium for survival, has a fundamental economic meaning. Bare subsistence rarely satisfies anyone. While some people have a deep psychological need to give up the comforts of civilization, most people find it a matter of compelling common sense to make use of them. The outhouse and the kerosene lamp have no enduring value of their own. There is no particular virtue in being poor. As the late Sophie Tucker once put it, "I've been poor and I've been rich, and believe me, rich is better."

The need for money is a basic reason for working, but not the only one. When a person is able to earn enough to meet his fundamental financial needs, then other reasons for working become proportionately more important to him. Thus many people prefer white-collar jobs at which they earn less than they might as skilled technicians, or prefer to work in a more elite downtown district than in a factory area.

Money is an important incentive to some, not for its own sake, but because its acquisition represents power, achievement, success, safety, public recognition, and many other things. In recent years, studies of motivation to work frequently have emphasized the importance of factors other than money, leading some executives to think money of little importance, with unfortunate consequences. Many businesses today suffer from inadequate leadership largely because they allowed men of initiative to be attracted away by higher financial rewards.

A study of the motivation to work by Professor Frederick Herzberg and his colleagues indicated that dissatisfaction with salary in middle-management ranks can make a person discontented with his work. However, satisfaction with salary alone is not enough to make one satisfied with his job.

For some people, particularly executives and unskilled workers, money remains the important incentive. Executives enter business rather than the professions because money more than service or function is an incentive.

Researchers Edward E. Lawler III and Lyman W. Porter, the former of Michigan and the latter of the University of California at Irvine, report from their study of executives' views of management compensation that the higher the level of management the less satisfied the executive was with the amount of his pay, regardless of the amount he was receiving. Unskilled workers have few other sources of gratification in their work than the money they earn, since their lack of skill deprives them of both esteem from superiors and a sense of accomplishment from skill itself.

THE NEED TO BE A MAN

Work has many social meanings. When a man works he has a contributing place in society. He earns the right to be the partner of other men. In effect, he is hand in hand with others, exchanging the fruits of his work for the fruits of theirs. The fact that someone will pay for his work is an indication that what he does is needed by others, and therefore that he is a necessary part of the social fabric. He matters—as a man.

The conception of what a man is and what he does varies from one culture to another, and from one social class to another. In every culture some form of work is man's and some is woman's. When, as in our culture, the difference sometimes becomes hazy as more women do what only men used to do, then some men become threatened. They see their role as men being diminished.

Often the definition of a man has to do with a specific skill, trade, or occupation. In some circles, to be a man means to do work requiring strength, or to work outside. An unemployed furrier, casting about for other work, snorted disdainfully at the idea of becoming a cashier in a restaurant. Even in the South Sea Islands, where, as Western fantasy has it, no one works, a woman judges the worth of a man by his skill as a fisherman.

To have a skill, trade, or occupation is to be a "who" and "what." That is, a man is identified in his own mind and by others by what he does. His work defines the nature of his partnership with others and the value of that partnership. In most cultures, the healer, the holy man, and the arbiter traditionally have been the most valued partners. Historically, those whose work was ruling or governing drew their surnames from the locales they ruled, and those whose power resided in a skill and trade became Goldsmith, Turner, Kaufman (merchant), Priest, and so on.

A man's work, therefore, is a major social device for his identification as an adult. Much of who he is, to himself and others, is interwoven with how he earns his livelihood.

THE NEED TO BE HEAD OF
THE FAMILY

In Western societies, work enables a man to meet another definition of manliness; the head of the family. Most men take this role for granted, and most can do so until they have no work. Then the meaning of work for this aspect of being a man becomes all too painfully clear.

During the extended depression of the 1930's a number of studies of the unemployed provided us with considerable insight into the meaning of work for a man's place as head of the household. One of the classical studies was done by Professor Eli Ginzberg and his colleagues at Columbia University. This and other studies disclosed that when a man lost his job and was on relief (called welfare today), often his whole family's picture of him changed. Not only did he feel himself to be less a man outside his family, but also within his family he was often regarded as less a man than he had been.

For example, frequently the children of the unemployed man would no longer accept his discipline or listen to his advice. After all, he was demonstrating to them by the fact of his unemployment that he was not successful or powerful. Welfare, not he, was supporting them, and they would flaunt this fact to him. His lack of a work position in the community deprived them of status among their friends whose fathers held jobs.

Sometimes, in his desperation to be doing something useful, a man turned to cleaning or cooking or making toys, as many men did. These activities further vitiated his role as the strong masculine identification figure for his children that every father ideally should be.

It is pointless for boys to try to be like unsuccessful fathers. They have to turn elsewhere for models. It is painful for fathers to feel that their sons do not want to be "chips off the old block," that they have no fundamental respect for their fathers. It is equally painful for the boys not to be able to consolidate their schooling, aptitudes and interests around a central core of identity which usually comes from identifying themselves with their fathers. Girls, too, need to be able to see their fathers as competent masculine figures, as the measure of a man, because such a positive experience with their fathers gives them a better basis upon which to choose both a mate and a work role.

There were problems with the wives, too. Some mothers, of course, would try to "pump up" their husbands in the eyes of their children, and to support the fathers in their positions as head of the family. Others used the occasion of their husband's economic defeat to emasculate them even further. Under the combined stress of being without work and losing some of their masculine self-respect, the sexual demands of the men tended to increase. Those wives who had merely tolerated sexual relations while their husbands supported them, rejected the advances of their unemployed spouses.

Thus a man's work not only makes it possible for him to provide financially for his children as in most cases still befits the adult male but, equally important, to provide for them psychologically as he should. Furthermore, his work is an essential ingredient of his ability to hold his place as a man in his family.

THE NEED TO SATISFY
THE CONSCIENCE

Much of a person's behavior is an effort to appease or alleviate the pressures of the conscience. He has to justify to himself much of what he does. The tradition of being "fair and square," of doing the right thing, of being our brother's keeper, are strong in the American culture. Among these traditions is the almost conscious belief that a person must earn the right to be alive.

Philosophers and theologians have debated for centuries the purpose of man's existence. Ordinary men do not usually debate such questions in so many words, but they do make certain assumptions about their purposes in life, and act accordingly. A man who reads meters for an electric utility company whose basic function is service and who devotes every spare moment to Boy Scout work, assumes, among other things, that a fundamental reason for living is to render service, to give something of himself to others. An English teacher who also makes furniture assumes that, in addition to communicating knowledge about language, it is important to use a part of one's life to create enduring items which increase comfort. A landscape gardener tacitly assumes that it is important to create beauty and thereby to enrich living.

Sometimes man justifies himself by his aspirations. He may aspire to a certain position in life, to "arrive," to provide a better social and economic springboard for the children, to protect himself from adversity, or even to make the world better. Sometimes a man's justification is a matter of trying to be loved, as when he seeks popular acclaim or prestige. Often he is uneasy because he does not have a justification. That leaves him dissatisfied with himself because no achievement provides any lasting internal satisfaction. Work goals and achievements can become both temporary and enduring justifications.

Work helps man to live with his conscience in another way. Through work he tries to achieve his personal goals and to live up to his aspirations. He feels inadequate when he is not doing quite as well as he thinks he can or should. Even though he may not yet have fulfilled his aspirations, so long as he is working toward them, he tends to feel more comfortable with himself.

A finding by J. Stacy Adams of the General Electric Company provides an interesting sidelight to the function of work as a mode of dealing with conscience. In the course of an experimental study, he made some hourly workers feel that they were overpaid and others that they were being paid fairly. Those who felt that they were being overpaid increased their productivity to justify to themselves the greater pay they were getting.

Work provides a means of reinforcing the conscience. Usually a person has to be at his job regularly at a given time and produce goods or services of a certain quality. The task itself makes demands on him for a level of performance, stimulating and reinforcing his internal desires to do well. People such as artists and commission salesmen who have no externally imposed schedules or demands often have a difficult time motivating themselves to produce. Those who become successful usually have had to discipline themselves to work consistently so that it seems as if the work itself is making demands on them. An interesting sidelight to this phenomenon is that people who are unemployed seem to lose a sense of time. It is as if work, work schedules, and work demands become measures of time.

Time is irreplaceable. When people devote significant amounts of time to anything, implicitly they are assuming that it is important to do so. They are justifying to themselves why they exist.

The need to justify oneself is so strong that many people have difficulty accepting welfare, charity, even social security or hot lunches in public schools. Yet all these forms of assistance are intended to help people overcome and prevent family disintegration.

If the purpose of the work is in itself not worth living for, if it does not meet the implicit assumptions of those who do it, if it does not make reasonable demands on people, then it should be no surprise if employees are apathetic and need constantly to be bought off with ever higher wages and fringe benefits.

Recent trends toward participative management in business and industry are one step toward increasing the responsibility of employees. Responsibility as adults for the success of the business helps many people meet the demands and expectations of their conscience.

THE NEED TO MASTER

Work, Freud pointed out, is an important medium for mental health because it is a consistent and fundamental means of staying in touch with the world and of mastering it.

Almost everyone has had the experience of being sick in bed. Before long he begins to lose touch with life beyond what he can see from his window. People whom ordinarily he saw every day at work, he sees only occasionally. The longer he is sick, the less frequently he sees them. The sick man is desperate *to do something* after a while, to use himself. In the museum of The Menninger Foundation there is a large ball of string, perhaps two feet in diameter. A state hospital patient plaited bits and pieces of string together over a period of years—because he had nothing else to do. It is mute but painfully eloquent testimony to a sick man's need to master some part of his environment.

People who are not working seem to lose some of their motivation to try to solve their own problems. It is as if they had lost both their skill and their confidence to contend with reality. A layer of apathy insulates a person from his own problems, as well as the pressing social problems of a city or the nation. This is one reason why it is difficult to motivate the chronically unemployed to seek retraining. The longer they are unemployed, the more afraid they are of going to work. Most people have a dread of being helpless. When man works, he demonstrates to himself that he is not helpless. To be without work is to increase the feelings of helplessness.

In addition to being a fundamental medium by which an adult adapts effectively to his world, work is also a major medium for mastering himself. Each person, as I have noted, has the continuous psychological task of controlling, fusing, and channeling the twin unconscious feelings of love and hate. Work is a central psychological device for this task. The mechanic who repairs a car is not only discharging his aggressions but also rendering a service to others. The carpenter who hammers nails builds shelter by doing so. The salesman who persuades a customer also provides employment for those who make his product.

Work helps one master himself in another way. People frequently say, "I'd go nuts if I didn't work." By this they usually mean two things would happen: they would become increasingly tense and restless, and they would have many fantasies ("I would think and worry too much"). In fact, in the Morse and Weiss study, one third of the men gave such reasons for wanting to continue working, even if they could afford not to. By concentrating on his task, a person pushes out of consciousness many thoughts and ideas he would just as soon not have. In some prisons there is a punishment cell called "the hole." Neither light nor sound penetrate "the hole," and meals are shoved into the cell through an aperture. Few prisoners want to talk about their experiences in "the hole," because, without stimulation from outside themselves, their own thoughts become "crazy" and frightening to them.

THE NEED FOR SOCIAL TIES

Many people find a means of socialization in their jobs. The work activity which people share requires interaction and communication. It is not unusual to find people who live lonely lives after working hours, particularly those people who do not make friends easily. In fact, in the rehabilitation of people who were mentally ill, often the most difficult problem to be surmounted is not quality of performance, but the loneliness of the after-work hours.

Work has another social meaning, too. A man's earliest and most fundamental experiences take place in his family. There he establishes his characteristic ways of relating to other people and his preferred ways of finding pleasure. It is a psychological truism that people tend to recapitulate their early family experiences in their subsequent activities. This truism is as valid in the workaday world as it is in other aspects of living. In fact, people often speak of their work group as being a "family."

As in the family, working with others usually involves a certain amount of friendly give and take, and sometimes not so friendly exchange. There are relationships to people who, like parents, have more power. Fellow employees can have greater, equal, or lesser power, depending on their seniority, experience, and skill; thus a man's relationships with them may be similar to relationships with brothers and sisters. Hiring and firing is psychologically similar to the parent's giving or withholding of love. To be hired is to be valued, and to be discharged is to be rejected.

As the family fostered social activities among its members, so does the work organization. Coffee breaks, lunch together, evening entertainment in each other's homes—all encourage social relationships among people whose basic tie is that they work together. Golf, fishing, hunting, and other group activities often stem from work associations. It is not uncommon for men to head for a bar as they leave the plant, to have a few beers together and to continue their discussions of the job and sports.

THE NEED TO MAINTAIN
PSYCHOLOGICAL BALANCE

In addition, work is one of the most constructive modes for transforming impulses, derived from the constructive and destructive drives, as well as for resolving problems of identity and dependency. In work, a person channels the aggressive drive, adequately fused with the constructive drive, into creating products, rendering services, and competing with others.

If work serves these many purposes, it is apparent that a man who finds gratification in his work has attained a harmonious co-ordination of experience, interests, capacities, skills, drives, and conscience. Thus work is essential to achieve and maintain one's psychological balance. It should be no surprise, therefore, that one of the indications of emotional disturbance is a man's inability to find gratification in work. For some men this means an inability to hold a job. Others seem unable to be happy no matter how much they change jobs. Still others are never able to find themselves or to realize their potential. Some manage to fail no matter what the opportunities.

The most trenchant evidence of the importance of work to psychological balance is a common clinical phenomenon. Psychologists and psychiatrists often see mentally ill persons whose friends and relatives are disturbed by their symptoms at home, symptoms which either never occur on the job, or become evident at work long after they have become an old story at home. The alcoholic, for example, will rarely come to work drunk. Work becomes a fundamental resource, something to hold onto until it is no longer possible to do so. It is at the same time a psychological glue which often holds a man together.

What are the implications of all this?

1. *The psychological value of work to a man lies largely in how much of a man it enables him to be in his own eyes.*

Every leader of men, therefore, would find it wise in his own self-interest and that of his men to look carefully at what it takes to be a man among the friends and families of his employees, and to encourage, support, and give pub-

lic recognition to the socially acceptable aspects of that behavior on the job.

2. *The psychological rewards of work are purchased
with the days of a man's life.*

An executive might then ask the question of himself,
"Do I structure work rewards and work achievements in
such a way that those for whom I am responsible feel that
what they do is worth spending part of their lives on? If
not, how can it be made so?"

3. *Work is a way of being "on top."*

If work is a fundamental device for mastery of self and
some part of the surrounding world, to have some idea of
what the future holds and to be ready for it, to be in touch
with the changing world, and to grow more competent and
secure in it, then the motivation to work is strengthened
with increasing opportunity of the employee to master and
control his work in keeping with the task to be done.

4. *Preferred work relationships recapitulate preferred
family relationships.*

To understand some of the deeper meanings of work to
his employees, an executive would do well to know the
kinds of families from which they come. If the work
process can recapitulate the style of family relationships
typical of his employees, so much the better. If it is radically different, he is likely to have difficulty keeping his
people. Conversely, he would be wise to select people
whose family experiences fit the kind of work processes he
must use. A highly mechanized work process in which
people cannot talk to each other because of the noise level
or the distance between them will hardly meet the needs of
people who are accustomed to close family relationships.

5. *A man's feelings about his work are closely related to
his conscience and his modes of psychological self-protection.*

Management must therefore understand that the events
of a man's job, however trivial they may seem to others,
are powerful barbs. They must not be treated arbitrarily or
casually; they must be respected for what they mean to
the man.

Folk wisdom says that to work is to live, and those who
do not work seem to die—literally and psychologically.
There is much psychological truth to this observation.

4

WHY WOMEN WORK

WOMEN WORK for essentially the same reasons that men do. Women have always worked. The pioneer farm wife and the immigrant mother toiled beside their husbands even as they bore their children. Women trekked westward with their men: rifle and bible were their protection and their hope. Women in early-day factories or at home doing piecework accumulated piece after painfully labored piece to earn a pittance to help the men support their families.

The same is as true in other parts of the world as it is in the United States. Developing nations in Africa encourage women to enter professional careers. Burmese women have managed the marketplace of that nation for a long time. In fact, Burmese women retain their own names rather than take those of their husbands.

However, the fact that it is necessary to write a chapter on why women work indicates that there are many dimensions of a woman's work-life which need special consideration and attention.

● *Women live with the residues of feelings about whether women should work*.

Only when it became possible for large numbers of women to work outside the home was there a question of women working. That question was a powerful one until World War II for a number of reasons.

In the United States women first left their homes to go to work because they had to, having lost their husbands, or because their husbands could not earn enough. Because they were denied access to higher education or training, they rarely had marketable skills and had to take the most menial jobs. Often they were exploited. Thus the working woman was identified as unfortunate and of the lowest socioeconomic level. When a wife worked outside the home, therefore, her husband and others viewed her working as a reflection on his manhood. In addition, while the man was the breadwinner, presumably he was the boss of the family. In the marriage oath his wife had promised to "love, honor, and *obey*." Since women have gone to work in increasing numbers, "obey" is no longer part of the vow. The working wife was, therefore, until World War II, a threat to her husband's dominant position in the family.

Actually, much of man's dominance began to yield when women, too, began to acquire education. World War I necessitated that every possible able-bodied person do war work, enabling thousands of middle-class women to justify leaving their homes for the workplace. Some tasks became defined as "women's work." Teaching and nursing were logical professions for women, and the needle trades and clerical work their almost exclusive province. World War II completed the cycle started by World War I. More millions of women went to work, many in the uniforms of the armed services. And when the war was over, wives by the thousands supported their husbands who went to school under the GI Bill.

As more mechanical conveniences became available and home ownership spread, the possibility of attaining both came within the reach of thousands of families—sooner if wives worked. Once the home was purchased and furnished, the same conveniences which were so attractive made it a simple matter to maintain the home. There was no good reason why a woman should continue to be bound by four domestic walls. At last she was free to come and go as did her husband. To match their freedom, at least some women demanded full equality of employment. "Equal pay for equal work" became their slogan and nondiscrimination against women their goal. Equal pay for equal work and nondiscrimination against women became federal law.

Still in many circles and among certain groups of men, there continues to be a serious question about whether women should work. Many men in high managerial ranks, for example, still consider it to be a reflection on them if their wives work, and still others feel that the woman's place is in the home, building and maintaining the family nest as well as being responsible for having and rearing children. For many men and in many cultures, the woman is still an inferior person, and women have had to contend with the residue of these feelings.

A corollary to these feelings on the part of men is another, namely that women cannot and should not do what men do. Out of a history of sex-role stereotyping, many men regard it as unfair that work which has been defined as such a significant component of their masculinity can and is being done by women. These feelings are especially apparent in managerial ranks, where to many older men it seems unfair that women should aspire to managerial ranks and to many younger men unfair that women should be competing with them for managerial positions.

A final problem that women face more keenly than men is the issue of having a family, because for women it usually means some interference with career pursuit and the necessity to evolve ways of managing family responsibilities, which still fall far more heavily on the woman. The balance between family and work is a difficult one to strike for most women and requires constant attention.

MARRIAGE AND CAREER

Although many young people live together without legal sanction, marriage has not yet gone out of style, nor, despite the cries of many, is the nuclear family defunct. The reason is a very simple one: human beings need close attachments to other human beings. These attachments must be on a continuing basis or there is no escape from the loneliness which, next to death, is the fundamental threat of the human condition. The casual sexuality of the swinging generation has resulted in the breakup of a large number of marriages and other relationships without a corresponding replacement for emotional attachment. Sex is no substitute for love.

As a result, even though a woman may be more comfortable now about going to work as soon as her schooling is finished, and identifying with her work and even with her work organization, she will need to devote a significant portion of her time to working at and maintaining family relationships, whether under the rubric of formal marriage or not. The same is of course no less true for men. However, there is a special problem for women, one which reaches its peak in the period roughly between twenty and twenty-seven years of age, and that is the problem of whether a woman will have a child. In my experience, many women agonize over this issue. Those who want to have children begin to have great urgency about marriage, but not without fears about the commitment and demands of parenthood and the greater dependency they will be likely to have on their husbands. Some are concerned about the interruptions of their careers and the difficulties they will subsequently have with respect to geographical mobility if they expect to move up in the managerial levels in large organizations. Some women resolve these issues by deciding they are going to stay put in one locality as the easiest way of juggling both family and occupational responsibilities.

Four forces have operated to make work more central in the lives of women than it was a generation ago. The first of these is identification with mothers who have, at one time or another, worked, or who, if they have not, have frequently verbalized the wish to have been able to do so. Second is a greater sense of approval by their fathers to do whatever they wanted, coupled with more education in a more affluent society, which increased freedom of choice. Third is the growing general humanistic thesis that each person should be able to fulfill herself, free of discrimination, stereotyping, and prejudice. The protests of minority groups and students were simply part of a general culture-wide protest against artificial barriers to meeting the demands of the ego ideal for anybody in any part of society. Fourth, with rising divorce rates many women found themselves to be at an extreme disadvantage because of their dependency on their husbands and their subsequent inability to earn, when separated or divorced, enough to support themselves at the level to which they were accustomed. Like other members of society, they could no longer tolerate dependency and helplessness. More and more began to feel that their only economic security lay in what they themselves could provide for themselves.

All this laid the groundwork for greater equality in heterosexual adult relationships, both within the family and in work situations.

The woman needs to work to support herself and, sometimes, her family. In addition, she must define for herself her adult role in society, a role which can no longer be circumscribed by the fact that she may also wish to be a wife and a mother. She must, like a man, serve as a model for her children, one who actively pursues independent, self-gratifying directions while at the same time effectively mastering the problems which confront her in determining her own preferred life-style and practices. Finally, she has to meet the demands of her conscience and to justify her existence to herself, which today involves using all of her capacities and skills; this in turn contributes to her self-confidence in coping with her problems.

In situations where both spouses work, there are sometimes special problems which can be solved only with a great deal of effort. If a man commutes to his work, his spouse may see him in a family relationship only 20 percent of the available time in a week. If she too is working, then that time together may even be further reduced. Thus family burdens may not be so easily shared, because despite much talk about equalizing responsibilities between spouses, wives carry a heavier burden of responsibility for and tension about the children than do husbands. While that may change in time to come, it is still the case: after a divorce, the children are most often the charge of the mother.

This problem is even more pressing for the working mother because of the intense demands of the nuclear family. In generations past, the Western family, like many of its counterparts the world over, was an extended family. The family consisted not only of father, mother, and children, but often also of grandparents and other relatives who lived in the same house or community. Children could turn to grandparents or other adult relatives as models, guides, even companions. Now one out of five Americans moves every year. Neither neighborhood nor community has the same psychological importance for children it once had. The result is that families turn inward more intensely. Children must lean more heavily on their parents, particularly their mothers, in a world in which they are often transients. Despite the limitations of time together, the relationships among parents and children are more intense and demanding.

Thus the wife and mother cannot find the same gratification in childrearing which once justified her existence, for the experience of motherhood is changed. It is also more difficult for her to maintain a continuing emotional partnership with her husband. Yet there is a greater demand on her to give of herself to both husband and children, while simultaneously pursuing her own career goals.

In addition to whatever gratification relationship with others at work and with work activities themselves provides, the woman sees that the tensions and pressures of the home are dissipated, drained of some of their urgency. If she can successfully balance work and family demands, gratifications at work recharge the woman to return to her home responsibilities refreshed by her absence and her diversion from them (providing that the work situation does not increase her tensions). She can have a greater sense of partnership with her husband, for, less burdened, she complains less. She is freer to be with him, to go places and do things which the second paycheck makes it possible to afford. She has more time to devote to the partnership, more freedom to listen to and support him, and less anger in her discussion of family problems.

Drawing a paycheck for her work, she has immediate and direct recognition of her value. No matter how much we may argue about it, value in Western society is measured in monetary terms. The working woman has direct evidence that she is in so much demand that someone pays for her services. Furthermore, she must be someplace at certain times and accomplish certain tasks. Others depend on her. Their work cannot go forward without her presence or help. These demands appease the consciences of women as they do of men. No one gets something for nothing in any culture. One way or another, people must work to earn it. If they do not do so, they often feel they are cheating or not carrying out their responsibility.

This attitude is so strong that one mother who was receiving Aid to Dependent Children, and therefore did not need to leave home to work, went to work when her small daughter asked, "Who works for us?" And with increasing separation and divorce, and independent careers, more women are their own financial mainstays.

One of the major problems for women at work is the absence at this time of sufficiently large numbers of models and mentors; another is the need for underlying parental and societal permission to succeed. People make it in organizations to the extent to which mentors—people who care about them—show them how to advance in the organization, eliminate organizational politics, and ease the paths to advancement. Women and members of minority groups often do not have mentors because frequently this relationship functions in the most informal of associations, figuratively in the men's room and the country club. It is difficult for women to have male mentors because such closeness between a woman and a man would create concern within an organization and lead to rumors that the woman might be paying for occupational favors with sexual favors. Thus the woman in managerial ranks frequently suffers from a problem she may not even know she has, namely the need for a guide or an instructor.

The second problem is somewhat more difficult to solve because it is often based on unconscious feelings. Dr. Matina Horner, now President of Radcliffe College, indicates that women who achieve high levels of attainment in competition with men frequently begin to feel that they should not go further even when opportunities are open to them, because unconsciously they feel it is not right for them to be attaining such heights. That right presumably belongs only to men.

Such problems will be with us for a long time. My guess is that it will be at least three generations before women feel themselves to be quite comfortable in managerial and professional ranks and on a par with men. Therefore, organizations must do something about these two problems. One of the ways of coping with them is through group discussions among women who are in the same relative organizational position and professional leaders who can help them in exchanging feelings and experiences and free them as much as possible from these problems, while simultaneously instructing them collectively as individual mentors might about the intricacies of the organization.

There is an additional aspect to the above issues. The major task is to provide psychological permission for the woman to proceed as her own best interests dictate. If she has family obligations, then there is the need to free her from irrational and therefore unnecessary concern about her family obligations. If she carries great responsibility for her children and hers is the major family responsibility, then obviously she will be worried if for some reason she cannot feel secure about her child-care arrangements or if there is inadequate supervision for older children. Sometimes organizations help in making arrangements for such problems, but beyond this issue for many working women are elements of guilt for what they conceive to be abandonment of their family, if only on a part-time basis. While many women deny having feelings of guilt, others do indeed have them. These too are best dealt with in groups.

A corollary to these group discussions should be similar group discussions for men who are new at supervising women in managerial roles and vice versa. Men have to deal with all their feelings about "a woman's place" and rivalry and attitudes about women's abilities. Women, on their part, for some time to come, will have to learn how to compete with men in a man's world. The reason I say "learn to compete" is because frequently women feel themselves to be at a disadvantage because they are women; sometimes they don't like themselves for being women, and they tend to overcompensate by intense competitiveness. That kind of competitiveness, usually denied, nevertheless undermines their relationships with their colleagues. They then blame their failure on prejudice. Although society is moving toward a condition in which sex roles may become less distinguishable, the facts of the matter are that there are men and there are women. There are sex roles. These in turn lead to expectations about how people should behave as men and women, derived significantly from attitudes toward mothers and fathers as parents. When women try to act like men or as they think men would in a given situation, they undermine themselves by not meeting these unconscious expectations. If women dislike themselves for being women and try and pretend they are men, their anger with themselves will spill over into their relationship with others and also undermine them. Such problems usually can be dealt with only by professional counseling.

PART TWO

Fear, Anger, and Self-Doubt

Relationships are the bonds which cover the distance from the tip of one's nose to the tip of the other's nose. A relationship is like the thread of a spider's web; it is part of a network which provides a structure for mobility, for relating to the world outside oneself, for a home base. But man must operate in that structure, and much of how he will operate hinges on his feelings. In this section we examine three of the more crucial feelings underlying behavior.

5

FEAR ON THE JOB

FEAR IS a fundamental feeling; it has a basic relationship to mental health. Fear is so commonplace that we take it for granted. Paradoxically, it is the feeling that executives understand least because so many of them deny their own fears and push such feelings out of consciousness. The failure to understand their own fears and those of others causes them more difficulty than any other single factor.

Fear is the experience of danger. It is therefore a necessary, built-in, protective device. Without the capacity to be afraid, we would be unable to sense danger and to protect ourselves when we are threatened. For example, a major petroleum company operating in North Africa taught Arabs to drive trucks. But the Arabs, not having lived all their lives with wheeled vehicles, did not grasp the concept of accident. They could not be afraid of what would happen and therefore did not realize that they might be in trouble until a crash actually occurred.

However, there is more to danger than physical threat; there is also psychological threat. In Chapter 2 we observed that the fundamental task of the personality is to keep itself in balance. The equilibrium of the personality can be jeopardized if:

- *Feelings of love or hate are overstimulated.*

No one wants to lose control of himself. Often people do lose control of their behavior and apologize with the words, "I wasn't myself then." Anything which might make a person feel, however remote the possibility, that he might lose self-control is a threat.

40

- *Feelings of inadequacy are exacerbated.*

As we noted in talking about the conscience, everyone has feelings of inadequacy. Such feelings are uncomfortable. We therefore try to avoid situations which make us feel even more inadequate, which lower our self-esteem. That can happen when someone makes a deprecating remark or when we commit a social error or experience some kind of defeat. We like ourselves less on such occasions.

- *The wish to master some part of the environment is thwarted.*

Most of us are uncomfortable when we are dependent on someone else. Some people cannot tolerate accepting favors; others find it difficult to turn to someone else for help, no matter how badly they need it. Still others will not take part in anything where they cannot be in control of whatever is going to happen, and some cannot tolerate lack of success.

Threats to psychological equilibrium are much harder to understand than threats to physical well-being. A hazard to safety is understandable because it can have the same effect for everyone. But different events are psychologically threatening to different people because each of us has had different life experiences. It is therefore hard to understand why someone else is fearful in a situation which causes us no concern at all. In fact, sometimes people are fearful or anxious without themselves knowing why, because their fear is unconscious. Anxiety is the unconscious experience of fear.

THE LOSS OF SENSITIVITY

Not knowing why they are fearful, they tend to think that it is wrong or a sign of weakness to have such feelings and try to suppress them. Often the more a person has to prove himself or herself to be a mature person in his own eyes, the more he has to suppress or repress his anxiety. He can't allow himself to see it. Unable to see it in himself, it is difficult for an executive to be sensitive to those circumstances which arouse anxiety in others. He loses his psychological radar. To illustrate, we may observe that a man treats his boss obsequiously although we know the boss to be a harmless fellow. We may note that one person fre-

quently has strong arguments with others while a second
leaves a conference the moment his temper begins to rise.
One seems to be frightened of something outside himself:
his boss. The other seems to be frightened of something inside himself: his anger. In neither case does there seem to
be an objective, external, physical threat to fear. In both
examples we would say that these people experienced anxiety. If we could give them a physical examination we
might observe that their breathing rate increased, their
hearts beat faster, their digestive processes slowed down, as
if they were getting ready to protect themselves. Just as in
fear, anxiety moves us to automatic self-protection—to get
ready to run or to fight.

Thus the obsequious man of our example apparently had
learned that people more powerful than he could hurt him.
He was alert to differences in power between himself and
others. He "knew" from his experiences that unless he
treated a more powerful person deferentially, he might be
hurt again in some way. He had put together in one class
all people who were more powerful than he, and his boss
symbolized that threatening class. Though we might know
that the boss was harmless, he "knew" something else from
his experience. What he "knew," however incorrect by objective standards, nevertheless aroused his anxiety. To protect himself, he acted in an obsequious manner.

Watch a group of strangers as they meet on a social occasion. At first they are somewhat formal and distant from
each other. Their conversation is halting, tenuous. They try
to find a common topic to talk about. They sound each
other out, as if watching warily to discover whether the
other is friend or foe. When the testing process has
proceeded far enough and they feel safer with each other,
they begin to relax. The unseen barriers are lowered. The
pace and volume of conversation increase. Some laugh.
Soon there is a steady hum of talk. The social occasion is a
success.

Why should a group of mature people, gathered to share
the pleasure of their mutual company, behave in this way?
Why can't they be more friendly from the beginning?
Logically, adults know they have little to fear from each
other on a social occasion. No one is likely to hurt anyone
else. Yet their behavior is guarded and defensive. They often act as if they were afraid that they might be hurt.

All of us behave defensively, as this example demonstrates. Living with other people, we must be prepared to defend ourselves against those who might hurt us by words as well as actions. We also must be alert to control our own feelings so as not to hurt or offend others. We must guide our behavior to avoid the painful feelings of guilt which the conscience can engender.

All of us experience a myriad of psychological threats every day. Some of them are so subtle we are hardly aware of them, and of some we are not aware at all. The flare of anger when someone drives recklessly too close to us is commonplace. Being accidentally bumped by someone on a crowded bus may make us angry for a moment, but that anger is quickly suppressed when we realize it wasn't anyone's fault. The echoes of a nasty remark by a colleague remain longer. But we only rarely become aware of the negative feelings we might sometimes have when we feel burdened by the responsibility for subordinates who are dependent on us for direction and guidance—because in our culture we are not supposed to think of responsibility negatively.

And everywhere there are symbols of support or threat. If a person is promoted to an office which has a rug, this simple symbol signifies that he or she is held in greater esteem by his superiors. Presumably then he is more secure in his position. If he is demoted or loses certain symbols of esteem, he is likely to think of himself as being less worthy and therefore in a more precarious position psychologically as well as economically.

Fear on the job, then, is not just a matter of worrying about having the job or losing it. More often, it is anxiety related to one's self-esteem and the feelings one has about being esteemed by others. Frequently it has to do with one's conscience, the way one judges oneself and responds to how others judge him. The trouble with repetitive anxiety is that, causing the person to mobilize his resources for defense again and again, it consumes energy which might better go into the work. Furthermore, defensive behavior, as we shall see, can become detrimental to the work process.

SITUATIONS OF THREAT

Many job situations precipitate anxiety. Four such circumstances occur repetitively. These are change, rivalry, increased responsibility, and role ambiguity. Each of these situations evokes feelings in people which have ancient, childhood roots. Often the person himself is not aware of the feelings which have been aroused. One may only know that one is tense, worried, restless, physically upset, excessively fatigued, irritable, or otherwise uncomfortable. Sometimes one may level off in performance—hit a plateau or slump. This is frequently a form of flight. One may, on the other hand, fight—attacking one's environment by becoming increasingly competitive or burying oneself in one's work.

Change. Human beings are like trees or plants; they are rooted in their environments. Relationships for people are the equivalent of roots for trees. We draw our psychological nourishment from other people, things, activities, and beliefs. We are attached to some more strongly than others. Seeing a tree, our attention is drawn to its height and shape. We are usually unaware of the complexity of its root system. Seeing a person, our attention is directed to his appearance and behavior; we are similarly unaware of the subtleties and complexities of his relationships.

The most common situation producing anxiety is change, for change always means some disruption of ties or relationships. Even a change for the better means loss—something has to be given up. All of us evolve characteristic ways of doing things—our preferred ways—and make use of our environments to meet our needs. We turn to different friends and resources for different needs. We know who can help with some aspect of the job, what professional people we trust for help with emergencies. Change means some alteration in our characteristic ways of coping with our world. As a result it may produce temporary feelings of helplessness. The experience of homesickness is a common example.

The change itself may not seem significant either to the person or to another who observes him—because we observe external appearances, not the root system. Even a seemingly insignificant change may awaken ancient, forgotten feelings of helplessness. In that case we have not only to deal with the feelings directly related to the change, but also with the old buried feelings. Of course the more radical the change, the less a person knows about what is coming next, the more helpless he feels and the more hesitant and anxious he is likely to be. The longer a person is unable to cope effectively with a change, the greater his tendency to withdraw from coping with his environment in the form of apathy or chronic illness.

We build broad curves into highways so that change will not occur precipitously. We post roadside signs to warn of approaching environmental changes. If we move a tree, we sever its roots gradually, adding more fertilizer, and then place it in an already prepared site. All too often executives assume people need no such attention—particularly grown adults. Then managements complain people are resistant to change, as if something were wrong with the people.

Rivalry. Everyone is an experienced rival and has had experiences of rivalry. Those who have brothers and sisters have known rivalry from infancy. Small children also have feelings of rivalry with parents of the same sex. Every child has had many strong feelings that he or she would like to be rid of his rivalrous brothers and sisters in order to have the parents to himself, and even to be rid of one parent to have the other to himself. Usually, however, he has been told that it is "not nice" to have such hostile feelings. Often, when he has persisted with his angry feelings or even open hostility toward his intrafamily rivals, he has been severely threatened or punished. He may then have guilt feelings and considerable anxiety about rivalry.

Rivalry is ever present in a competitive culture and is a necessary component of a competitive business system. But because it has these ancient roots it is a most difficult psychological problem to deal with.

Up to a point, rivalry has a constructive place on the job. The competition for advancement and achievement moves both people and organizations onward. But the executive usually does not realize that a rivalry situation duplicates the competition of the children for the attention of the parents, and old unconscious feelings are stimulated. If the rivalry is between an older and a younger person, ancient feelings of competition with the father are awakened. In all too many companies, the leader, like the parents, increases the hostility of subordinates toward each other by comparing them with each other, particularly when he has put them under pressure. What the executive may see as friendly rivalry, intended to make people more effective, usually bcomes an intra-organizational war. As anxiety is increased, defensiveness increases, and fights ensue. Then the boss cannot understand why sales and production cannot get along, why different divisions won't help each other, why people cannot seem to communicate with each other, why old colleagues become bitter enemies, why men guard their prerogatives and perquisites with fierce intensity.

Professor Abraham Zaleznik, of the Harvard University Graduate School of Business, speaks of two kinds of anxiety related to rivalry. One is "status anxiety," the feeling which results from the need to exercise authority over others and the simultaneous wish to be liked. The second is "competition anxiety," the fear of failure and the fear of success, both of which can lead to withdrawal from competition. Withdrawal takes many forms.

One form of withdrawal, a cardinal sin in management's eyes, is a person's failure to compete after showing promise. Often a person is told he can have a senior's job if he outdoes the latter. What management does not see is that, unconsciously, to many people this can seem to be competing with father again, with all the implicit threat— and therefore anxiety—of that ancient competition. One way out is to withdraw from the competition unconsciously by hitting a plateau or by failing to live up to one's talents and capacities.

For some people, any success arouses such feelings. They simply cannot tolerate it. Dr. Lionel Ovesey, of the Columbia University Psychoanalytic Clinic, points out that such success phobias can be traced to threatening childhood competitions with the father or siblings. Such people see aggression as inherently hostile, yet they are extremely ambitious, and often come to the point of success before failing.

Another form of withdrawal is to stay out of positions in which one has to work for someone else. Some people have such difficulty with feelings of rivalry that they are unable to work for someone else at all. Professors Orvis F. Collins, of Michigan State University, and David G. Moore, of the New York State School of Industrial and Labor Relations at Cornell, did an intensive study of 150 small businessmen. These entrepreneurs, they report, often start businesses themselves because they are uncomfortable under strong male authority figures as a result of unresolved fears of their fathers. The fear may remain, unconscious but so strong that special success will be avoided to escape the imagined possibility of jealous wrath.

Of course the fear of jealous wrath is an unconscious memory from childhood. But man can bind time. Not only can he act now in anticipation of the future, but also the unconscious memories of unresolved problems which he carries continue to be alive within him as if they were yesterday's events. That is why the unconscious aspect of the personality is such a powerful force—because it makes people act in the present, using symbols, as if still living in the past with the real thing.

Professors Collins and Moore add that for entrepreneurs the business becomes a "mistress." Often the wives of such men will complain that the business seems to come before the family, that they have "married the business." The entrepreneur wants exclusive possession of this "mistress" just as he, as a child, wanted exclusive possession of his mother. With these attitudes, however, such men are lonely, isolated, detached, and unable to develop subordinates or to let others assume responsibility. Their work is sometimes a monomania.

This is not to condemn entrepreneurs or to minimize their contribution. Without such men we would have little enterprise in our free enterprise system. But their experience does tell us something about the powerful dynamics of rivalry and the need for managing rivalry situations carefully.

Responsibility. Anxiety about responsibility has somewhat more complex sources than rivalry. Some people, who might well have been overcontrolled by their parents on the one hand or pushed too hard before they were ready on the other, find responsibility difficult. In both cases they are likely to be more frightened of failure than most people. The image they carry of themselves is one of incompetence. Many nevertheless pursue success avidly, in fact achieve it because of obsessive devotion to the job. But, as Dr. Robert N. McMurry, a psychological consultant to management, observes, their technical competence obscures their underlying weakness, which lies primarily in their inability to accept responsibility for their decisions. The result of this is that they are rarely on top of the job; rather, the job is the master.

Such people also have difficulty permitting others to depend on them, which means they make poor bosses. Having difficulty enough with their own wishes to be dependent on someone else, the burden of being responsible for someone else simply increases anxiety. This is one reason why first-level supervisors have a higher incidence of ulcers than any other level in management, and why many supervisors irritably reject the requests of subordinates for help.

Responsibility, in the form of promotion, also precipitates a cultural problem, what Professor Zaleznik referred to as status anxiety. Some sociologists would call it role conflict. A newly promoted man soon notes that his old colleagues treat him differently. He may want them to continue liking him even if he now has power over them. But he cannot have it both ways—both power and affection—because sometimes he has to exercise power in a way that some may not like. If anxiety is great enough, he will repetitively try to have it both ways by trying to avoid using his power and by bending over backward to be liked. That only undermines his position and increases his anxiety.

In addition to the cultural problem of relationships downward in the hierarchy, increasing responsibility poses another in relationships upward. Some people are just not comfortable moving into higher socioeconomic brackets where they will have to dress differently, speak differently, act differently—in ways unfamiliar to them. Their modes of organizing and coping with their world call for different techniques. Some, of course, see themselves as incapable of learning new ways and are afraid of making fools of themselves. "I don't want to have to mix with all those people in the front office," a foreman in an electric utility company once told me, indicating why he did not want to be promoted. To have accepted promotion would have increased his anxiety. What would happen to him? Probably nothing. He might in fact do very well. But he had classified management as being above him, as critical, and he would interpret every possible cue as a symbol of that conviction. His anxiety would not let him move.

Worse than simple, possibly painful, contact with higher authority is having to deal with conflicting authorities. Such a situation also reawakens problems of dealing with conflicting parents and evokes severe stress in the subordinate who has had such a parental problem and is now responsible, as he was then, to both parties. Conflict between authorities demoralizes the subordinate work group, increases the feelings of helplessness of the person caught in the middle, and provokes his hostility to both warring parties.

Apart from personal and cultural considerations, the handling of responsibility in an organization is a pervasive management problem. Among the most frequent complaints in American business is the protest against having responsibility without authority. Too many people are expected to get a job done without being given the power to do it. Giving a person a title or a position is fine. That says where he or she is on the organization chart. But the position is essentially honorific if the person has no authority; a figurehead simply hasn't the power to do a job. Anxiety is likely to mount when one is responsible for the work of others over whom one has little or no control. I can still remember the anxiety of a marketing co-ordinator of a large company who was expected to get six plant managers to use the same package for the same product when he himself was a staff man who wielded far less power in the organization than any one of them. A similar bind is the lot of the first-level foreman in a shop where employees can do no wrong and the foreman's actions are consistently undercut by higher management. In such situations people have no control over what may happen, so the future is necessarily foreboding.

Role Ambiguity. A job can be viewed as a role, a part to be played in an organizational drama. Included in the concept of role are the definition and requirements of the role, the expectations held of how the role will be performed, an outline of the relationship of any given role to other roles in the organization and to the organization's goal. Most large companies go to great lengths to delineate roles within the organization by organizational charts, job descriptions, performance appraisals, and so on.

Despite extensive use of performance appraisals and job descriptions, a number of research studies shows that there is considerable disparity between what a person thinks his or her job is and what his superiors think he is supposed to do. A study of organizational stress by Dr. Robert L. Kahn and his associates, of the Survey Research Center of the University of Michigan, discloses that role ambiguity is widespread in business organizations. Simply put, most of the people studied in that research project said that they were not sure what they were supposed to do and what was expected of them. In such a situation a person can only feel too anxious to move in any direction. Apathy, withdrawal, anger, passing the buck, and other defensive maneuvers are natural consequences.

Even in those situations where management does define the job role more clearly by stating what is expected of the person in that job, there is usually one flaw: management fails to clearly delimit the job. It does not tell where one job stops and another begins. It may seem ridiculous to say that people should be told where their responsibility ends. But, as my colleague Dr. John A. Turner points out, in a competitive business culture, where problems of rivalry are acute and where people feel keenly their responsibilities, many conscientious persons will try to cover every eventuality. This means that they may well overwork themselves unnecessarily, sometimes intrude into the work of others, and waste endless hours in protective effort.

Another anxiety-producing aspect of role ambiguity is inadequate support from higher management in doing the job. If one is being judged by superiors, and knows it, one needs continuous feedback on one's performance. Usually one does not get enough feedback, which is why the most frequent complaint in business is "I don't know where I stand." As Dr. Herbert H. Meyer and Emanual Kay, of General Electric, and Professor John R. P. French, of the University of Michigan, have shown, continuous feedback from superiors is conducive to growth on the job. Annual appraisals are not. This is particularly true when one sees an appraisal situation as a "court" where one is being judged, rather than an occasion in which one will be helped to accomplish tasks better. Too many times, people complain, the boss doesn't really understand the problems of the job. He or she does not know what the person on the firing line is up against, and thinks that pressure will force the subordinate to get the job done. Sometimes it may, but not without considerable fear and anxiety—and even failure.

A few simple steps can reduce anxiety on the job—yours and your subordinates'—considerably.

1. *Plan all change together with the people who are going to be involved in it, to whatever extent is possible.*

That way they are continuously in charge of what is happening to them and they have less to fear that is unknown. They are less likely then to be hostile and rebellious toward you and to threaten your position.

2. *Make the collective goal the target, not competition with each other in a given company.*

Recognize individual improvement or achievement for its own merits. Don't introduce guilt feelings into one person's achievement by making it the condition of failure for another. When you promote or transfer someone, or bring someone new into his or her area, talk with that person about the likelihood of feelings of rivalry and the fact that everyone is likely to have them under such conditions. Do the same with an older person who is being asked to bring along a younger one. He doesn't like to see someone take his place either. Let the objectives of the company and the immediate goals upon which superior and subordinates have agreed together, not your personal pressure, be the motivating forces. Personal pressure will only increase rivalry. It may produce short-term results at the cost of long-term gain. Even those results will be at your expense because from then on people will be on guard against you.

3. *Maintain continuing contact with subordinates to both define in practice the limits of their task and to support them in accomplishing it.*

Every executive wishes for a self-starter, the person who will do the job without coming back to bother the boss. Such a person is indeed a find—but his weakness is likely to be that he is a one-person show and not able to supervise or develop people. In a team operation, it is necessary for the team to function together and for the coach to be guiding his team as they play the game. That way the coach, too, always knows what is going on and remains a part of the team.

4. *Provide opportunity to talk things over, day in, day out.*

This is not an argument for talk rather than action. But a lot of waste motion can be prevented if people can talk about their actions before undertaking them. Much defensiveness and protectionism can be eliminated if people can be helped to realize that certain feelings of rivalry, hostility, disappointment, helplessness are everybody's lot in some circumstances. When people can let themselves be more aware of their feelings, there is less likelihood of letting unconscious feelings govern their behavior. Furthermore, the boss is rewarded with greater productivity, less friction, and fewer negative surprises.

The function of the executive is to organize people to do

a task together and to facilitate their doing it. Preventing anxiety not only serves the purpose of getting the task done more efficiently but contributes to people's well-being as well. This is one way—perhaps the only one—to have power and affection, too.

6

ANGER

LIKE FEAR, anger is a universal experience. Fundamentally, anger arises from the continuous operation of the destructive drive and the consequent feeling of hate. As we noted in Chapter 2, the aggressive drive, ever present and ever necessary as motive power for the personality, perpetually seeks expression.

Hate is closely associated also with fear because impulses to aggression or hate are necessary for self-defense. Furthermore, all of us fear the possibility that our hostility will burst out of our control. As we noted in the previous chapter, anger tends to rise in any situation where a person feels he may be defeated, even if such a feeling is so subtle that he or she is unaware of it. Possible loss of self-esteem, rivalry, threat to a person's autonomy or power—all tend to arouse anger. Every person has his psychological weak spots, those particular situations and problems which are more provoking for him or her than for other people, and everyone at one time or another turns his anger on himself in self-defeating ways.

By being aware that anger is always a part of his or her personality and by understanding some of the ways he can deal with it, the executive can reduce his own tendency to excessive anger and the harmful effects which anger can have on the work group of which he is a part or which reports to him. To accomplish these two aims, the executive should consider how and why anger arises in himself, and how it can manifest itself in a business situation involving other people. Review of the previous chapter on fear will help him understand the how and why. Here we will consider the manifestations.

● *Anger most commonly manifests itself in hostile with-drawal from others.*

It is a common experience among executives to be disappointed in or angry with a subordinate about his or her performance. It is equally common to have differences with colleagues. When they feel guilty about their anger, particularly if it mounts and they have strong impulses to punish the other person, executives will not talk about their feelings of anger with those at whom they are angry. They act as if the anger will go away if they do not discuss it with the person. Sometimes it does. But much of the time it continues to fester. The executive finds himself avoiding the other person or pretending joviality, or quibbling about minor matters. He or she continues to be irritated. Here is an example, typical of many such situations:

> A corporation financial vice-president is apparently unwilling to implement several programs the president wants. He has failed to select a cost control man, to decentralize the accounting functions to the divisions, to utilize data processing equipment more fully, and to replace some of the weaker managers in his organization. As a result, the relationship between the two is strained. Each is gradually communicating less with the other, and the close-working relationship they once had is no longer apparent to those who work closely with both. On the contrary, each is becoming more openly critical of the other, and this breach is causing considerable concern among other top-management executives. The president is now bypassing the vice-president to avoid further friction.

● *Anger manifests itself more subtly in the displacement of hostility onto others.*

Because so many people have frequently repeated provocations to anger without being able to discharge that anger at their *provocateurs* or in solving the problems which created their frustration, there is much readiness to discharge anger. Many people are just waiting for a target—one which is helpless or anonymous or both. An ordinarily gentle man, once behind the wheel of a car, may show his worst snarl to other drivers—because in a few moments he will escape the other and never see him again. Like animals who develop a pecking order among themselves, executives find easily available targets who are less powerful than they are, or who must, for some reason, take their hostility, or from whom they can easily escape. Thus store clerks, public officials, waiters, housemaids, children, or subordinates are frequent victims.

The manager of a large savings and loan office, now in his mid-fifties, has been highly successful in his company and is widely known throughout the industry. He sees himself as a firm disciplinarian, and an exacting taskmaster—the best kind of a boss for developing others. His subordinates, however, regard him very differently. They find him unjust and intemperate. They are particularly aware of his apparent need, at all times, to have a "whipping boy" in the organization. The manager is always highly critical of at least one of his subordinates and "rides" him so hard that the subordinate quits. Within a few weeks after the departure of the old subordinate, the manager transfers his highly critical attitude to another one.

• *Anger which is overcontrolled reflects itself in tension, irritability, and pain.*

It is easy enough to know when you are openly angry with someone. It is much harder to be aware of anger when you hide it from yourself. Much of the time we overcontrol our angry feelings or direct them unwittingly to ourselves.

Some people are past masters at overcontrolling their angry feelings. The person who is always clapping a lid on his or her anger, pretending to himself and to others that he does not have any anger, constantly holding it within himself, is a good candidate for psychosomatic illnesses. He is like an automobile driver who is racing the motor with one foot and applying the brakes with the other—most of the time. A person who is constantly sitting on his own feelings loses some of the sparkle, spontaneity, and initiative he could have if he let himself be more free. To restrain or deny his feelings forces him to keep up his psychological guard continuously, an effort which requires much of his energy and literally wears out some of his body organs, increasing the likelihood of such illnesses as hypertension, headache, coronary disease, and intestinal disorders. Repressed anger is an important factor in almost all emotional illness. To use another analogy, when you overload the circuits you are likely to blow a fuse. When you overload the body with emergency demands, something eventually has to give. Besides, sitting on anger contributes nothing to solving the problem causing the frustration.

Here is a fairly typical example. A fifty-five-year-old department manager fulfills the obligations of his job well, but seems to be unable either to train a successor or to assume greater responsibility. He is ill at ease with top management, reluctant to express himself or present his views. He says he has no desire to advance. He has had two "serious illnesses" which originally were thought to be heart attacks, but subsequently the cause of his illnesses proved to be more obscure. No one really knows what he suffers from. His superior and his doctor both have urged him to slow down, although there is no indication that the work pace is sufficiently strenuous to be a pressure for him. It seems apparent from his uneasiness with his superiors that his stress is psychological. He is both fearful and angry. He seems to have great difficulty dealing with his own feelings of hostility, particularly toward his superiors. Apparently he goes to great lengths to control these feelings by containing them, and this unconscious process of containment ultimately results in his illnesses.

One of the reasons man is his own worst enemy is that so often he is hurting himself and is unaware of it. He has many ways of doing this: putting his worst foot forward or, as the saying goes, in his mouth; provoking others to anger against him; deprecating his own value; having accidents; and, in extreme form, killing himself. Obviously, this mode of handling anger does not solve the real problem either. Some modes of self-destruction, like suicide or alcoholism, are evident to everyone. Most self-destructive behavior is not recognized as such. It is often passed over as poor judgment or immaturity, like this example which occurs frequently:

An experienced and conscientious assistant to a corporate vice-president seems not to know or be able to accept a decision as final. He continues to talk about the issues. His persistence, which goes beyond good taste, is very annoying to his colleagues and superiors. Occasionally, when he pursues the subject in the presence of others who are not members of the firm, his talk can be embarrassing. He does not mean it to be so, and he is

not consciously trying to be difficult, but he continues
this undesirable behavior even though it has been pointed out to him. The self-defeating aspects of his actions
lie in the fact that he will not be given more responsibility. One day someone is likely to become angry
enough with him to fire him, despite his conscientious-
ness.

People who characteristically handle their anger in ways
which are destructive to themselves, to others, and to the
organization, and who cannot change their behavior when
its destructive aspects are pointed out, need professional
help.

• *Anger is often an avowed technique for controlling
others.*

Some people pretend anger as a control device; others
become angry for the same purpose, thinking they are doing so deliberately but in actuality they do not know what
else to do with their anger. Both kinds of people systematically use anger for cowing or testing others. They know
that most people back off from anger and angry scenes.

The assistant to the president of a machine tool company constantly overreacts to minor deviations from
personnel procedures, policies, and practices which he
finds in operating divisions. He exposes these deviations in an accusatory manner, implying either purpose-
ful disregard of policies or inexcusable negligence, and
threatens to report them to the president. Though the
president supports them, line executives react fearfully
and defensively to such criticism and spend considerable
time trying to justify their actions. They continue to let
the president's assistant bully them, responding not to
his power, which is limited, but to his anger.

This is not to say that there aren't times when a person
must become angry to make a point emphatically clear. It
may be necessary to clarify a position with considerable
emphasis in order to dispel anxiety and confusion. The late
Irénée Du Pont, one of the three brothers who led the Du
Pont company from a small explosives manufacturing
concern to the position of the world's largest diversified
firm, had as one of his basic principles of management the
thesis that sometimes a man has to swear at his colleagues
to drive a point home. But this does not mean that anger

should be used as a whip or a club, for that will only produce fear.

THE ADVERSARY SITUATION

These multiple manifestations of anger become most evident in adversary situations. The adversary situation is basic to law, politics, business, and government, because out of the clash of ideas, points of view, and interest come agreement, consensus, and justice.

Such situations range from collective bargaining, to hammering out a merger, to debating alternative courses of corporate action, to arriving at a financial agreement. There are people who have an innate aptitude for the give-and-take of adversary engagements. But most must serve a long and painful apprenticeship before they become comfortable with them. Some find the experience so stressful that they never acquit themselves adequately and prefer to leave negotiating, bargaining, and compromising to someone else.

There is, of course, the reward of using aggressions constructively and with benefit. There is the pleasure of matching wits, the stimulation of competition, the achievement of victory, and the resolution of problems.

In an adversary situation an executive may or may not be arguing for himself. If not, he is in an ambassadorial role. As an *instrument* of power he is only as strong as his support, and often this support is equivocal. The power sources behind him can undercut him even while he is vigorously representing them; they may not accept the agreement he reaches, or may even reach another agreement behind his back. His self-esteem is always on the line if that is the case.

Adversaries characteristically find themselves targets of their opponents' wrath. Moreover, they are frequently blamed by their own constituents if the agreement they achieve is not as advantageous as the constituents would wish. They are likely to be criticized for holding out too long or giving in too easily. In the heat of argument and frustration, they are likely, too, to be accused of nefarious objectives or themselves to feel their opponents are tricking them. This is the mechanism of *projection*. Displacement is seen when the adversaries bring to their discussions feelings about many problems which do not belong there.

For instance, the principals negotiating a merger may have long-standing feelings of hostility toward each other; that anger can only intrude into the process of reaching an agreement.

For those who become comfortable with it, the negotiating process is a welcome arena for their aggressive impulses. Those who already have considerable difficulty controlling their aggressive impulses may find the increased stimulation to aggression in the adversary situation intolerable. Those who have control difficulties may react prematurely with impulsive anger, or, conversely, may so overcontrol their aggressions that they become passive and permit their opponents to victimize them. Still others may have particular difficulty if they are required to advocate a position they don't believe in or to adopt a style of behavior that goes against their grain; i.e., the cautious, conservative man who is forced into "brinkmanship." The less well the social role fits the characteristic behavior of the person, the greater his stress is likely to be.

The task of mobilizing and managing one's own aggression can have another consequence of a different nature. The person who devotes considerable time in adversary situations perforce spends much of his or her time expressing much of his aggression toward others directly. To be constantly at odds with opponents may leave a person pugnacious. However, those who do not retain such an attitude may well be strengthened for higher responsibility.

All these problems, taken together, constitute a tremendous psychological drain on the people involved, which in turn is felt as a severe physical fatigue. The longer the adversary situation continues, the greater the exhaustion. There are other frustrating possibilities which increase anger. Older, more highly educated people are likely to be more frustrated with less sophisticated, less knowledgeable opponents. Those who are more sensitive to feelings of people are prone to being more frustrated with adversaries who cannot recognize the reality of such feelings. When there is a third party in the situation, the adversaries may act like competing children lest the third party show favoritism. Failing to understand the childhood roots of such irrational behavior, an executive may only become more angry with it. There is danger, too, in achieving a good agreement. We all have mixed feelings about those on whom we depend. If we feel we are too dependent on another or that he puts us under an obligation to him by doing too much for us, we are likely to become resentful. Thus a person's boss may strike back at that person if he or she has been too successful, making the boss feel unable to do without the subordinate, to the detriment of self-esteem.

TURNING ANGER TO GOOD USE

The most constructive way to deal with rising aggressions is to try to sense them, capture them, and use them to further the communications and problem-solving processes. Here are some possible steps to aid that process:

1. *Try to become aware of your own readiness to become angry and to learn to recognize how you handle your anger.*

Make an effort to discover the more subtle sources of frustration and difficulty which induce your anger, as they are reflected in the manifestations described above, and direct your energies toward solving those problems rather than in useless gestures.

2. *When you are aware that you are becoming angry, try to control your anger until you can decide how to handle it, rather than letting it handle you.*

Any *apparent* threat mobilizes one to a defensive posture, ready to attack or run. But when you are angry, your judgment is impaired and you are not likely to act constructively. When a person is stimulated to anger he or she is like the old-time fire horses who jumped into harness position the moment they heard the fire bell. Sometimes, of course, there was no fire, but from the bell they could not tell a false alarm from a real one. A person cannot tell a false alarm from a real one either until he has had a chance to take a good look at the situation—and some people, once aroused to defense, are never able to take a second look. Like soldiers on the front lines who fire at every sound, they are too busy defending themselves by attacking.

Another reason for trying to control your anger is the tendency to lash out at convenient substitute targets. When you attack easy blameless targets, you make your own problem evident to others. "Where love rules, there is no will to power; and where power predominates, there love is lacking. The one is the shadow of the other." So said the famous Swiss psychiatrist, Carl Jung. In short, in this form of angry display, a man bares his hate blatantly.

3. *Be particularly alert to ways in which you may displace your anger onto helpless targets.*

If you aren't aware of when you do that, ask your spouse, your secretary, or your subordinates. Most people will be surprised to discover how often they do this. Some, who don't know how to control their anger, try to joke themselves out of their discomfort, saying, "I don't get ulcers, I give them."

4. *Understand, too, that sometimes when people become angry at you, they are not necessarily angry with you, and the same may well be true of their anger with your subordinates.*

If you are in a position where it is easy for others to attack you, some will displace their anger on you when the real cause may be themselves, their spouses, bosses, or someone else. If you supervise people who are in such a vulnerable position, you should help them understand that one of their occupational hazards is the likelihood that customers or clients may at times become inappropriately angry at them. This does not mean that you should disregard customer complaints about your own or your subordinates' work performance, but it does mean that you will have to take this point into consideration in deciding upon a course of action.

Another way of making constructive use of aggression is *not* to respond to attack with counterattack. Rather, it is more often conducive to progress to point out that you can understand some of the reasons why the other feels angry. Being human, you, too, feel angry at times, but the purpose of your being together is to deal with the problems at hand, and your joint efforts should be focused on that task.

Another side of this problem is the manner in which you and your subordinates take criticism of your work. Everyone's performance is evaluated in some way. Even the most powerful executive has his or her management judged by the board, the stockholders, the creditors or financiers, governmental bodies, or the customers. Criticism of performance is not criticism of the person as a person, although it is extremely difficult for people to keep these two ideas separate. Unless they do, they will have problems in their relationships, for no relationship is free of differences and criticism. No person can know how well he or she performs without getting some form of criticism. So criticism is a necessary precondition for growth, provided it is directed to the way a job is done and not to the person himself. If you are evaluating a subordinate, focus on job performance. If you are being evaluated, try to help your superior concentrate on how you do your job. You might even ask what your superior thinks of various aspects of your work if he or she has difficulty recalling some of them.

5. *When someone else loses control of his feelings and becomes angry with you, that is his problem, not yours. Stand solidly on your own equanimity.*

There is much psychological truth to the children's saying, "Sticks and stones will break my bones but names will never hurt me." Words will not hurt you. If you are wrong, a simple apology and whatever amends are necessary are enough. If the other person persists in criticizing you or in trying to make a continuing fight of it, something is itching him or her. You do not have to respond to this itch. If you understand such behavior to be the problem, you will be less likely to respond with anger to the anger and become a partner in his emotional battle. Neither lash back at him nor bend over backward trying to appease him. Both reactions will merely add flame to the emotional fire. Extended apology tells the other person you feel you were wrong, guilty, and therefore merit his anger. It also communicates to him your fear of his anger. Like lashing back, it tends to provoke more attack.

Many people, experienced in adversary situations where such outbreaks are likely to occur, are masters at tempering hostility by injecting humor into the situation. In a completely serious, highly emotional atmosphere, from time to time it is important to take the emotional kettle off the fire before it boils over. Sensitive to one's own rising tension, one can call for breaks in the discussion when tension increases and one cannot find a way of using it constructively.

6. *If hostility becomes severe, make it clear that though name-calling and hostile remarks fall on deaf ears, you will not permit yourself to be exploited or physically attacked.*

Nothing reduces those who use anger as a manipulative

device to good manners more quickly than stating in a calm voice that you will not let yourself be attacked, and not being impelled to take retaliatory action as a result of their anger. If they become inappropriately or consistently angry, you should make it clear that while you are willing to hear their criticism of your performance or ideas, you are not willing to serve as the butt of someone else's anger. When someone is victimized as the subject of attack by others, often it is because the person permits himself to be and sometimes even unwittingly encourages it.

7. *If anger threatens the stability and effectiveness of the work group, it is important to control its expression immediately.*

Failure to control anger which arises within a group simply lets it mount in intensity until it becomes destructive. Once control has been established, then you can do something about the anger. In such a situation you must be careful of the tendency to concentrate on finding out who is to blame and to think the problem has been solved once the culprit has been found. (See Chapter 17.) It is too easy to find scapegoats. If there are problems in a work group which give rise to anger, it is far more constructive to have people talk the problems out, clarify them, and suggest ways of working together more effectively.

For example, a common business problem is the pressure to cut costs. Frequently a management decision to intensify cost-cutting efforts results in pressure on first-line supervisors who in turn put pressure on the work group. Work groups often see dozens of ways in which money is wasted, ways which management cannot see because it is too far from the work situation. When the waste they see usually costs far more than they can save, the work group is likely to respond to cost-cutting pressure with considerable anger. If the work group becomes turbulent in its anger, management is prone to blame inadequate supervision. And the supervisor, representing management, is the closest managerial target to the work group so the employees find it convenient to protest his or her methods. The upshot is often the discharge or transfer of the supervisor. The employees may be temporarily pacified by the sacrifice of the supervisor, but the anger will recur until the underlying problem is resolved.

8. *There are times when becoming angry is a step toward the solution of a problem.*

Sometimes subordinates or business associates are testing to find out how far they can go and when someone else will take a firm position. Often they do so unconsciously. Taking a firm stand in such circumstances clears the air. When it is important to be angry in order to make one's position clear or to take a stand against another's position, this can be well timed to move the problem-solving process further rather than impede it. If this occurs in an adversary situation, one needs a sense of the rhythm of the give-and-take process and, like an orchestra conductor, call for the cymbals to clash when that sound is a proper component.

Another way in which becoming angry can be a step in the solution of a problem is to channel the anger into competition. A person whose competitor gets ahead of him or her in some way wastes time just being angry about it. But if the anger becomes a stimulus to finding new competitive advantages for the firm, in the form of innovations in products and services, then that person has turned it to constructive use.

9. *Develop activities which you can use regularly as channels for draining off your excess aggressive feelings.*

Athletics, hobbies, home projects, travel, all serve such a "safety valve" function. Volunteer or service activity often enhances a person's self-esteem and provides gratifications which foster the constructive forces in the personality. The stronger the constructive forces of the personality, the easier it is to deal with anger. A change of pace—new activities different from the ordinary routine—is usually helpful in this respect. Some can find this variety in their regular jobs; others find it away from work. In either case you are refreshed by new forms of gratification which compensate for the extraordinary drain on energies which anger induces.

10. *If you are in a hostile situation, remember that many of the feelings of your antagonist are likely to be much like your own.*

Sometimes a situation can be eased if you can pause to ask yourself, "How does the other person feel behind the words he says? How can I ease his anxiety?" This is not easy to do, particularly in the heat of dissension, but it is important psychologically to maintain perspective.

Of course, psychological understanding will not magically solve all the problems of handling aggression. The aggression is still there; but understanding may take some of the sharp edges from the hostility and make it possible to deal with the hostility more reasonably.

7

SELF-DOUBT

FEAR AND ANGER combine to create painful psychological burdens for a person. Behind much of the difficulty in human relations in business—behind the tendencies to be autocratic, unduly rivalrous, selfish, hostile, inflexible, and evasive—usually lies someone's feeling that he is not as good or as strong as he thinks he should be. Self-doubt is an exacerbation of feelings of inadequacy stemming from the pressures of the conscience. Those aspects of a person's behavior which make life difficult for other people usually are that person's ways of protecting himself against his or her inner doubts—the self-criticism of his conscience—his fear, and his self-directed anger.

Many people have achieved great heights as a way of proving themselves in their own eyes and in the eyes of others. Self-doubt, paradoxically, can hold people back or prod them to proud achievements. Unfortunately, in both cases, the price of self-doubt can be high, for self-doubt is probably the greatest crippler of executive ability.

Although executives by definition are supposed to have self-confidence, even many of the most successful do not. A group of young executives attending a conference were asked to write anonymously on slips of paper the one deficiency, of which they were most keenly aware, which they tried to keep from other people. These were the replies:

Not as confident of my ability as others are confident in my ability.
Cannot understand that associates expect *all* the answers—or a position on the answers *all* the time.
I cry at emotional stories or movies.

I believe that I am unusually sensitive and understanding of others—but don't know how to use it well.

I judge people too extensively on moral characteristics.

Frequently I react to an emotional impulse, and then spend a good deal of time finding seemingly objective reasons to rationalize the action. Before it's all over, even I am convinced I acted objectively.

Seen by others as knowing where I'm going—but don't.

Fear of failing to communicate ideas to others.

I take some satisfaction in the failures of those whom I see as rivals or competitors.

Desire for complete authority and no sympathy for the direction of others.

Fear of losing face in a ridiculous situation.

I think I have a genuine desire to help people, but coupled with a reluctance to develop the emotional investment that comes with a strong personal relationship. Consequently others see me as cold and unresponsive, and not really interested in helping or understanding.

I was once told, "You are the most indifferent person I've ever known." This isn't true (I don't think) but is a result of a reluctance on my part to become involved in other persons' personal lives.

Inability to deal as ruthlessly, to put it bluntly, as I know I should with the subordinates who have erred or failed.

Shyness—difficulty in meeting new people; coldness—reserve.

Uneasiness in new situations with new people—a question of whether I will be accepted. In established groups where acceptance has occurred, I enjoy meetings—in new groups I am apprehensive and retiring. This is true both socially and in business.

Have not revealed that I believe Christian principle must be remembered and used during the work week.

Fear of failure—resentment of less than peak efforts by my associates.

I do not like to meet new people.

I fear being disliked or hated.

I do not have sufficient self-insight right now to be specific about a "known-to-self" area I should reveal —this in itself is, of course, a revelation.

Nothing hidden that I would not discuss with the group.

I am considered a "poker face"—have been told that I never get excited in a crisis—I "never worry." This is far from true. However, I feel that keeping this inner worry or turmoil hidden is an asset in coping with the particular crisis in that I am better able to guide other people.

Lack of self-reliance in newly created situations, particularly in strange locations.

Fear of people or of being accepted by people has led to a high degree of aloofness in my personality.

Not really interested in what or how someone else might feel. No attempt to be sensitive to other feelings or viewpoints.

I have a compelling drive for power over other people —in directing, counseling, and controlling their activities.

Lack of ability to judge other people in the same light I wish to be judged.

Insecure feeling when dealing with persons presumed to be of higher intellect.

Can be insincere deliberately in situations in which I feel it necessary to accomplish an important goal for the organization.

Feeling of insecurity, risk of failure, concern about loss of income.

Doubt of ability to clearly express myself spontaneously in groups.

I am a decided introvert. I tend to avoid contact with others, to be alone, e.g., for lunch, on trains, etc. This applies even to friends. I also dislike having to push myself forward in any way and resent those who do sound their own horn.

I am not satisfied with my total effectiveness—use of time, stimulation of others, etc. Perhaps my standards for myself are higher than others expect them to be.

Being held up as a specialist by others and being expected to give expert advice—I often question and lack confidence in the soundness of my judgments and my professional competence.

Fear of not being personally accepted by my superiors —peers—subordinates and fear of not having ideas accepted, really accepted rather than receiving lip service, particularly from peers and subordinates.

This group was not a representative sample of all executives or even of some well-defined segment of the range of executives. Their replies therefore cannot be considered anything but responses by thirty-six young-to-middle-aged men who have important reponsibilities in the business world. They are promising men who supervise others, who have proven skills, and many of them will go far. What they wrote may not be really the most pressing issues for them, but even if they were only the ones the men were willing to reveal, they deal with self-doubt in one way or another. Some men merely doubt, and struggle along as best they can. Some withdraw from other people, others attack. Some are guarded, others impulsive, still others overcontrolling, disdainful, and hostile.

I have no doubt that any group of people asked the same question would give similar answers. Of course, this does not mean that people have *no* confidence in themselves. Obviously, this group of men and many others would not be where they are if that were so. Nevertheless, all of us have doubts with which we struggle and which handicap us in various ways.

There are two conspicuous ways in which self-doubt handicaps an executive in his or her work role:

• *Inability to trust oneself to undertake a larger responsiblity for which one is qualified and capable, and to which one keenly aspires.*

Most people are more constricted and inhibited by their own fears than by objective limitations. We are often afraid to do something because we think we are not good enough or that we can't possibly accomplish it when, as a matter of fact, all of us can do far better than we are doing.

In the course of interviewing employees in a client organization, I talked with one man who had completed two years of college but who had resigned himself to working at a relatively unskilled laboring job for the rest of his life. He couldn't go back to college, he felt, because he had to support his family. In that same community there was a municipal university which provided night courses, and extension classes were offered by the nearby state university as well as the local high school. Furthermore, his company paid for both academic and correspondence courses which its employees completed. Yet, there he sat, paralyzed by his own sense of inadequacy. There he will continue to sit, disgruntled and unhappy for the rest of his life. At that point he was still in his mid-twenties, with forty years yet to go before retirement.

Although this book is directed to executives, I use this example deliberately because it illuminates so clearly the same psychology which affects some executives. The executives' underlying feelings can be more easily disguised; they can offer more acceptable reasons to themselves and their associates for their reluctance to use themselves more fully, like these:

The president of the company was approaching retirement age, and the board wanted to select a successor from among his subordinates. Three men were approached with the same offer: that he become executive vice-president and succeed the president on his retirement. All three refused in turn. The vice-president, finance, refused because his children had finished their schooling and he liked the work he was doing. The vice-president, manufacturing, refused because he did not want to move from the city where the largest part of his manufacturing was done and where he had lived most of his working lifetime. A promising plant manager, not yet a vice-president but long recognized as officer material, also refused because he did not want to move.

While there is more to one's life than one's work, and reasons like these are often not mere rationalizations, in this case each person could say privately that he or she did not think he could carry out the president's role. Each, however, recognized the abilities of the others and each had a commendable performance record.

By way of contrast, the president of a small company near this one quit his $30,000 job to go to medical school. Though he was then thirty-seven and going to medical school was no easy task, he had little doubt that he would make it; if not, that he could always get another good executive job.

● *The feeling that one has reached an occupational dead-end, that one has done all one can do, and that one is destined to remain in the same rut for the rest of one's life.*

This feeling is part of an early middle-age crisis experience for many people. It cuts across all professions, businesses, trades, and callings. It is part of the process of aging. By the time a person is thirty-five, usually his or her children are well on their way to growing up. The initial spurt of spontaneous creativity has tapered off. By that time, too, one has formed an experienced idea of what one's particular business is about. One has established the occupational track on which one is going to run. The combination of having reached that vantage point and of coming to the realization that there are only so many week-ends left in life stimulates sober thoughtfulness which ideally becomes wisdom. But with the end of occupational novelty, one also begins to be bored and to wish for new stimulation.

Even those executives who have been promoted quickly often feel they have leveled off in a barely comfortable rut on an extended plateau. They have, it seems, no reason to be dissatisfied with what they have done with their lives so far, but they live with the feeling that there is so much more that they could enjoy doing if only they could start off again in another direction. Continued promotions temporarily relieve some of their inner discontent; larger homes, fancier cars, and more extended travel serve as external badges of status and achievement. Few of us, however, are satisfied with our achievements alone.

There is nothing wrong with collecting badges of success. The problem lies in the fact that the badges rarely assuage the underlying self-doubt. The pursuit of the badges often becomes like playing football with baseball rules and plays. You cannot score touchdowns by playing baseball harder. In fact, the harder you try, the more frustrated you become.

To illustrate, take the person who has reacted to inner doubts by making intensive efforts to achieve great success. In such a case the overcompensation is evident in the fact that he or she cannot stop competing even when he has won his rightful achievements. He cannot regulate his own efforts. He is not in charge of his competitive behavior. He *must* compete whether he wants to or not. This is not to deny that there is pleasure in competition, which most people enjoy. Nor is it to say that one should stop exercising one's talents because one has achieved some goals. But when one feels one *must*, when one cannot voluntarily choose to relax or do something different and feel comfortable with oneself, that is a different problem. The driven quality indicates that one is "possessed" by his motivation. Under such circumstances, one is likely to get no real pleasure from one's achievements. Such a person is like an alcoholic who does not enjoy drinking but cannot stop. In neither case is self-doubt relieved. From this point of view, the strenuous lifetime effort is useless, despite its successes.

Put another way, such people have many satisfactions but few gratifications. In my psychological conception, the difference between the two is significant. Satisfactions are temporary pleasures: a thrilling ball game; a striking vista; an unusual dinner; an academic or business achievement. The reward in each of these, important in itself, pales as times passes. The memory of the experience loses its capacity for evoking repeated or continued pleasure. By contrast, a gratification is an enduring pleasure. It may be a "peak" experience, something which provided one with unusual insight, or a deeply felt relationship whose pleasure is re-created every time it is remembered. Gratification, by my definition, is something which leaves one feeling continuously good about oneself and about living.

THE REASONS WHY

As we have noted, the agent of self-doubt is the conscience. In the first instance of occupational limitation the conscience is too harsh a judge. In the second, a person does not please his or her ego ideal sufficiently. How does self-doubt arise and why are its consequences so high? There are at least three contributing factors:

● *Many self-doubts have their roots in the early feelings of inadequacy of the helpless child.*

Children, after all, are completely dependent upon their parents for many years. For too long, at least as they experience it, there are always bigger and more powerful people around them who keep telling them how much they still have to learn. It is painfully obvious to them that they cannot dress themselves, open the door, cut their food, control their impulses, understand big words, or win fights with bigger people. Their feelings of inadequacy are often reinforced when parents demand of them more than they can do, or criticize them too harshly for their failures.

● *Frustration precipitates feelings of anger.*

Such feelings are sometimes extremely painful for children to handle. It is hard to be angry with someone who loves and cares for you. It is even harder when, in anger, the child feels he or she would like to do away with the parent ("I wish you were dead"). For the small child, the wish is tantamount to the act. The small child cannot distinguish between reality and fantasy like an adult. To wish something is the same as doing it. He then tends to feel guilty or no good for having such wishes, particularly if he is repeatedly told that to feel angry is bad. But he still has the feelings. More often than not, he represses them or "forgets" them. To repress feelings is not the same as erasing them. They remain, unconscious, and he continues to feel inadequate because he has them. As we saw in the preceding chapter, some people are so afraid of their unconscious anger that they cannot tolerate the ordinary give-and-take of relationships with others which, from time to time, must stir up their feelings. Others feel so guilty about their hidden anger that they constantly seek punishment in the form of failure, accidents, or even imprisonment. Some are afraid that others will discover how angry they really are under their mask of compliance, and punish them. Such people find it difficult to compete openly.

• *There are also cultural problems.*

The poor boy may be ashamed of his poverty in the face of the wealth of his richer neighbors. The girl of foreign parentage may be ridiculed by her friends for her parents' strange ways or accents. The boy who lacks the physical capacities to compete with his peers in communities where competitive athletics are highly valued may feel himself to be a failure.

The person who experiences himself as inadequate will have his or her guard up—to keep others from criticizing him and making him feel more inadequate. The person who experiences the outside world as hostile will also have his guard up, ready to be hostile in turn. The effect of both styles of behavior—styles which were evident in the responses of the young executives listed at the beginning of this chapter—is to fend off close and intimate relationships with other people. There is a consequent tendency to treat other people as things—objects to be manipulated, avoided, pleased, rejected, exploited, attacked, controlled—or whatever is the person's characteristic mode of coping with these feelings. The result is a pervasive feeling of distrust, intensified in companies by the competition for power and status.

In turn, lack of trust makes it difficult to maintain continuous and effective relations with others for the purpose of getting the job done. As Jacques Barzun, former provost of Columbia University, has pointed out, "... nothing in this world can be accomplished without trust, however rudimentary. You cannot buy a box of matches without entering into a tacit trust agreement with the tradesman to the effect that when you have handed him the coin he will hand you the box. Deception and ruthlessness are not 'Machiavellian' wisdom as the vulgar think; they overshoot policy and recoil on the user."

The cost of self-doubt in dollars and frustration is beyond computation. Despite their capacity for zest and spirit, uncounted numbers of people endure what they experience as dead-end traps with quiet desperation. They want to do something bigger and more exciting than they are doing, but they are either afraid or don't know where to begin. They are trapped by barriers they cannot see and hindered by psychological glasses that distort their perceptions of themselves. The tragedy of having given up on themselves is that so many could use what seem to be barriers as steppingstones to gratification. Too much self-doubt blinds us to the opportunities around us. Without knowing where to start pulling oneself out of the psychological trap, even the person with considerable self-confidence has difficulty doing so.

SOME POSSIBLE WAYS OUT

What, then, can you do about your self-doubts?

1. *Recognize that self-doubt is widespread, if not pervasive.*

It is no stranger to the notorious. William Shirer writes pointedly in *The Rise and Fall of the Third Reich* of Hitler's doubts—a man who appeared so self-assured and invincible to so many. It is equally familiar to the famous and respected as well. The late Professor Edwin G. Boring, one of the most esteemed of American psychologists, writing of his own career, tells why he undertook his own personal psychoanalysis: "I told (Hans) Sachs (a noted psychoanalyst) that I was insecure, unhappy, frustrated and afraid. I told him that I could no longer work, that I had to be rescued to productivity, that my honor was involved since I owed achievement to Harvard." The man who has doubts about himself is not alone.

2. *If your doubts are about your work and you want to take a different career direction, first find a model.*

Look for someone whom you want to emulate. Ask for the opportunity to talk with him or her about his experience for the purpose of reexamining your own career alternatives. Find out what was involved in doing what he had done, what problems there were, and how he resolved them. See how his business or occupational world looks through his eyes, what kinds of pitfalls must be avoided. Don't be dismayed to discover that he has doubts, too, and don't let that discovery deter you. Your concern is not to discover a doubt-free vocational direction, but one which is more gratifying. Of course, don't plague the person or you will wear out your welcome. If they are not made to feel exploited, most people are flattered to be asked for such advice.

3. *Supplement the consultation with a model by vocational guidance, if necessary.*

Many people don't have a clear grasp of what talents and capacities they have and how these relate to possible career directions. In some communities there are private guidance bureaus which for a relatively modest cost will give you a battery of psychological tests and interpret for you where your talents, skills, and abilities lie. Such services are provided under the auspices of the YMCA or fraternal lodges in some cities. In smaller communities they may not be available publicly, but, with the growth of vocational guidance activities in high schools, there are often local guidance personnel who, on their own time, might perform the same function for a modest fee. Sometimes such services are available in college departments of educational psychology. (Caution: don't fall for mail-order testing.)

The usefulness of vocational guidance is not limited to young people. It has much to offer those who are already mature. One of my colleagues went into sales work for some years after college. During World War II he spent enough months in a hospital to do considerable thinking about the limitations of his job. The upshot was that he sought vocational guidance, discovered that he was operating far below his capacities, and despite his years, went to medical school. Following medical school, internship, and three years of psychiatric training, he began working with executives on management problems. His mature years made it possible for him to be accepted readily by these men as soon as his training was finished. Other younger men with the same training probably would have to practice for several years before they could gain equal acceptance.

4. *Once you have found a model, talked with him or her,*

*and evaluated the extent to which you can follow his path,
next lay out a plan for self-development.*

What is the goal you want to reach? What are the steps,
in the form of courses or experiences, one must have to
reach that goal? Can the courses be taken at night school?
By correspondence? Are there scholarships available which
will permit you to take time off from your work and still
support your family? Will your company pay for completed courses as many companies do? There are an
increasing number of schools and specialized programs
especially for people who want to get a new start.

In addition to the formal steps that can be taken, what
informal steps are there? What kinds of magazines and
books should you be reading? What meetings that have to
do with this occupation or profession can you attend or
should you be attending?

5. *There is no alternative to perseverance except failure.*

When you have laid out a plan for self-development,
checked it out with your model and vocational guidance
counselor (and by all means, if you are married, with your
spouse), then take each step one at a time. The mere fact
that a person starts to work on a problem brings it down
to manageable proportions.

The prospect of spending years in learning frightens
people. It seems to require too much time or perhaps they
will have to endure feeling ignorant for a while. What they
fail to realize is that they are going to live those years anyway and the learning itself, if one has made the right
choice, can be enjoyable. In the process of taking one step
at a time, the going may seem slow and difficult. Progress
can be adequately measured only in retrospect. The biographies of all successful people are filled with periods of
failure, self-criticism, self-doubt, even outright defeat.
These are the times to talk with your model, or counselor,
or spouse. By and large, you will find that you underestimate your progress and undervalue your capacities and
ability. As Al Smith used to say, "Let's look at the record."
One important difference between those who succeed and
others is that the former did not admit defeat. What passes
publicly for self-confidence is often only an unwillingness
to give up.

A corollary to this is that you cannot expect other
people to understand what you are doing. Many, who
would look upon you as a model, or envy what you have,

will find it impossible to identify with your wish to pursue your own direction. Learn what you can from the criticism; disregard the rest. It happens to the most competent of people.

Self-doubt occurs frequently with respect to one's work itself, without raising the question of possible career change. Perseverance is just as important in that instance. Leopold Infeld, one of the world's outstanding mathematicians, worked with Albert Einstein for three years at Princeton. Although by then Einstein had made the four great discoveries of his life for which he was justly famous, many of the distinguished professors in the same center thought the work he and Infeld were doing would come to nothing. Einstein knew he was regarded by some of his colleagues as "an old fool." Yet, Einstein and Infeld persisted, through mistake after mistake, until they produced the *Evolution of Physics.* Every creative person has had similar experiences.

There is a difference between perseverance and dogged stupidity. Sometimes the difference is hard to distinguish. One way is to have a trusted critic. For decades, Sigmund Freud carried on a correspondence with Oskar Pfister, a Protestant minister, in which they discussed Freud's developing conceptions.

6. *When you find yourself being aloof, hostile, unduly compliant, practicing "one-upmanship," or behaving in ways which you know will cause others to distrust you, ask yourself if there is not a more constructive way to cope with your self-doubt.*

Will it really be to your disadvantage if you try to help the other person clarify the point he or she is trying to make rather than to argue? Will it really shake the world if you yield a point, rather than having to win them all? (You might win more of the big ones by giving in on the little ones.) Do you really get enough out of taking another person's credit to compensate for making a thief out of yourself? Or would you get much more giving him or her some of yours? Will the subordinate you help really take your job as a result, or will you gain a reputation for helping others succeed? Do others really "have it in for you," or is it easier to blame your shortcomings on them? Whatever the problem, start first by what you are contributing to it and why.

7. *If you find that, despite your best efforts, your self-*

doubt keeps you from moving ahead, or make you too defensive in your relations with others, or cause you too much anxiety which results in physical symptoms, then it might well be time to see a psychologist or psychiatrist for help.

When you step on the accelerator of your car with the brakes on, one of two things happens. Either the motor dies and the car is immobilized, or the brakes begin to burn while holding back the car's momentum. In neither case is the automobile's energy available for the getaway of which the car is capable. Self-doubt has the same crippling effect. If you cannot release the brakes yourself, it may take a mechanic to do so.

PART THREE

On the Way Up

Having discussed the manner in which one's inner self-protective concerns affect one's behavior as an executive, we turn to some of the issues and problems of moving toward increased authority and responsibility. The upward path is fraught with many complexities. There are few sources of information and guidance with respect to them. The aspiring executive, therefore, would do well to think as much about the process of getting where he or she wants to go as of the end point itself.

8

THE PROBLEMS
OF PROMOTION

FEAR, ANGER, AND SELF-DOUBT become focal issues in promotion. This case is illustrative.

Arthur Robinson, at thirty-four, was energetic, ambitious, neat in appearance, pleasant in manner, and well educated in both management and law. He was chosen over several of his colleagues to become departmental manager. Within six weeks, his superiors observed that despite his experience with his company he was operating in a way which made it difficult to co-ordinate his work with others. Not that he was violating policies and procedures. Rather, without consulting any of his associates he took actions which disrupted the flow of the department's business. When his boss talked to him about this matter, he seemed to understand the problem and things moved along smoothly for the next few weeks. But then he reverted to disruptive actions. Once more his boss took this up with him. This pattern was repeated over the next several months.

Robinson's superiors were at a loss to understand why a man of high intelligence, qualified by experience and training, and easy to get along with—in short, a man who presumably was ideally ready for this promotion—should fail. Had their decision to promote him been wrong? Reluctantly they removed him from his post.

And Robinson, how must he have felt about his failure? What had seemed to be an opportunity turned out to be a setback.

But isn't the American way aimed at trying to get ahead—and staying ahead? Young people everywhere pursue opportunity. Undeterred by such forbidding phrases as "organization man" and "pyramid climbers," their slogan might well be "The future belongs to those who work for it."

Opportunities for growth are highly desirable. Without them people would stagnate; without competition they would remain undeveloped. Yet promotion for any given person may not be opportunity; instead, it may be like Arthur Robinson's experience, a big step toward failure.

As with every other major decision about one's life, a person should do some serious thinking when he or she is faced with the opportunity for promotion. It is elementary that he does not want to fail, nor does he want his company to fail by choosing him. Moreover, he has only a limited number of years during which such opportunity is available. Failure to make the right choice at the right time can severely limit his subsequent opportunities.

The commonsense questions which determine acceptance or rejection of a promotion are usually fairly easy to answer: Will the increased pay be worth the move? Is this move upward, or will it lead to a dead end? Will it bring me closer to the power center of the organization, or will it give me a better chance to show what I can do?

The more important questions, those which have the most to do with success and failure, are much harder to deal with. These call for what Dr. Karl Menninger has often described as uncommon sense. Much of the time they are not even formulated as questions because the defense mechanisms each of us uses to maintain his own idealistic picture of himself hide from his awareness those aspects of his personality he is unwilling to face. We go to great lengths to hide from both ourselves and others what we feel are our most painful deficiencies and weaknesses. Sometimes we simply deny what we think are our limitations. (Who has not pitied people whose aspirations so far exceeded their capacities that their goals were mere foolishness?) Sometimes we try to cover our deficiencies by making extra efforts with the talents we have. (Many people have made important contributions by just such compensatory efforts.)

Contrary to the old maxim, what we do not know about

ourselves usually does hurt us. There is no substitute for a cold, honest, self-appraisal.

What then are some important psychological questions one might ask of oneself as one considers accepting a promotion? *These will have to do with how one handles the need to love and be loved, the aggressive drive, feelings about one's own wishes to be dependent, one's conscience, and one's modes of self-control.* The triangulating points which confirm one's decisions are one's experiences in the past and the *psychological* specifics of the new position being offered.

Our actions and experiences in the past will indicate possibilities for the future because the dominant features of our personalities are relatively enduring. Our characteristic behavior patterns are our preferred established ways of meeting our underlying psychological needs. Some people are characteristically outgoing; they make friends with almost everyone they meet. Others are more reserved, more controlled in their relationships. Some like to work in a group, others by themselves. Some have very high standards for themselves, others are less demanding of themselves and those around them.

As we look back on our own experiences, we can easily describe ourselves in these and many other terms. Our patterns of behavior are enduring since each person doggedly maintains those kinds of behavior which early in life proved to be most successful for him. Such patterns become our personal trademark—we and others recognize who we are because of the continuity of our behavior. In a sense we are how we behave, and what we mean by personality is the totality of our needs, feelings, and behavior.

A fundamental axiom in considering promotional opportunities, therefore, is that one should not accept a promotion which requires one to behave in ways which are quite different from the manner in which one customarily prefers to act.

1. *A new position should permit a person to maintain his or her preferred emotional distance from others.*

Consider, for example, how a person handles the need to love and be loved. If one characteristically prefers to be somewhat aloof from others (that is, to deny or avoid the need to be close to others), one will have difficulty when accepting a promotion which requires him or her to work closely with them.

This is a case in point. A man who was promoted to supervising engineer is now in his mid-thirties. He had never been married, and throughout his tenure in his organization before his promotion, he had had little contact with his family who live less than one hundred miles from his workplace. He worked hard in his earlier job, sometimes seven days a week. As a result he built up a reputation as a fast and effective worker, even though he spent little energy on consulting with his superiors. When he took over his present work group, it became isolated from the rest of the organization. He personally devotes as much energy as ever to his work. He has continued his lone-wolf approach, opposing any attempt at teamwork, and is in constant conflict with other department heads. He knows he is irritating to others, but he says he does not care. Despite his relative success, as reflected by the profitability of his unit, he has had frequent trouble with customers, overcontrols his subordinates, and has had continuous conflicts with his superiors. Every three or four months he threatens to quit. His superiors are almost ready to let him do so the next time.

From this man's own personal history, he himself could readily discern that his characteristic mode of giving and receiving affection is one of keeping his distance. It should have been evident to him that the supervision of others, continued relationships with customers, and teamwork necessary in his new job all require a man to be closer to other people. Straightforward comparison of his preferred behavior to that demanded by the new job would have told him the fit was a poor one.

Quite another problem exists for the person who so much needs the warm affection of many people close to him or her that it is difficult for that person to exercise power appropriately.

There are many variations between these two extremes. In moving up, will a person be cutting ties to friends and associates? Are such close ties important? Will there be adequate replacements if those ties are important? If one denies the need for such ties or assumes they will continue to be available in the new post, one should carefully double-check lest the brilliant attraction of this opportunity obscure the realities of one's own personality.

2. *A new position should allow one his or her characteristic ways of expressing aggression.*

The second major issue, how a person handles his aggressive drive, is one which tends to be grossly ignored in business. All of us must deal with our aggressive impulses. Executives must be able to invest considerable energy in their tasks to capitalize on opportunity, to overcome obstacles, and to lead their organizations on. People who compete for advancement know that they must demonstrate their abilities in their own achievements. There is considerable validity to the belief that a good executive must be aggressive.

Frequently, however, though a person can direct his or her aggressive impulses into the accomplishment of an excellent, even brilliant job on his own, he fails miserably when he is then promoted and must work through others. The same drive which stood one in such good stead in one's own individual performance cannot easily be transformed into indirect support and guidance of other people who carry on the direct efforts.

To avoid deceiving oneself and inviting failure one should ask oneself in considerable detail how he or she handles his aggressive impulses most comfortably. Does he do best when he can organize and carry out a project firsthand? Does he have trouble when he has to let other people do the task? Has he little patience with the human limitations of others? Does he complain about the need to pay attention to the details of relationships with other people in the organization before plunging ahead?

Some people, such as accountants and engineers, handle their aggressive impulses by tightly structured control of their work. Others, such as some salesmen, do so by vanquishing customers. Still others, such as advertising and public relations men, do so by persuasive efforts. A man or woman considering promotion will therefore have to ask what new demands the prospective position will make in terms of handling aggression. Will it be more constricting and therefore will the candidate chafe restlessly? Will it demand more frequent open confrontation of others, and perhaps thereby be somewhat frightening to someone who needs to be more friendly?

One important consideration here is the focus of aggression. Does a person direct his aggression toward himself and consequently make himself fail? This happens more often than most people realize.

One man, for example, had dropped out of college in his third year. He then held a succession of jobs, each lasting from three to six months, quitting each in turn because it did not offer opportunity or because he felt his superiors did not want him to advance. He then became an office manager for the local store of a chain. He was so competent in his job (when he could lean on the boss) that he was soon promoted to a similar job in one of the company's largest stores. There he had to function independently. In a few short months, though he worked hard and did his job well, he made a simple "stupid" error which caused the company to question his integrity, and he was promptly fired. Again he felt he had been done an injustice. What he was unable to see was his repeated pattern of failure and self-defeat.

All of us have our unique ways of putting our feet in our mouths or of spoiling our own efforts. Some people do so by talking too much, some by being sloppy in dress or appearance, some by putting their worst selves forward and some by "stupid" mistakes. The reasons we do so are complex, and I have discussed them in detail elsewhere.* The important consideration here, however, is that a person must examine the ways in which his or her self-directed aggressions can result in self-defeat. What has he done before when his responsibility was increased? Did he run away from it, as did the office manager? Did he fumble it to prove to himself he could not handle it? Did he become so ill as to have to be reassigned? Did he start drinking too much? Did he fail to deliver what he was capable of delivering? Did he try to cover over his insecurity with bravado? Making a mistake once or twice is not necessarily an indication of self-defeat. Continuing blindly to make the same mistake is.

The difficulties inherent in dealing with both affection and aggression in promotion are reflected in classical managerial failures: the supersalesman who becomes a terrible sales manager, the shop superintendent who cannot keep away from the shop floor when he or she becomes plant manager, the plant manager who is miserable as a vice-president.

The salesman in his continuous contacts and interchange with others draws on those relationships for much of his

* *Emotional Health in the World of Work.* New York, Harper & Row, 1964.

gratification and channels his aggression directly into the sales task. As sales manager his contacts are limited to supervising salesmen, and his aggressive energy finds inadequate outlet in shuffling papers.

The new plant manager who formerly was directly involved in production not only had worked closely with his men and women but also did something about the problems on the floor. As plant manager, he is necessarily further removed from his old colleagues, and he can no longer directly solve a production problem. When he tries to do so, he avoids the new broader responsibility which is now his. In each of these instances, sources of affection, regard, esteem and personal ties are diminished sharply. Avenues for the more direct discharge of aggressions also are narrowed. Taken together, such changes can constitute psychological losses and, if they are experienced as losses, the person who suffers them may well wish he or she had never accepted the proffered promotion.

3. *A new position should be congenial with established ways of handling dependency needs.*

The third issue, that of dependency needs, is also unrecognized by many executives. Every move upward in the organization structure usually requires increasing independence of thought and action. Most people would say, if asked, that they welcome the opportunity for greater independence. A person can rarely admit to himself that he or she really wants to remain in a subordinate position for, as he perceives it, that would be to admit failure and damage his self-image. Yet many people neither want nor can handle independent responsibility, for their own needs to be dependent on someone else are paramount. In pursuing the satisfaction of these needs they become too preoccupied with pleasing their superiors, are reluctant to make decisions or to act by themselves, and are unable to accept the dependency needs of their subordinates.

The last problem is particularly widespread. Many people have all they can do to cope with their own wishes to be dependent. They dislike intensely having other people depend on them. Consequently they avoid, reject, overcontrol, or attack their subordinates, to the detriment of themselves, their subordinates, and their companies.

This is a typical example: A company officer is described by his president as brilliant, hard-working, and generally personable. However, says the president, he is overly influenced by and attentive to the ideas and whims of his superiors. This results in his setting aside important projects to find immediate answers to questions which come from an influential source, even if the issue is unimportant. In contrast, he is close to despotic with his subordinates. Both he and his superiors are in frequent turmoil about his behavior which changes not at all despite repeated discussion. Given what we know about the relative immutability of characteristic personality traits, his behavior is not going to change.

In considering promotion, a person should take a close look at how he or she has dealt with dependency needs. How much independent action has he really sought in the past? Was he actually more independent each step up the ladder or, despite increasing responsibility, did he subtly continue to lean just as heavily on his superiors or selected subordinates? Did he become increasingly anxious with each promotion? Despite obvious talents which seem to send him forward, would he be far happier being a good contributor than an unhappy, unsuccessful leader?

This issue needs extremely careful consideration because a significant number of people fail when they are moved from a No. 2 position to the No. 1 job. Dependency needs can become more acute if the new job is not adequately structured so that a person can continue to have ready access to superiors, or if the job is not clearly defined, or if the person has not had enough experience to cope with it.

Dependency needs are not bad, though the word dependency has acquired negative connotations. Everyone has dependency needs. The very fact that children have such a long period of dependency and go through a long process of separating themselves from their parents makes these needs a problem for everyone. Each of us works out his own way of dealing with them. Some people seek out highly structured organizations which are well routinized; others go to great extremes to stand on their own feet and never lean on anyone else. No one has to apologize for his or her particular mode of dealing with these needs. Rather, if a person is to make rational decisions about promotion, in his or her own self-interest he must be brutally honest with himself about what degree and kind of support he needs to function well. Ideally we resolve such a problem by being *interdependent,* equal give-and-take with others, but it is rarely possible for practice to be the same as the ideal.

4. *A new position should increase one's positive feelings about oneself.*

The fourth major psychological issue to be confronted is the ego ideal or the image one holds of oneself at one's future best. People often have conflicting images of what they would like to be, some of which are unconscious images. As a result, they are not sure themselves who they are or what they really want to be. This is part of what I described as self-doubt in Chapter 7. The consequence is that they tend unwittingly to pretend they want to do a certain kind of work when basically they would much rather do something else.

Sometimes people follow a given occupation for many years before deciding this is not for them: a number, for example, have gone from business into the ministry or into professional training of one kind or another. Sometimes the conflict has to do with a person's values. Whatever the reason, if a person is not certain in his or her own mind that he is following his own basic wishes, then he will have great difficulty in his work. He may not be able to invest himself fully in his job; he may vacillate between one activity and another; he may find no real satisfaction in what he does. He drains his energy fighting both himself and the demands of the job. If he accepts promotion in a field about which he has considerable question, he is asking for trouble. Promotion demands increased commitment to his task and to the organization, and thereby is likely to increase his conflict.

It is commonplace that some people do what their parents want them to do, rather than what they want to do. Such a conflict is relatively obvious, and therefore fairly easy to deal with. When the conflict is more obscure, it is more difficult to resolve. One way of taking a look at the possibility is to raise the question I pointed to in Chapter 2: "Do I want this promotion because of what I want to *be* or because of what I want to *do?*" If, as I said earlier, one's motivation is to *be* something, one is likely to be pursuing a will-o'-the wisp, for usually nothing one attains really gratifies one. If, however, one's motivation is to *do*—to sell, to manage, to invent, to cure illness—then the gratifications lie in the doing and, if one does it well, achievement is a consequence.

Here a caution is required. Conscientious people often feel less capable than they really are. They are all too aware of some of their shortcomings and expect themselves to perform extremely well. The distance between their ego ideals and their daily performance tends to be astronomical, and therefore the gap between their assessment of themselves and what they really are is too large and therefore false. To avoid depreciating one's abilities a person should review what he or she has done. His past performance will realistically reflect his ability.

There is a second caution. Just as promotion is not necessarily the high road to happiness, so it is not necessarily a threat to happiness. Increasing responsibility does not mean increasing stress for everyone. Some will fail with it, some will thrive on it. Whether one will succeed or fail depends on oneself, the structure in which one will have to work, and the kind of supervision one will have. If one considers promotion in these terms, and begins one's consideration with an intensive, frank look at oneself, one will considerably improve the chances for doing what is best for oneself and one's organization.

Basically, one has to ask, "Will I continue to be me in this new post or will I have to be someone or something different?" Such a question is not intended to reinforce a rigid position (once a salesman, always a salesman), or to prevent growth and change; but it is to recognize that although we grow older, wiser, more capable, and more responsible, we cannot and do not change our personalities drastically.

There are two final considerations.

● *It is not easy for one to look at oneself.*

If one wants to take a good look at oneself, one would do well to talk to someone in whom one can confide, and whom one can trust to help oneself find honest answers—a spouse, a superior, a minister, or a professional consultant.

● *In the last analysis, one must trust one's judgment of oneself.*

Usually if a person decides a promotion is not for him or her, then that is the wisest decision. Most people know more about how they feel and their assets and limitations than those who seek to persuade them. Even if a person underestimates himself, he or she must live with his judgment of himself, and how one feels about oneself is more critical in success or failure than what one is objectively.

9

THE RACE
TO THE TOP

THE PERSON who chooses successive promotions accepts the dominant business value. One word characterizes competitive American business: "Go!" From the time young people are recruited into managerial ranks, they understand themselves to be in a race for position, prestige, and power. They speak of "making a track record" and of "waiting for the telephone to ring" with an enticing offer. Companies spend millions of dollars seeking them out, more millions training them, and still more evolving better systems of supervising, appraising, and keeping track of them.

The cynical observer of this post-World War II phenomenon compares corporate manpower specialists with racetrack touts, and their records of executive performance with form sheets. Peter Drucker complains that there are not enough responsible positions in management for all of the young people who are being promised challenge. One major company, noted for its rapid expansion and therefore its executive opportunity, still promises fast promotion; it is apparently unaware that the average stay in one of its positions has lengthened from eighteen months to four years.

Nevertheless, many move and some do so very quickly. According to studies by Professor Eugene E. Jennings, of Michigan State, a majority of executives who move through the corporate hierarchy to the presidency do so in three stages: the technical level, the managerial level, and the executive level. The last stage includes the presidency and the two immediately lower positions. The average president spends three years in the technical stage; one fourth of them begin to move up within a year. The next stage, through middle management, which he calls the *developmental* stage, is characterized by rapid movement from one experience to another for rounding-out purposes. The last stage, *arrival,* is characterized by interaction with top management. The fastest moving people arrive at their presidential positions between forty-seven and forty-nine years of age, half of them from fifty to fifty-three.

Today's president, another survey of 492 of the heads of the largest companies shows, assumed his post at forty-nine and is now fifty-five; in 1962, his average age was fifty-six, and he had reached his position at fifty-four. Two thirds of the contemporary presidents had been in office five years or less.

Thus, among those who are moving up more young people are advancing; they are advancing more quickly; they have a shorter span of time within which to reach the top. The quickened pace is gratifying to many; the inevitable tensions, however, need more careful attention. There are several sources of tension, which will vary in their importance from one person to another:

• *Change in social status.*

Drs. William N. Christenson and Lawrence E. Hinkle, Jr., of New York Hospital-Cornell Medical Center, studied 139 young (twenty-two to thirty-two) managers, 55 of whom had graduated from college and the rest from high school. In a single year the high school graduates suffered twice as many illnesses as the college graduates, suffered more deaths, and showed more beginning signs of coronary disease. The college men were fourth-generation Americans from middle-class families; the high school graduates were sons or grandsons of poor immigrants. The research team concluded that the relative ill health of the high school graduates reflected the increased stress for them of pursuing success in a social world far different from that in which they had been reared.

That this stress is indeed cultural and not a function of being in the business world is reflected in a study by Professors Robert A. Ellis and W. Clayton Lane, of the University of Oregon. Their study of lower-class young men entering a high-status university shows that those men encounter a disproportionate share of isolating experiences and personal strain. They conclude that their study confirms the contention of the late Harvard sociologist Pitirim A. Sorokin that upward mobility itself is a disruptive social experience which leaves the individual for an appreciable period without roots or effective social support.

He or she is like a person driving an automobile through several different countries, each with a different language, different road signs, different driving customs, and different traffic patterns. Anyone who has lived in a small town and then has had to drive in a large city for the first time knows the anxiety of the first days. Put in simplest terms, a person who uses grammar incorrectly may fit well among blue-collar people, but that deficiency may make him or her feel inadequate among managerial colleagues. Not only are there different forms of speaking among various social classes within the same culture, but also what constitutes acceptable behavior varies widely. The glibness of a salesman, and his hail-fellow-well-met manner, so necessary to the selling task, may be viewed as lack of dignity in executive circles.

An added stress in upward mobility is the likely conflict in values. A person who cherishes family life is torn when he or she must sacrifice family relationships for career goals. One who judges himself on his stability as a friend will be angered in circles where he is gauged on his judgment in wines, his club memberships and his political beliefs. The young executive who values personal integrity will be in conflict about practices in some companies. One who wants to be evaluated on job performance alone will be angered when he or she discovers that political maneuvering is rewarded.

The stress of social mobility becomes even more acute when so much of a person's career success depends on how well he or she negotiates the social shoals. Almost every executive who has followed this path has had to deal with this problem. Sometimes he has done so with only dim awareness, but he has only to look back on the people he has left behind in his ascent up the hierarchical ladder to note the differences between them and himself.

That same retrospective observation will also demonstrate how much he or she has become separated—from old friends and favored activities as well as former behavior. One poignantly painful separation he will observe is the distance between himself and his children as they follow social paths he cannot traverse. His preoccupation with career goals diverts his attention from their worlds to his own.

There is yet another stress in mobility. The rapidly moving young executive is repeatedly reassigned to take charge of ever larger units. These are composed largely of others who are not moving so quickly. As Professor George Strauss, of the University of California at Berkeley, has pointed out, the permanent nonmoving employees will tend to look upon the young executive as a carpetbagger. Envious of his or her achievement and knowing he will move again quickly, they are reluctant to depend on him. They are more likely to be united in their defense against him than to offer him support in his new role. If they still retain loyalties to other former leaders or have chosen informal leadership from among themselves to counteract the repetitive loss of the leader, they may even be hostile.

Mobility also increases risk. The higher a person rises, the harder he or she is likely to fall if he errs. Errors are likely to be bigger, more costly, and, even more painful, obvious to an increasingly wider range of people. As if that alone were not threat enough, the higher one climbs the closer one is likely to come to the limits of one's competence. One runs the additional danger of demonstrating to oneself that one will not be able to move farther. Each higher step carries with it the risk of demonstrating some deficiency in training or experience which will be exposed by the demands of the new position. Each also increases the person's isolation from those below him or her. Arthur Goldberg once described this painful experience when he became a Supreme Court justice: old friends were reluctant to call until he called them first.

The farther up the hierarchy a person climbs, the more he or she is called upon to shift his leadership style. With each higher step he is likely to be responsible for a larger number of more competent people and activities. He therefore will do less himself, both in the sense of action and decision making. Instead he will have to create a climate which facilitates the work of others. This poses a problem for many executives because they are held responsible for results but cannot simply command or direct that something be done without being accused of authoritarianism. Futhermore, those who are less secure psychologically are likely to find it difficult to delegate authority. Promotion tends to increase the tightness with which such people hold on to their power and that makes their lack of flexibility more obvious.

At a certain point in the upward climb, perhaps close to the top, many executives experience a specific disappointment. Looking upward from the lower rungs of the hierarchy, it is easy to view distant bosses as having almost omnipotent qualities. They have a powerful impact in executive meetings. They cajole, inspire, punish, exalt. They seem always to know what they are doing and why, and, so the rumors and legends go, they are even uncanny in their judgment. To the young person on the move they seem to be virtual giants. When he or she reaches their levels, he discovers they were only human after all, and he will not acquire omnipotence from them or from the fact of being in a high-level executive post. Thus he confronts the painful reality that he will always have to live with his frailties and inadequacies. This frightening experience is not insurmountable. But it does point up the fact that one of the consequences of mobility is that one soon reaches one's own personal frontier. From there on there are no maps, no guides up ahead—only the experience of the past, which has its limitations for the future.

In a word, rapid upward mobility means repetitive breaking of old attachments—from the world of the family to jobs, colleagues, activities, locations, and sometimes even a professional skill as well—and their limited replacement with tenuous new ones. This means that psychologically it is easy to concentrate one's attachments into a focus on the image of the organization itself, to become a company person. That can be a tenuous thread, too, for many different reasons. Taken together, all this may be summed up in one generalization: *The sharper the differences between hierarchical levels, the more rapidly a person plunges through them, the more likely he or she is to feel the loss of customary ways of behaving and the greater will be his or her anxiety about unfamiliar practices and values.*

• *Blocked routes.*

If rapid changes in social status constitute one source of stress for the young executive, another lies in its very opposite—the failure to move up. Apart from the limitations of one's own competence, there are two major roadblocks to upward mobility: One may be detoured on side roads rather than continue on the open routes to achievement. One may also be held up if one's superiors are delayed, and if one is part of a trusted team with them.

There are several kinds of side roads. One is to be assigned to a department or activity which is not the main thrust of the organization. Fewer personnel executives become company presidents than manufacturing or sales executives because in most companies personnel is incidental to the other two activities. Another is to remain specialized beyond the optimum time for moving into management, or to be in a key position which is difficult to fill, or just to stay too long in the same job. Still another is to limit oneself to becoming expert in a given area on the assumption that that is the golden road, while simultaneously closing off other knowledge. Thus one limits oneself when one should be wide open to diverse information. Finally a person may try to continue the brilliant broken-field running of his or her early career when in later years wisdom is called for. If so, that person will find himself running with the pack instead of riding with the master.

The second kind of blockage, being stuck behind superiors who are not moving, is much harder to cope with—and at the same time retain the trust of others and a comfortable conscience. When one person moves up, several others tend to move with him or her, either as part of the same team or closely allied to the key man. A person's future in an organization is interwoven with that of others. Says Jennings, "Few arrive at the top not already trusted by those who are already there."

Thus if a person tries to go around the blocked superior, or cut loose from him, he or she may well be cutting off his own career nose. If he becomes too impatient he may alienate the very superiors on whom his future depends. Careful evaluation of such situations is called for.

If a person is delayed behind superiors who have been detoured or blocked for political reasons, there is no telling how long the other side will be in power. The question then to be decided usually is whether to stay in the organization or leave it. This is particularly difficult because the odds for reaching the top are in favor of the person who remains in an organization, according to a study by San Francisco psychologists Patrick Sullivan and Shepherd Insel. Of 120 top-level executives whose careers they analyzed, three fourths had been employed in fewer than three companies.

If one is held up by superiors who are blocked for technical reasons, then that may mean the company is shifting its direction. Discerning this shift, one may then re-educate oneself to follow suit. Most large organizations want to conserve their manpower and will reach for competent people who have prepared themselves. However, there may be an alternative technical reason: there are not yet enough responsible jobs for all of the people who are ready for them. In some businesses this may be because the company cannot expand fast enough; in others it may not have won the contracts it expects; still others may be delayed in expansion by a tight money market. The task here is to estimate the company's potential for movement and its initiative in pursuing growth.

Perhaps the most painful circumstance of this kind is to be blocked, invisible, behind a superior who has reached his maximum competence. Such people often do not know what competence is required above them. Even if they do, it is extremely difficult to push one's subordinates when one has stopped moving up. This kind of situation is more complex in organizations which depend on the superior to develop his or her subordinates and keep them informed. The problem in this instance is to gain visibility.

Intense young people with pressing aspirations will be impatient with such blocks. *The greater the tension of delay, the more likely one is to be angry in one's frustration; and the closer one is to one's goal, the more likely one is to act impulsively toward attaining it.*

• *Symbolic deprivations.*

As I have noted elsewhere,* for those who are affiliated with it, an organization is symbolically a "good parent." People, particularly executives, are asked to identify with the company, to be a part of the "one big family" which is the company and to sacrifice a certain amount of their self-assertion for the greater good of team effort. Commenting on the psychology of this relationship, Dr. Stanley Lesse, of the Columbia University psychiatric faculty, observes that it is conducive to becoming dependent on the organization. Since the young executive is simultaneously stimulated to compete and be a team member, he or she is

* *The Exceptional Executive.* Cambridge: Harvard University Press, 1968.

frequently caught in the dilemma posed by the choice between demonstrating initiative or maintaining a protected role in the company. Giving more emphasis to the latter has its own problems. Dr. Edwin A. Fleishman, of the American Institutes of Research, and Professor David Peters, of Yale, summarize their conclusion succinctly: conformity is not success.

Dependence on the company as the "good parent" makes the executive vulnerable to the evocation of deep-seated unconscious feelings. If, for example, a person has played the organization game well and then fails to move upward as expected, his or her conscious feeling is that "someone up there" has failed to recognize, appreciate, or reward loyalty and effort. Unconsciously he is likely to feel that he has been deprived by an untrustworthy parent. The unconscious feeling is far more powerful, and the reaction is therefore likely to be equally powerful. This is one of the reasons the reactions of some people to temporary setbacks seem so disproportionate to their colleagues.

Dr. Lesse calls attention to a similar phenomenon among ambitious people who are passed over. These are persons who are "stranded" or "left behind" not because of incompetence but because, for a variety of reasons, others have been preferred by higher management. Too old to leave, pained to have become subordinates to their contemporaries, such people feel rejected, lose their zest and their identification with the organization. Their self-images are often shattered. They, too, have experienced loss and deprivation.

The experience of deprivation usually leads to recalcitrant and sometimes retaliatory behavior. The problem with symptomatic behavior is that it can become a barrier to advancement where none might have existed before. Such feelings of deprivation are fostered by performance appraisals which are almost universally inadequate.

A personal loss often becomes a symbolic deprivation as well. While I was studying an organization, one of the senior vice-presidents died. He was loved by many in middle management, and some had hitched their futures to his star. Shortly after his death one of the middle managers had too much to drink, made a fool of himself in public, and was promptly fired. The loss of a man who had been "like a father" to him was a severe one. His intoxication and exhibitionism were forms of self-flagellation. In effect, in his sorrow he destroyed himself. Such reactions tend to occur when a person has staked his own career heavily on the fate of another and then loses his father-confessor-protector-guide-promoter.

For some few people there are problems of clinical proportions in upward mobility because for them success itself is a deprivation. These are the people who fear success while striving for it, usually without being aware of their fear or the reasons for it. These reasons stem from ancient childhood problems. Some may feel they have attained heights they do not deserve and should not have. Some may fear their increasing vulnerability to competition or attack as they rise higher. Some may feel that each step away from their parental families is that much more lost.

To some men, having exceeded their fathers' achievements means unconsciously that they have defeated their fathers as they had wished to do when they were children. In the mind of the small child to defeat someone is the same as to destroy him. If a man still retains much of that unconscious feeling, success will mean symbolically destroying his father. There are yet too few women in management to generalize about their experience.

In each of these instances, the achievement of success means that a lid has been lifted from deep-seated feelings. The achievement is simultaneously the loss of a protective barrier. As long as they are busily competing, their feelings are held in check. When they win, there is nothing to hold the feelings down. Some people fail dismally at this point, some destroy themselves. When success precipitates symptoms, that kind of loss requires professional help.

Thus failure to move upward not only increases tension and frustration for ambitious persons but also the circumstances surrounding such delay tend to be experienced as deprivations. *For the person who fails to move, in the absence of unequivocal feedback on his or her own performance, it is as if an unkindly parent had favored his rival and given to his brother or sister something which was rightfully his.*

There are many different ways a person might deal with

these problems. The specific ways will vary with his or her own position and his unique setting. Here are some generalizations which might be useful as anchor points.

1. *Your life is yours.*

You have to take charge of it, manage it, assume responsibility for it. No one else can do it, nor can you leave that responsibility to someone else. There are no corporate trust departments to manage one's life as there are trust departments in banks to manage one's funds. If a person does not manage his or her own life, then it will be managed inadvertently by others. That is, he or she will be buffeted about by this wave and that current to land upon distant career shores—or be swamped—by chance. The more one manages one's own life, the less one will experience psychological deprivation because of the actions of others.

2. *All careers have their specific stresses.*

There is no such thing as life without stress, occupation without tension, or career without problems. If a person has chosen an executive career, he or she will manage his career more wisely if he is alert to those stresses which are part of being an executive. Then he will try to evolve ways of counteracting them.

Among the most prevalent are those delineated here having to do with mobility. One mode of anticipating and counteracting them is to consider in detail with one's spouse where one wants to go in one's career and what that ambition will mean for the other and the children, if any. It will mean, for example, that they must build their lives around the concept of mobility and transiency. That, in turn, will mean that they must plan together to give more attention to their family life than do nontransient families. The latter can count on the continuing support of community relationships, old friends, and local professionals whom they know and trust. The mobile executive cannot. Stationary people do not have the problem of dealing repeatedly with the experience of loss; mobile families must again and again establish, then break, ties. They must make specific provisions for their children to talk about the loss and to mourn it, or they will find it increasingly difficult to adapt to new situations.

If a person cannot maintain a consistent relationship to

one geographical community, then he or she must establish other consistencies. One critically important consistency is a stable set of values, to have something to stand for, and to stand for it. That is an internal stability which will remain with one and will serve as an enduring criterion by which to judge oneself and one's alternatives regardless of where one is and what criteria others use.

Another important consistency is a network of friends. I use the word network advisedly because among people who are highly mobile there is no specific locale of friends. People travel long distances easily these days; the telephone makes instant communication possible. Intentional efforts must be made to maintain friendship ties. These can be sustaining in the face of other losses. It is easier today to go three thousand miles to help a friend than it was to travel three hundred miles a generation ago.

3. *Think out and plan your own future.*

If you were to take an extended automobile trip, you would use a road map; if the trip included mountains you would want to be certain your car could negotiate them. So it is with a career in a company. The more complex the route, the greater the number of alternative routes, the more necessary a map and advance planning.

Specifically, an aspiring executive needs to know how people move up in his or her organization and to be able to compute his own chances. He must judge how well his own skills and talents serve to traverse those routes. For example, an engineer is likely to have far greater opportunity to reach the top in a company where engineering is a dominant function than in one where engineering is incidental. If one has doubts about this issue, one need ask only one question: Who brings the money in?

Assuming that one is clear about the possible routes and one's own potential, then one must recognize the importance of two concepts: team and organization. There is no question but that one will have to work with others and that, if he or she is to move up, someone will have to be ready to take his place. If one takes the initiative in implementing both of these concepts, the odds are one will increase the chances for advancement. If one is too afraid of competition to do so, that fact will become evident and undermine one's aspirations.

4. *Use incidental guides.*

Every new job increases anxiety, no matter how old or experienced the executive is. Allow for it. Expect isolation and the temporary fear that you won't make it. You will have to make certain of two things: that you are in charge and that you have a reliable guide.

Whenever a person moves into a new job, someone always wants to take him or her in tow, to take charge of him, show him around. It is important that he or she not be viewed by others as anyone's person but his or her own. In practice this means one will choose one's own time and route to find one's way around; others may accompany him or her if they wish.

If one is to remain in charge, how does one get the lay of the land? From an observer outside the power structure. In almost every unit or department there is an old hand who knows his way around but who isn't going anywhere. That person, sometimes a secretary, sometimes an innocuous clerk, is free to speak yet not in a role to exploit his boss. Senior medical students and interns are taught as much about their functions in the operating room by the nurses as they are by their surgical mentors.

Having established one's role and learned one's functions in each new setting, a major part of one's task will be to help those who report to one look good in their own eyes for accomplishing their tasks and fulfilling their responsibilities. That will require that one create modes through which people can work together in complementary ways. The more effective the machinery for complementarity, for confronting organization problems together, the more people will feel esteemed by their boss and the more they in turn will esteem him or her. The superior will then leave a reputation behind in the form of models for problem solving and memories of respect. That reputation will travel ahead of him or her to ease his future course.

5. *Get feedback.*

Executives have a difficult time telling their subordinates how they are doing. This arises mostly out of guilt for the hostility of being critical. Some executives are reluctant to "play God" in judging a person. Others do not want to hurt the subordinate. Still others are afraid of the subordinate's possible anger, and many feel the subordinate does not really want to know. As a result, few people in organizational ranks really know how they are performing.

This means that many people entertain fantasies of the effectiveness of their performance, and the esteem their bosses hold for them, which are far from reality. When, at some point, they come up against the hard reality, as in the choice of someone else for a job they thought was theirs, they then feel deprived.

No amount of effort to improve performance appraisal, coaching and counseling efforts and supervision will surmount this problem adequately. The feelings of guilt are too strong to be completely counteracted. The aspiring executive therefore will have to manage his or her own feedback.

Specifically, this means that one will have to inquire actively of one's boss about the boss's judgment of one's performance. One will have to make it easy for the boss to speak up, to express his or her feelings, and one will have to take the boss seriously. If the boss can feel safe (free of guilt) in making hypercritical comments, then the subordinate will get accurate information. If one makes the boss feel defensive for judgments, one will be certain to cut off all but angry or disguised comments.

In addition, one should cultivate and maintain contacts with the personnel department for additional feedback. Most executives do not use personnel departments adequately to support themselves or their activities. Continued contact with the personnel department will help overcome the problem of being invisible or being held up behind an immobile boss. This is an ethical and responsible way to maintain visibility, particularly if the executive takes advantage of the company's willingness to pay for further education and if those courses are noted in one's record.

When you are getting accurate feedback, then you will have an accurate picture of your own reality. That, in turn, will counteract the natural tendency to hostile fantasy—"someone up there has it in for me." It will also give you the opportunity to work constructively on your limitations of knowledge, skill, and personality to whatever extent you wish. Most important, it will tend to constrain your impulsivity when you are delayed along the way and to soften the sense of disappointment when you are not the chosen one.

Moving up fast does not foredoom one to premature failure. But, the faster one is going to drive, the more one had better be certain both about the vehicle and the road. That way one has a better chance of getting where one is going. So it is with a career.

10

THE PROBLEMS
THAT WALK
IN YOUR DOOR

A MAJOR FUNCTION of the executive role is support of subordinates. This often includes support of others who do not report to the executive, but who turn to him or her for help or guidance because of his position or his disposition. This places the executive in two kinds of binds.

1. *From the moment one gets one's first promotion, one is "in the middle."*

For the rest of one's business career there is always someone for whom one is responsible and someone to whom one is accountable. (Even if one reaches the top there are stockholders.)

2. *Some jobs place an executive more "in the middle" than others.*

They are collection points for the problems unresolved at lower levels. While these issues are not the kind to be dealt with at higher levels, failure to resolve them will have repercussions in those ranks.

No formal names designate such positions. Their location on the organization chart varies from company to company. Frequently they do not even coincide with the "chain of command." Much of the time no one but the person in the middle knows that an undue proportion of the day's problems—particularly the problems of and with people—lands on his or her desk.

A department manager, for example, frequently found himself exploited and demeaned by the president of the company, who acted impulsively in embarrassing ways. He would burst into a departmental staff meeting, not only disturbing the meeting but also often contradicting the manager. He would make critical remarks about the manager both to the man himself and to others. Then, in an abrupt turnaround, he would praise the manager publicly and privately and reward him with higher salary than others in comparable positions. The manager's superior felt powerless to cope with the situation and told him as much. For his own mental health, the manager turned to a senior executive who was not in his reporting chain but whom he knew and trusted. That senior executive was equally powerless to change the president. But he became a man in the middle for there was no one else to whom the manager could express his frustration.

Such jobs are full of headaches. The one in the middle must become involved in spite of oneself. When one listens to people who are suffering, one suffers with them. When one is confronted with the consequences of managerial insensitivity, problems created by heavy-handed actions or rigid interpretations of company policy, one is resentful. One experiences unrelenting frustration with people who cannot seem to get along in any position. Often one has little tangible to show for a day's efforts. Often, too, one may feel something less than an adult for not being able to solve problems by direct action. Sometimes one feels oneself reduced to the position of an amiably spineless politician. To complicate matters, this part of what one does seems unrelated to the organization's goals and is without much prospect for recognition.

This unrecognized and unrewarded function is an abrasive, draining task in which one must suppress one's own feelings and serve as a cushion for those whom one must help. The unheralded job is to untangle the human knots in the thread of organizational continuity. When one gets home in the evening, emotionally laden with the difficulties of other people, one finds oneself in another double bind: not only must one meet demands of his or her family for participation, but also one must guard oneself especially carefully to avoid displacing job tensions onto them.

Thus, at the end of the day, the person in the middle

may often wish for a way out. Short of quitting the job, there is none. But there are some ways of easing the burdens, incorporated in these principles:

• *Recognize that compassion and altruism are normal feelings.*

There is nothing wrong with feeling sorry for someone and wanting to help. Though latter-day Scrooges may believe that in a business there is no room for compassion and altruism, effective human relationships are impossible without such feelings. In fact, following their experiments with monkeys, Drs. Jules H. Masserman and Stanley Wechkin, of Northwestern University Medical School, concluded that "protective" or "succorance" behavior is observable throughout the animal kingdom. Drs. Masserman and Wechkin observed that monkeys in an experimental situation would go without food themselves rather than push a button which would give another monkey a mild electric shock. Similarly, the person in the middle often takes considerable psychological punishment in order to ease the difficulties of others. But one need not punish oneself additionally by criticizing oneself for being "soft" or sensitive.

• *Develop and maintain a conception of psychological distance.*

It is natural to have feelings of compassion and altruism and to make personal sacrifices to help others, but neither the feelings nor the actions by themselves will necessarily solve the problems. In fact, when acting only out of compassion, altruism or self-sacrifice, a person may complicate matters.

Anyone who would help another must understand the difference between *sympathy* and *empathy*. In sympathy what affects one person affects another similarly. A person feels badly because a friend is hurt or sick. Empathy, on the other hand, is the ability simply to put oneself in another's shoes—to understand how another might feel and why he might feel that way without oneself experiencing a similar emotion. (One might understand, for example, the anger of a man who has been fired from his job without agreeing that it was wrong to fire him.)

The person in the middle can simultaneously ease his or her own psychological burdens as well as be most helpful to the other person if he will grasp this difference. One must distinguish clearly between what are one's *own* problems and what are not. More often than not, the problems which people bring to one are not one's own problems.

There are two reasons why this distinction is important. First, no one can ever really *solve* someone else's problems. Everyone is entitled not only to his or her own problems, but also to find his or her own solutions.

Second, only a person who is relatively objective about a problem can be of much help to another person's problem-solving efforts. The greatest difficulty people have in solving problems is the fact that emotion makes it hard for them to see and deal with their problem objectively. If the person in the middle loses his or her objectivity then that person cannot help either. The person who needs help needs the objectivity of the helper; he does not need someone who has been sucked into an identical emotional morass.

There is a long and essential tradition of objectivity among physicians, attorneys, and others who render services that involve deep and complex feelings. Yet even the best of professionals is an amateur when it comes to dealing with his own problems. Physicians do not treat members of their families because they fear their judgment may be impaired by their feelings. Every psychoanalyst must himself be psychoanalyzed to minimize the possibility of his own problems intruding upon the problems of the people he is trying to help, and also to assure that their problems will not touch him so deeply as to affect him and cloud his judgment.

If the person in the middle does not consciously try to maintain an appropriate psychological distance from the problems which come to him or her, then in self-defense he will tend to become hardened. His callousness will simply be the best way he has of covering his pain. Then he will no longer be able either to sympathize or empathize, and his primary concern will be to rid himself of whatever problems come his way just as quickly as he can.

● *Help people to formulate their feelings.*

Though it would seem to be simple enough, one of the most difficult tasks for people to face is to express how they really feel. This candor becomes even more difficult when they are distressed or upset. Since human feelings are behind most interpersonal problems, it is essential to sort out these feelings—to get from what is said to what is meant and to deal with it constructively. The first task of the person in the middle is to try to understand how troubled employees really feel about what they are saying.

EMOTIONAL DECOMPRESSION

One way to do this is simply to let the other person talk, in the course of which he or she is apt to undergo an experience of psychological decompression. Once the emotional pressure is reduced, the person can see how strong his or her feelings have been, and then is often able to talk more objectively about what he is struggling against.

The executive who is listening can often put names on feelings that are not clear to the employee. For example, a person may be extremely angry about a supervisor's behavior, but unable to admit even to himself how angry he is. As he first expresses his feelings of mild anger, the executive can indicate that he or she understands that the employee is irritated. The person who is speaking may agree or disagree. If the executive is right in identifying the feeling, the employee is likely to express himself more openly. The executive may then pick up and identify some feelings of disappointment, annoyance, or anger. The employee may continue to deny such feelings by saying, "Oh, it didn't bother me." Nevertheless, the attentive listener will note that as he or she identifies feelings, the expression of the feeling will tend to mount. This tells him or her that the employee really was bothered by such feelings, and that the executive's recognition and understanding of them, without judging their validity, made it possible for the employee to open up and express himself frankly.

● *Open courses of action.*

When an employee is able to identify how he or she feels about a situation, alternatives then tend to become much clearer. The person in the middle can facilitate this process by summarizing the feelings and incidents discussed in such a way that both parties are clear about the issues. Together they can then examine the alternatives, both those for the person experiencing the problem and those for the person in the middle.

For example, suppose a department head is having problems with another department head. Has he or she talked with the other department head? Why not? Is it because he can't or because he won't? Is he fearful? Of what? How realistic is the fear? How often has the same thing happened before? These elements of the problem relate to the person's own actions and alternatives. The person in the middle may have others. Is this particular problem being presented as a displacement from other problems which the employee cannot talk about? Is supervision adequate? Is supervision of the other party to the problem adequate? Is the problem a chronic one, the product of failure to confront the issue directly? Has the problem been dealt with by manipulation? By transfer? By failure to confront the issue? Should the person in the middle talk to anyone else? If so, how and to what end?

Several alternatives will offer themselves for action:

1. *The situation may call for no further action.*

If ventilation of feelings has been enough, you may invite the person to see you a second time. Make an appointment for this so you can see whether the situation has in fact been resolved by simply talking about it.

2. *It may be necessary to direct the person to the responsible party, that is, the one who has control over the situation or who must deal with it.*

3. *It is often helpful to talk with both parties to a conflict together or have their immediate superior do so, which will bring the problem to the appropriate arena.*

The superior must not be permitted to evade the problem. If superiors are allowed to pass problems on without taking action, or if the person in the middle allows himself or herself to be used as a messenger of feelings between parties, then he or she will get an increasing load of unpleasant—and unsolvable—problems. Besides, helping a superior work out a problem both strengthens his skills and spares the person in the middle additional burdens.

4. *If there have been two or three discussions with no resolution, it is time to refer the employee to a source of professional counsel.*

Some companies have counseling services, as part of their medical or personnel departments, which can be a first source of help. If one must refer to sources of help outside the organization, the person in the middle would do well to cultivate the acquaintance of a social worker, a psychiatrist, or a clinical psychologist whom he or she can call upon for advice and guidance.

5. *If the question is one which has to do with job placement, then it may be well to review the psychological tests*

if they were made and other data used in the employee's initial placement.

It will be important also to review the employee's work history to see whether the problem is a chronic one which has been repeatedly passed off or whether it is something which has happened relatively recently and if there are events to which it can be traced. The principles suggested in Chapter 8 should be carefully considered.

One caution: Don't be in a hurry to transfer a person. Transfer sometimes, but rarely, solves problems; some people have a record of repetitive—and fruitless—transfer. An executive should be particularly wary when transfers are requested and take a thoughtful look into such a request. If you do agree to a transfer, be certain in your own mind that that is the best solution. There is so much buck-passing by way of transfer that such a dodge should be exposed because it only makes for chronic problems for both the employee and the organization. You should ask yourself, "What's hidden behind this transfer request?"

6. *Don't overidentify with the person so that you feel so guilty for what has happened to him or her that you want to make amends.**

Among the most difficult problems the person in the middle must face is that of dealing with employees who turn repeatedly to the organization to help solve personal problems. These are problems that often tempt the person in the middle to involve himself or herself and the organization in situations outside the scope of business relationships—e.g., the chronic domestic quarrel. When these situations come up, appropriate psychological distance is imperative; referral is the best recourse. Furthermore, the job is still the basis for the person's relationship with the organization, and come what may, the job still must be done.

7. *If the person cannot meet the demands of the job, then usually he or she must leave it.*

Unless the job is poorly structured or makes inordinate demands on a person, the job itself is unlikely to be changed. The requirements of most jobs tend to remain relatively constant and are not too amenable to significant

---

* See *Emotional Health in the World of Work*. New York: Harper & Row, 1964. Chapter 18, "Management by Guilt."

change unless there are radical changes in other parts of the organization.

THE DANGERS

For the person in the middle who follows such a process of meeting problems straightforwardly and who must also exercise authority, there are a number of dangers. In taking a stand, one always runs the risk of being undercut by higher management if people go beyond one to complain further. The one in the middle must decide for oneself, *before* encountering the specific problems which make such a decision necessary, whether one is going to stand on an ethical position or devote one's energies to defending oneself.

If one deals honestly with the problem, one assumes the risk that a negative judgment about a person may have to be defended through appeal channels. Often this process is painful and difficult. The person in the middle may feel it is not worth carrying through. But if he or she chooses this dishonest course that appears "safe," the whole job environment becomes a threatening situation with high psychological costs.

A third danger is the human tendency to procrastinate to avoid the unpleasantness of confrontation. This is particularly a hazard in supervisory relationships. The person in the middle must decide whether he or she wants to take the continuous psychological beating of working with an incompetent or unsuitable subordinate, or take the pain in one big dose. Most people choose the former course, despite the fact that the internal wear and tear over the longer run is higher.

The fundamental question in these three situations of danger is simply what psychological price do you want to pay? Each alternative has its cost. The wisest choice is the one which costs the least over the longer pull.

If the person in the middle chooses to deal with a problem directly, he or she must be certain to clear the channels beforehand. He should talk with appropriate supervision and personnel people so that those who may later be faced with decisions about his decision know what was going on, what the problem is, and what should be done about it. The better prepared they are the stronger support they can and will give.

Where doubt is involved, an outside consultant may be helpful. For example, an executive recently called me about some technicalities in re-employing a man who had left his employ for another organization. As we talked, it became apparent to both of us that, despite the executive's strenuous efforts to dissuade him, the man had deserted him for seemingly greener pastures. He was still angry with his former employee whom he needed but now distrusted. As the executive's feelings became clearer to himself, he decided he didn't want the man that badly after all.

A consultant's view is often a support for an action that must be taken. But even though a consultant may help define the psychological problem clearly, the executive is still left with a decision which no one else can make. The managerial decision often hinges on how much one is willing to tolerate. That is an economic and psychological question which only the person involved can answer.

The most pressing danger, however, is the tendency to judge oneself too harshly. Too often we tend to act as if our decisions involve life and death for the other person. The person in the middle must make a decision on the basis of available facts. He or she will make mistakes; everybody does. Even procrastination is a mistake. All one can do is use one's best judgment at the time the decision must be made. In the final analysis, the greatest sense of comfort for the one in the middle is the knowledge that one has been honest with oneself.

11

GETTING ALONG WITH YOUR BOSS

THE OTHER SIDE of the person-in-the-middle relationship is the boss. Every executive is not only someone's boss, he or she also has one or more bosses. Even a president must deal with others who have certain kinds of power over him—a board, representatives of financial institutions, and officials of governmental control bodies, to name just a few.

Many executives give considerable attention to effective supervisory practices and modes of successful leadership; few give the same careful attention to being a subordinate. The principles of establishing and maintaining effective relationships with superiors are much the same as those for similar purposes with subordinates. The key question for every subordinate is, "How effectively do I use my boss as a resource?"

An executive who would learn to make effective use of his or her boss as a resource should have in mind how and what he or she might learn from the boss, and how the boss might help him do the job more effectively. Both factors are important for every executive who aspires to advancement because promotion hinges on increased competence and demonstrated achievement. If one's relationship with one's boss is instrumental for these purposes, the executive must focus attention not on the boss alone, but also on the relationship between them. That means one must look first to one's own behavior. While one may be only half of that relationship, and even the lesser half of that, one can do more about one's own behavior than about the boss's. As one has greater leverage on oneself, that is logically the place to begin.

The executive will feel the first barrier to an effective relationship with his or her boss as he reads this sentence. His hackles were raised just before he started this paragraph; the previous sentence threatened his own carefully fashioned self-image, which is supposed to be guaranteed to make him look good to himself. For most executives, two feelings are likely to be stimulated by such a statement:

• *If only the boss would change, I would change too.*

As Professor Richard C. Hodgson, of the University of Western Ontario, has pointed out, this statement is made repeatedly in management development courses. It has great validity, for, as everyone knows, the boss sets the emotional tone for the organization. But, as everyone also knows if he or she thinks about it for a moment, says Hodgson, the boss has plenty of his or her own problems with the attitudes and feelings of subordinates. Every executive is highly experienced in the frustrations of leading, motivating, and supervising others. The assumption that everything would be fine if only the boss would change, therefore, is only partly true.

• *Who, me?*

There is a tendency to feel helpless in the face of a difficult situation, to perceive oneself as the victim of Fate or forces beyond one's control. My former colleague, Dr. Prescott Thompson, has noted that this sense of helplessness must be confronted in every psychotherapeutic situation. The implied, if not direct, question posed by every psychotherapist is, "What are *you* going to do about your problems?" Behind this question is the recognition that every adult is responsible for his or her own life and only he or she can act in his own self-interest. The same problem, fear, the tendency to feel helpless, and the subsequent reluctance to assume responsibility for problem-solving action, is the second factor which contributes to raising the reader's hackles.

Once the executive is aware of this resistance to looking at his or her own behavior, the way he influences his relationship with his boss, he is on the way to improving that relationship. The next step is to try to understand some of the reasons why he behaves in that relationship as he does.

The roots of one's relationship to one's boss lie largely in one's own personality development. From one's most helpless infantile experiences through childhood, adolescence, and into maturity, each person has always had to deal with others who were more powerful than he or she and who exercised authority over him. As everyone knows from his own experience, and has learned again from whatever experiences he has had with adolescents, coming to terms with authority is a path fraught with conflict. Apart from the issue of who is going to control whom how, such relationships always involve feelings of love and hate, the wish to be cared for or to be dependent and the contrary wish to be independent, and to be master of one's own life—the fundamental issues outlined in Chapter 2.

These often conflicting wishes and feelings are also closely related to a person's ego ideal—one's image of oneself as ideally one would like to be. A person therefore always brings to his or her relationship with the boss a picture of who and what he thinks he is. One presents oneself in a way which is characteristic for that image of oneself. Some present themselves as "nice" or "agreeable." Others proudly assert their righteousness. In presenting oneself according to one's own self-image, each person tacitly anticipates that the boss will act or react in certain ways. That is, one tends to have a fixed picture of what a boss is and how a boss is likely to behave.

These two "pictures" are formed out of a lifetime of experience in coping with one's feelings in the context of relations with authority. However, just as no one photograph of a person represents that person fully, so no single image or conception does. The more rigid one's self-image, the more fixed one's conception of what authority is, the more likely there are to be difficulties in supervisory relationships. The person who believes that he or she is virtuous, upright, and correct in every situation and that every boss is someone who is out to get him or her, to take an extreme case, will be unable to get along with any boss. He will provoke each successive boss to hostile rejection, which will "prove" how correct he was in the first place. Psychologists speak of this as a self-fulfilling prophecy. It is just such self-fulfilling prophecies which get us into recurrent difficulties, the tendency to repeat the same behavior again and again.

These distortions of self-perception and perception of

the other are one of the reasons why supervisor-supervisee relationships are so thorny. Next to child-rearing, probably no other single subject has been given such detailed attention.

If the executive can become aware of the danger of the "fixed picture," particularly if he or she can understand that psychological images can become just as distorted as physical images become in the crazy mirrors of an amusement park, then he can begin to reflect on his own behavior. That is the third step in improving relationships with one's boss. How does one do that?

Professor Abraham Zaleznik, of the Harvard University Graduate School of Business, notes that there are two themes or dimensions in human behavior which help us understand the problems in authority relationships. One dimension is the continuum from activity to passivity, the other the continuum from dominance to submission.

• A person who is both highly dominant and highly active will tend to be impulsive, to exert initiative, to move things along. Without adequate self-control, such a person can be irritating, rebellious, and injudicious.

• A person who is dominant but passive tends to be compulsive, attentive to detail, and to use indirect and manipulative methods which serve both to hide his or her aggressive feelings and to avoid responsibility for his or her actions.

• A person who is submissive but active is likely to direct aggressive impulses to himself or herself and to provoke others to do so also, as in failing to complete work adequately or in inviting criticism.

• A person who is both passive and submissive will withdraw from others because he or she does not trust them, and therefore has little interest or investment in work.

These dimensions, together with the tendency to repeat the same behavior, provide an executive with a method for self-examination. He or she can look back on his or her previous relationships with superiors and ask what forms of behavior occurred in each relationship. That is, how did he behave the same though the superiors were different? What "picture" of the boss was he holding in all those relationships, and what self-image? How was he likely to provoke negative reactions with such images? The greater the manipulation, provocation, or withdrawal, the more likely there will be difficulties in relationships with superiors.

This implies, then, that the more initiative one can assume in one's relationship with the boss the greater the likelihood of using the boss as a resource, of correcting one's distorted images by interaction with the boss, and of coming to creative solutions to one's personal and business problems. One demonstrates strength and self-confidence; one can be open, constructively aggressive, and trusting enough to be interested in the work and to maintain effective relationships.

The problem then becomes how to control one's self-assertion so that it gives rise to spontaneous creativity, new ideas, and forward motion rather than to hostile, negative reaction on the part of the boss. Here are some starting points:

1. *Start with yourself, not the boss.*

When there are differences and you find yourself angry with "what he did," before developing a logical case to yourself for your position, ask yourself how it looks to the other person. Beware of the universal tendency to attribute blame to the other person. Our consciences are always ready to tell us we are not living up to our ideal self. That makes it difficult for us to tolerate an image of ourselves which does not meet with our approval. We therefore tend to attribute our worst faults, attitudes, and behavior to a person whom we see as threatening or opposing us: "It is not I who is hostile, it is he. Therefore I have every right to be hostile." Such a stance may serve to justify one's hostility to one's boss, but it may well obscure the very behavior which provokes the boss's hostility—one's own anger. When in doubt, reflect on past behavior to learn whether your behavior in this situation is a repetition of difficulties you have experienced before. Sometimes you can learn what particular feeling is stirred up in you and consciously take that feeling into account in relationships with others.

2. *Enhance the boss's sense of adequacy in his or her own eyes.*

This does not mean being Pollyanna-ish with your boss or being a sycophant or being manipulative. Those forms of behavior may serve temporarily to curry favor, but it is difficult for anyone to trust people who behave in those ways. The boss knows well that business affairs are not always rosy, that he or she is not always right. He may marvel at the manipulative skill of a subordinate, particularly when the subordinate manipulates in the boss's interest, but he will always wonder if and when he is being manipulated. So enhancing the boss's sense of adequacy does not mean overpraising, being deceitful, buttering up, or conning him or her.

It means trying to help the boss and the work group move toward its responsibilities. It means being open and honest but diplomatically so. People are most uncomfortable when someone exacerbates their feelings of inadequacy; when criticisms tear them down, when arrogance and contempt convey a judgment that they are stupid, when double-dealing makes them feel they were foolish for being trusting. Each of us, sensing his own anger as he recalls experiences of this kind, can appreciate how they might make the boss feel.

> Here is an example. A young executive was newly placed in the job of assistant to the president. As one of his first tasks, the president wanted a report on morale. The young executive talked to a wide range of people. One of their major complaints was that they did not see and talk to the president, that he did not know their feelings, that he was aloof and distant. Had the assistant reported to the president that there was low morale because of his aloofness, the president would either have rejected the report or have received it with superficial politeness and filed it along with three previous reports. Instead, the assistant recognized that the president sensed a problem or he would not have asked for a report. He recognized also that there must be a reason why the president was aloof, that probably he was fearful of closer relationships, that to urge him to get closer would fail. Acting on that assumption, he emphasized that part of his findings which enabled the president to feel more comfortable in his subsequent actions. He reported to the president that his people wanted to talk with him, to see him, to know that he knew about them. All of this was true; it gave recognition to the positive side of the president's relationships with his subordinates and opened a door to action which the president could take. He was not made to feel further inadequate and therefore more paralyzed in action or even further withdrawn.

3. *Do not provoke the boss's anger unnecessarily.*
Some people, like adolescents, are still trying to prove

how smart they are and how dumb the boss is. Nobody wins when you play one-upmanship with the boss. Perhaps you will prove that you are smarter, but that is likely to cost you your job. This is a difficult issue to deal with these days because young executives are entering companies with far more technical education than their superiors. In many ways they do know more than their bosses. Often they literally have seen more of the world. Certainly they have had many more advantages and fewer material worries. They also have the advantage of hindsight; they can see the boss's errors of the past and have not yet made enough of their own to be second-guessed or to have learned from them. Wisdom is learning from errors. No one becomes wise without error so the important issue is not how many errors the boss has made, but what he or she learned from them. If you can learn from the boss's errors without having to repeat them yourself, you have used him or her effectively as a resource and saved yourself much pain and headache.

This means that you have to talk with your boss to hear what he or she has to say, not because you want all the answers from him, not because he has them all, not because you want to please him, but to learn. It also means that a person should examine his or her own feelings before he talks with the boss, if he has any sense of uneasiness or anger about their prospective meeting. If one is angry with oneself or one's boss, that will interfere with communication; if the boss is angry and cannot talk about it, that, too, will interfere with communication. If a person can help the boss voice his feelings without having to feel guilty for doing so that will open communication and enhance learning and problem solving further.

This is not to make a case for tolerance. Tolerance implies condescension, putting up with someone else's thoughts, feelings, and behavior out of one's generosity. Instead, it is to call attention to the need for acceptance. Acceptance means that one understands that people are different, therefore see things differently, and each therefore has as much right to his distorted view as you have to yours. Tolerance makes understanding, and therefore compromise, impossible. Acceptance, putting all views on an equal plane to be examined on their merits, makes for give-and-take.

4. *Support the boss whenever you can.*

Subordinates know well enough how much they need the support of the boss to get their own jobs done. Rarely do they understand how much support the boss needs from them. Support means more than doing one's own part or being part of the team. Often it means opening psychological doors that are almost impossible for the subordinate to see unless he thinks about them.

For example, a vice-president and his group executive vice-president were reviewing a new responsibility the latter had just assumed. The new task required the senior man to bring together a number of community leaders over whom he had no power and to have them formulate a common program of civic action. The vice-president, having had considerable experience with such problems, outlined a range of possible actions and goals. He was dismayed when his boss did not pick up any of his excellent suggestions. The boss could not. He had had little experience dealing with such problems and hardly knew where to begin. The vice-president could have supported him by indicating his willingness to work with his boss on the project. The boss would then not have to admit his self-doubts; he could easily have accepted an ally.

This happens frequently with suggestions from subordinates to superiors. The subordinate may make a suggestion, then expect the boss to be able to act on it. There are many invisible psychological barriers to action. One is simply not being as familiar with the problem or the idea as the person who suggested it. Offer to go the next step.

Another psychological barrier is the multiplicity of bosses. The higher the boss the more political considerations and conflicting forces he or she must take into account. The subordinate can help by anticipating some of these, particularly when it comes to expecting a fast answer to a seemingly simple request.

Finally, the subordinate can support by touching bases frequently with the superior. This may be only a casual hello daily or taking extra pains to keep the boss informed. Many things, particularly feedback about negative or irritating matters, can be easily communicated if there are frequent occasions for doing so. If not, they tend to be stored up for an explosion. This does not mean plaguing the boss—just keeping in touch; do not put the boss in the position of having to look for you.

5. *Accept the reality of risk.*

All life is a risk. No one knows whether he or she will be alive thirty seconds from now. People who are passive, withdrawn, or manipulative are more fearful of the risk in relationships and therefore choose to relate in other than direct and forthright ways. They may think they avoid risk by doing so, but they really put their lives and fates in the hands of others. As Professor Zaleznik points out, the active person stimulates the environment; the passive one waits for the environment to stimulate him or her.

The risk in relating honestly has several components. We have already discussed the most difficult one in previous chapters: people's fear of their self-assertion, as if to be aggressive in interaction is the same as destroying others, or inevitably to incur their wrath. A second component is the possibility of being exploited; being open makes one more vulnerable to exploitation and requires one to be more aggressive in one's own defense. A third is the possible loss of one's job because not all bosses can tolerate openness.

Yet these risks are psychologically no more severe, often less so, than the risk one takes in letting others determine one's life for one. Either way there is some degree of concern and turbulence; better that it should be in the interest of being one's own master. Each person has a right to his own position and judgment. He or she will be acting on that judgment anyway, so it might better be aboveboard and subject to examination. If one is clear about one's position, that gives one a psychological platform on which to stand. A person may then be criticized but it will be more difficult to manipulate or exploit him or her. He may come to a definitive difference with the boss or the organization. However, the differences will then be clear and allow for choices to be made about alternatives, rather than to be confused with angry name-calling and blame. Furthermore, firm self-respect will foster the respect of others. Failure to respect oneself leads the boss unconsciously to form an alliance with you in victimizing yourself.

6. *But, if the boss would only change . . .*

True, but the boss is not likely to—much. Some people cannot take straightforwardness, some must be in absolute control, some are afraid of their own shadows. Some are intensely rivalrous with their subordinates. No matter what you do, it will not make any difference in your relationship with such people. After you have made a reasonable effort, examined your own history of relationships, and tried to discern ways in which you can remove the barbs from your own way of doing things, and still have made little progress, then it is time to think of other alternatives. If, on the other hand, you find yourself repeatedly getting into the same difficulty with a series of bosses and you are unable to change your own behavior, then it is time to think of professional help.

PART FOUR

When You Arrive

The higher the executive moves in the organizational hierarchy, the more he or she must focus his thinking and efforts on the organization as a whole, and assume responsibility for the work of others. Policies and practices are increasingly his or her professional instruments, the dissonances within the organization the source of irritations and stresses. The executive's modes of leadership can result in either increasing his or her own psychological stresses or alleviating them. Now we turn to considering those alternatives.

12

ON BEING A LEADER

By AND LARGE, executives are a serious lot, as much concerned as professionals in medicine or teaching, with learning how to do their jobs better. Of the many with whom I have worked, a few were paralyzed with anxiety: they simply didn't know what to do about the problems they faced. Some manipulated everyone and everything that came in sight, like a child for whom the world is one vast playground for his pleasure alone. Some were tyrants; a few were rivals of the gods. Too many struggled with a sense of their own inadequacy. Too often they were burdened with guilt for not being good enough in their own eyes. I have yet to meet one who is certain he or she has all the answers (although some will pretend that), or even one who, deep within himself, knows the secret of his own success.

I have watched executives curse in desperation the forces which, in moments, vitiated years of their efforts. I have listened to them protest the loneliness of their sometimes opulent offices, the distance from old friends. I have seen them cry out their pent-up fury at unloving spouses and disguise their tears with alcohol. I have been awakened by the insistent harshness of the midnight telephone to hear across the distant miles the heavy, slow depressed tones of a voice crying for help—now. I have learned that conflicts in family businesses cause a searing pain which is more chronic, more debilitating to an executive than being exploited by piratical manipulators. I have seen only one who became a bum by way of alcohol. Conversely, I know one who was literally a bum and became a successful executive as a result of religious conversion.

I have watched some build towering office monuments to themselves, and others emblazon their names around the globe. I have seen still others, no less competent, hide themselves behind monolithic company images. Some, I have observed, run to their tasks; others flee repetitively to distant meetings and conferences which only confirm what they fear—that they don't know enough. Some have given up in disgust to become teachers or preachers. Some should never have been teachers or preachers.

I have known some for whom attaining high position unleashed hidden psychological volcanoes of self-destruction. They died; some by their own hand, some by sudden fatal illness.

The happy ones? They are the ones who love their work, who accept its challenge, who want to leave something behind. They have one other characteristic enunciated in Chapter 2: they can turn their backs on their jobs when they want to relax.

For all that, when I am asked by insistent reporters to characterize the executive personality, I find myself at a loss. In that I am in good company.

Not long ago a managerial magazine polled a sample of corporation presidents to learn what it took to be one of them. The answers were as diverse as the faces of the respondents.

The several hundred managerial books and periodicals on my library shelves have much to say about the talents required of the ideal executive. A summary of that subject in those volumes would read like a combination of the Boy Scout oath and the Sears catalog. Furthermore, by the time I have read half a dozen of them, I begin to wonder where the human being went.

The literature of psychology and psychoanalysis discusses, often with complex profundity, what makes people tick, particularly what makes them miss a few beats now and then, and even what makes them fail. It has precious little to offer about what makes them succeed; and that, by comparison, is like the difference between a shallow mud puddle and a large beautiful lake. The fact is that we don't know much about creativity, artistry, and the difference between psychosis and genius.

The late Vannevar Bush, himself long experienced in major governmental and educational leadership posts, put it well: "The good manager is the practitioner of an art, and art in any form does not yield to analysis." Analyzing the executive personality for lessons in predicting executive success is about as useful as dissecting a cadaver to learn about the behavior of a living man, and it produces the same results: one learns the names and features of bits and pieces of deadness.

So executives are too diverse to be lumped together under one rubric. There is no such thing as an executive personality, though it is easy to recognize a competent executive when one observes him or her in action. You can see the competence in the style.

What is the style? On any warm Sunday afternoon in any one of a thousand parks you can observe it in microcosm. Watch a parent playing with his or her child—showing the child how to skip stones across the surface of a lake, practicing catching a ball, pointing out the hazards of poison ivy, refusing an ice cream cone too soon before dinner. The names may be different, the characters in the play older and unrelated by blood ties, but psychologically in every *good* business the drama is the same. By good, I mean a business built to ensure its own survival. By a successful executive, I mean one who builds an organization with that goal in mind. The executive who does so emulates quite unconsciously the behavior of the good parent.

The successful executive creates the conditions that enable his or her subordinates to identify with the executive's competence. Implicit in such executive behavior are three assertions:

- I stand for something; my cause is good.
- We can surmount our common problems if we work on them together.
- I care about you as a human being; because I do there is a bond of trust between us.

Let's see how these assertions are carried out in action. Although the specific behavior varies widely from executive to executive, it is governed by the same principles, derived from these assertions.

Every successful executive I know has a sense of where he or she is going and how he or she is going to get there.

The executive may not have every step in his or her route mapped out, but the broad outlines of the path are clear. Furthermore, the executive has a conviction about the necessity for having taken that path, which serves like a sparkling star in the firmament to pull him or her ever onward. The executive has a mission. Those who follow are really magnetized by his or her star. They are not simple imitators of executive behavior.

The sense of knowing where one is going and how one is going to get there must be leavened with a modest dose of self-doubt or it becomes arrogance. Lack of self-doubt also impairs the executive's capacity to get and use information. From his MIT study of heads of research and development organizations, Harry Schrage reports that the most significant difference between the more successful presidents and the less successful ones was that the former were more keenly aware of themselves, the market, and their employees than the latter. Furthermore, the more successful presidents readily admitted their weaknesses, uncertainty about their work, the many things they had failed to do. They were more self-critical of their own performance. The less successful presidents more often regarded themselves as successful by contrasting their position with others who had not done as well as they. Thus they were less able to assess what they were doing and their results.

I have observed that successful presidents have patterns of behavior similar to those reported by Professor Floyd Mann, of the University of Michigan, from his research on effective supervision.

For example, the successful executive is not very satisfied with what his or her predecessor has done, no matter how good it was. If an entrepreneur started his own company (rarely have women built large organizations), usually he was dissatisfied with the way his former superiors operated the old one. The enterpreneur knows his company can be managed better and he, with a determination that approaches passion, wants to do it. He is not much worried about being in a rut; he's too busy learning new things and working with his people. He thinks his people are more competent and capable than those in competitor companies and are doing better work.

Psychologically speaking, discontent with the past and with oneself, combined with respect for one's work group, with an element of self-doubt, and with sufficient self-confidence, is indicative of a strong ego ideal—a more effective self-image toward which to strive—without pervasive guilt feelings. This is a healthy kind of discontent. Its theme is, "I am good but I want to be better." That's the advantage of having a star. One's aggressive impulses are channeled into creative pursuit of goals.

Such executives, because they are not unduly rivalrous with their subordinates, can teach, guide, and psychologically support younger people, and take pride in their increasing effectiveness. Later we shall see how important these activities are to an executive.

By contrast, the executive who is more worried about his or her own technical competence than about his people is usually less satisfied with what he is doing, his preparation for doing it, where he is going, and what he is earning. Conversely, he or she is more satisfied with what his predecessors have done and is preoccupied with his own forward movement at the expense of concern with that of the organization and subordinates. A corollary is that such an executive is more likely to have or be worried about many health problems.

Such a style of operation suggests that its possessor is highly self-centered and has considerable unconscious hostility toward authority figures. The underlying tone of his or her attitude is one of deprivation. He acts as if nothing that he has now is any good, and further, as if someone else hadn't given him the resources he should have to do the job. At the same time such a person denies his or her self-hostility by maintaining positive conscious feelings toward the very persons who presumably created the unsatisfying conditions of work: predecessors, superior, chairman, the board. In an executive who has already achieved far beyond his or her fellows, chronic worry about failure to get ahead and about being in a rut indicates underlying dissatisfaction with oneself, reflecting an unduly punitive conscience. The underlying repressed anger takes its toll in generalized disappointment with oneself and others. The fact that the hostility must be overcontrolled and denied means that effort must be devoted to that control and denial, which in turn means that the person is continually in a tense rage. Such a psychological experience frequently underlies "heart symptoms" and actual coronaries. The tense rage makes it difficult for such people to establish and maintain supportive relationships with others, although frequently they are driven to achieve technical excellence in a usually fruitless effort to perform their way out of their discomfort.

Executives who give disproportionate attention to their

relationships with their colleagues and subordinates, as contrasted with the technical dimensions of their jobs, worry more often about not being liked. In Professor Mann's study supervisors who had such a behavior pattern complained more frequently about stiffness and arthritis than did other supervisors.

Psychologically, these people would be understood to be the more dependent, frightened ones, who probably try too hard to please their subordinates. Being overdependent on others, particularly for approval, such executives cannot discharge their aggressive feelings toward others, even when that is both necessary and appropriate, as in taking a stand or giving orders. Instead, they must hold on to such feelings tightly. A lifetime of such holding on becomes the psychological basis for stiffness and arthritis. It is also the basis for the inability to demand high quality performance. Such an executive's relative lack of concern for getting the job done only increases the superego or conscience pressures—the guilt feelings—of subordinates, demoralizing them. They feel guilty for not doing as good a job as they know they can and should. They then become angry with themselves, their boss, and the company.

Professor Mann concludes that there are three kinds of leadership skills: To co-ordinate the activities of one organizational group with another, the leader must have *administrative competence*. To accomplish other assigned tasks, including the performance of technical operations, the leader must have *technical competence*. To integrate organizational objectives with individual member needs, the leader must have *human relations competence*. As I have elaborated above, these various competences are closely related to how an executive manages his or her own aggressive feelings.

These findings are supported by the results of a study by social psychologists Edgar H. Schein and Douglas T. Hall, of MIT. They asked two classes of students in the Sloan School of Management to rate faculty members from whom they learned "a lot" or "very little" by using thirty-six pairs of contrasting adjectives. The good teachers were rated high on three dimensions: *competence, personal potency,* and *supportiveness.* When there were peaks on one or another dimension, teachers whose high point was *competence* (clear thinking, unconventional, humorous, original, scientific) were most often found in the good set.

Teachers whose high point was *potency* (active, ambitious, aggressive, confident, enthusiastic, sophisticated, deep) were categorized equally often as good or poor. Teachers whose high point was *supportiveness* were more often found in the poor set.

As in the Floyd Mann study, the men described as competent invest their energies in becoming more effective in their work. Those who are described as being personally potent, or whom Mann called technically competent, invest their energies in themselves. Those who are described as supportive inhibited their aggressions, bending over backward to win the affection of the students and earning their disdain instead.

Schein and Hall report from their survey of the literature that these three dimensions of skill occur repetitively in research studies on leadership under many different names. They conclude that these dimensions are the key style components of any authority role. Thus the more successful leader devotes equal energy to task effectiveness, personal effectiveness, and people. He or she combines them in everyday work as special executive power. The successful executive uses that power in a uniquely identifiable executive way in pursuit of his or her star. He manages the *organization*.

I make a special point of this because in my judgment too many executives manage the P&L sheet, which they view as a measure of their personal potency. And those who abhor the singular P&L focus tend to go to the opposite extreme on the thesis that everything will work out all right if they only take care of their people. These two foci miss the main point, that the task is to build the *organization* for survival, which means to build competence and flexibility into the company. That, to me, is what leadership means.

Sir Geoffrey Vickers distinguishes between administration and management. Administration, he said, is merely making established relationships work better. Management, by contrast, is changing the nature of the relationships within the organization. The successful president does the latter. He or she is more concerned with making the organization effective than pleasant. This thesis is confirmed by studies at the Institute for Social Research at the University of Michigan. Professor Rensis Likert, who headed that group, summarized the many studies on leadership which they have done by saying that the higher performing managers in all kinds of organizations build a social system in which there is a greater capacity to co-ordinate the members toward accomplishing the goals of the organization. Such managers usually involve their subordinates in setting standards, and allow personal psychological motivating forces to reinforce economic motivation. An individual's desire for a sense of personal worth and importance, as repeatedly demonstrated in research, is a fundamental psychological force. In terms of our present discussion, this is what we mean by meeting the demands of the ego ideal.

So the successful executive is going somewhere and taking his or her people along. He or she turns self-doubt to advantage. His people go with him because they identify with his goals and know-how, and because he supports them in their efforts. These factors alone, however, are not enough. The leader exerts his or her power on the organization. That is, he also organizes a working arrangement which makes it possible for their efforts to be effective. It is this latter activity which separates the professionals from the amateurs managerially.

Every successful executive I know invites engagement with himself.

In fact, taking one's people with one requires engagement. However, some executives are afraid to invite engagement or participation in managerial decisions. They fear that they will lose control of their organizations, or that productivity and profitability will be sacrificed to committee meetings. They don't trust their people, and even if they did, they don't know how to go about instituting the ideas which seem so simple in the textbooks and lectures. Furthermore, many presidents attained their positions because they are hard-nosed, hard-driving, directive men. In terms of our earlier discussion, their motivation is to control others. Conversely, they cannot let themselves be dependent upon others. Their strong point is personal potency; they cannot operate in any way other than by the sheer force of their personalities or the power of their positions. With that kind of personal motivation, and the attitudes which result from it, they interpret participation to mean chaos—letting everyone do what he pleases however he wants to do it.

But, ever since the end of World War II, there has been

a growing trend toward greater participation in managerial decisions by the people who are affected by those decisions. Participative management is now a commonplace theme in both business schools and company management development programs.

Furthermore, participation, or engagement with the leader in some form, is necessary for the regeneration of organizational leadership and survival. That's why the research studies show that the most successful executives are motivated to seek task effectiveness more than power over or control of others. As we have also seen from the studies referred to earlier, participation in decisions about the work and the organization—decisions which affect the people who are doing the work—does not mean extreme permissiveness. The executives who needed too much to be liked and therefore did not provide enough direction simply demoralized their people.

Thus, like it or not, those who would be successful executives must learn how to engage their people. Otherwise they will never be able to manage their organization. This means they must understand what engagement or participation means.

The concept of participation in decisions which affect them recognizes three fundamentals about human beings. It recognizes that those who are doing a given job are more likely to know more about the details and experiences of that job than someone who is not doing it. This is often true even when the boss at one time did that very job, although most executives are reluctant to accept that fact.

Participative management operates also on the assumption that one is motivated most and best by what one feels inside oneself, by self-motivation, rather than by external incentives which seek to pull or squeeze out of one what he or she is capable of giving.

The notion of participation recognizes that most people have strong consciences which demand of them that they do a responsible piece of work. It recognizes also that, given an opportunity to take pride in something which they have done and which represents them, people are likely to do so.

Many people quarrel about the last issue, complaining that employees no longer care about pride, detail, or workmanship. Few look at the environmental factors which often make it impossible to do so. A person cannot pay much attention to quality if he or she is paid for quantity. One is hardly likely to be much concerned about whether the work is done well if one's only relationship to it is so much per hour and there are no other gratifications. One cannot value the company's product if one feels manipulated or exploited in work situations. And one is likely to feel that way if one is implicitly treated like a grown-up infant who must be directed in every aspect of the job. Or, if an executive, as if one had to be whipped like a race horse into a competitive frenzy. The anger which mounts from such feelings takes its toll in sabotage of the product, of the work organization, and of the person himself as in sickness, accidents, and job failure.

Why? In a society which values independence, any person who does merely what someone else tells him or her to do or operates in robot fashion must inevitably build up considerable anger toward himself and those who make him or her work that way. In an organizational society any person who is judged by the number of pieces he or she produces, rather than for his or her contribution to the operation of the organization which the boss speaks about as being "one big family," tends to see himself or herself as a piece of a person. If management is going to talk about "joining" an organization, becoming a "member" of it, then it must recognize the assumption behind joining and membership: voting partnership.

This assumption is violated the very moment one sees how to help the organization function more effectively but has no way to make oneself heard. Any person who sees a hundred ways of doing a job better, but must limit himself or herself to the rigidly defined way somebody else has thought up, can only fume in contemptuous hostility for what is seen as the stupidity of the organization. It is primarily with these feelings of degradation, inadequacy, resentment, contempt, and hostility that both employees and executives must struggle.

When a manager at any level, let alone an executive, takes the time to sit down with those who are reporting to him or her to ask them how they feel about their work and how it is going, how they feel about what he or she is doing to facilitate their work, or even what he or she is doing that may hinder it, how the work might be improved, what the whole picture looks like, and what is necessary to meet the demands on the organization, then people begin to feel respected as human beings. This means that the boss must state the goals and resources, that he or she must take suggestions and ideas seriously, consider them honestly, allow open discussion of them, and, if additional information is necessary or if decisions have to be referred for the consideration of others, that there be prompt, accurate, and honest feedback about them.

Participative management is not a matter of throwing something to the group to chew on as a dog might worry a bone. It does not mean assuming that meetings and discussions as such will solve problems. The leader, too, must contribute—information, a perspective, a point of view, a statement of the realities the organization faces, value judgments. Otherwise there is no engagement.

Those who are participating in the decision making can do so only to the extent to which they have knowledge. To ask them to contribute where they do not have knowledge or competence is only to bait them. However, attributing lack of knowledge to employees is often used as an excuse. Executives frequently forget that subordinates have much more knowledge and competence than they are credited with. Executives forget, too, that subordinates will have feelings about whatever will affect them, and that such feelings frequently are data that no one else has. Those feelings constitute important knowledge for they are too often the invisible shoals on which change flounders. They belong on the table for discussion and consideration.

People should know the boundaries within which their participation in decision making can take place: the funds available, the market conditions, the relationship of their decisions to deliberations undertaken elsewhere. They should know also what the executive cannot share, and how the limits of their engagement vary from one problem to another. Not everyone can be in on everything. No one but the executive can make some decisions.

Participation means further that, in whatever ways it is possible to do so, the results of increased effectiveness become a return to be shared with those who have helped make it possible—the participants themselves. There should be a direct relationship between the collective responsibility assumed by organization members and the returns yielded by exercising that responsibility. That is not only the fundamental thesis of a free enterprise economic system; it is also a necessary condition for stimulating internal motivation and establishing common cause among organization members. They follow the star together.

Engagement in this fashion fosters the development of cohesive work groups, of people who need each other to accomplish their mutual tasks. People who need each other help each other. They support each other both at work and in times of crisis. As the work of Eric Trist and his colleagues in Great Britain has shown, people who are intimately familiar with the task form more efficient work groups than management itself could shape. Such mutual support increases the maturity of the subordinates and decreases their dependence on the leader. They learn to manage themselves.

The executive who undertakes participative management efforts for the first time must expect a period of testing. When people have been operating in one style of relationships and that is then altered, they will be reluctant to believe the new style until they have found it to be more than a gimmick. The testing may take many forms. They may suggest all kinds of irrational ideas. They may fail to respond to the opportunities opened to them. They may be erratic or listless in their participation, or quarrel with each other.

It is at this point that many executives give up. They had expected placid co-operation and enthusiastic approval for their progressive ways. What they got instead was turbulence. They are then able to say, "I told you so." By this they mean that they knew all along that the subordinates were irresponsible or didn't care or couldn't possibly make decisions that previously had been made by higher management alone.

It is at this point also that many employees become impatient and angry with themselves for testing the boss, their colleagues, and themselves, and for being otherwise hostile to each other. These bristling experiences make them wonder about their own capacities and to suspect that something lies behind management's efforts. Is this another form of manipulation? Is someone trying to kick them? Is the boss trying to get them to stick their necks out so they will then be vulnerable? Just what does it mean?

However, if the boss can be patient, keep the guidelines clear, and provide continuous feedback on performance as well as the results, then the aggressive energies which previously had gone into sabotage, anger, and resentment can be funneled into a more creative contribution toward the organization's tasks.

Participative management, or engagement, is not a panacea. For heavily dependent people it may even be frightening. It is a mode of operation which recognizes the inherent capabilities of people and their willingness to use those capacities in a common, mutually profitable purpose. The emphasis is on the *mutually* profitable purpose. And profitability means more than money—for what does it avail a person to buy bread with his or her pride?

Engagement has important advantages for the executive. The engagement process is like slipping a car into gear; it effects a connection between the source of energy and the driveshaft which makes the wheels turn. If the clutch is not fully engaged, power is wasted.

Engagement also has noneconomic advantages. In the engagement process the executive maintains a focus on managing the organization by exercising simultaneously the three competences discussed earlier. Furthermore, he or she also combats feelings of isolation. He talks with people about mutual concerns, reducing the insulation of the office suite and executive perquisites. He is required to come into contact with people of varied skills, interests, and perspectives. Continuous confrontation with a wider range of phenomena forces him to recognize the need for varied inputs, for breaking narrow modes of thinking with national, even international, perspectives. The need for survival compels him to focus increasingly on the long run. Not needing to be so tough to ward off subordinates, he communicates more easily with the more democratically minded youngsters who are entering management ranks today. He is more readily available to accept the legitimate dependency needs of his subordinates, to enable them to look to the boss for guidance.

Under such circumstances he is also more easily able to accept his need to depend on others, to form closer ties, and to more readily accept his own anger and disappointment. When one feels safe among others, one need not strive so hard to hide one's feelings from oneself and them. Thus one lessens one's loneliness. One also reaps greater satisfaction from teaching and from rearing others to be managers. With such a network of relationships and shared responsibility, the executive has greater protection against manipulation by one or another person whom he or she feels to be a powerful rival, or to whom he or she has a sense of paternalistic obligation. And any executive who has been in an organization for even a brief period of time finds himself caught up in such issues: the person who was a contender for his post; the aging, loyal deputy who has long since been outgrown by the job but who cannot be discharged.

Engagement therefore reduces what Professor Dale Yoder has called the threat of "automation, quantification and humanization." The essence of the executive's engagement lies in the recognition of the potential of his or her subordinates, of their need for a style of leadership which brings that potential to fruition, and of the executive's need for both their stimulation and protection.

Every successful executive I know cares about people and builds a bond of trust.

According to a study by Opinion Research Corporation, employees want to communicate about things closely related to the job itself and to their own future. This desire to get through to top management exists at all levels. Many feel that it is difficult to get the ear of higher management. Surprisingly, this feeling is stronger among white collar and professional employees than among hourly ones, perhaps because they believe they have a greater right to be heard and that they know more that higher management should hear. Such feelings contribute to poor attitudes toward management, particularly to the conviction that management does not care about people.

In the face of that kind of conviction, all communications efforts from the top down must fail. People will not trust what information they get from above, no matter how beautifully printed or frequently distributed. Conversely, when asked for their ideas, they will be reluctant to speak. Lack of trust exacerbates the conviction that expressing their true feelings could be dangerous—and, furthermore, what's the point if they believe management is not really interested in their problems?

Bonds of trust are the sinews that tie people together and hitch them to the distant star. Those bonds become even more important for organizational survival in an era of changing expectations, career mobility, and loyalty based on respect for the leader's expertise rather than on his or her power, prestige, or age.

But the meaning of caring about people has been widely misunderstood. As we have already seen, bending over backward to be nice to people is not the same as genuinely caring about them. They neither like nor respect that kind of behavior. The reason is that bending over backward and paternalism imply making the other person dependent and placing him or her under obligation. In one's own mind's eye, and in conflict with one's ego ideal, one sees oneself being treated like a child, or at least as other than an equal. A person may temporarily enjoy the benefits of being dependent, but soon dislikes himself or herself for the role he must assume to get the rewards. What's worse, he begins to hate the person who puts him in that position. He understands full well that he is being exploited to alleviate the conscience of the "big daddy" or to meet the goals of the organization. That is why paternalism failed as a device for motivation. In one's anger one must ultimately bite the hand that feeds. More than a few paternalistic managements have experienced this phenomenon when their employees have turned to unionization.

How then does one build trust and demonstrate that one cares? There is only one way: by creating the conditions under which each subordinate can become more competent, more capable, and more mature. No executive is satisfied with himself or herself as a parent unless his or her child becomes capable of standing on his own adult feet, and even of exceeding the achievements of the parent. No executive should be satisfied unless his or her subordinates become increasingly capable of standing on their own occupational feet, of relating to him or her as adult to adult, out of respect instead of fear.

The executive who distributes his or her energies equally to task effectiveness, personal effectiveness, and people is, as the research demonstrates, already building trust by enhancing organizational competence as well as his own and that of subordinates. In this engagement with people, the executive joins and supports them in mastering the problems they confront together in the organization. They in turn support and protect the executive. Such integrative relationships are as important for an organization as they are for a family. But good relationships are not enough in a family; children must go to school to learn skills. They aren't enough in an organization either. If the organization is to survive, it must increase the skill competence of its members to meet the ever more complex demands of an increasingly scientific and sophisticated society.

That means that the executive must be concerned with the step-by-step growth of people. One cannot turn them loose to drown if they sink or to be rewarded if they succeed, because too many will thrash and too few will survive. Those who succeed will have demonstrated only that *they*, as individuals, were capable of surviving. That may not require the same talents as building an organization for survival; indeed, it is a rare successful individual *entrepreneur* who can create the conditions for the organization's survival.

The executive should be certain that there are plans for the development of people, that he or she supports immediate subordinates in such a way that they in turn can psychologically support theirs. Development means formal training on the one hand, and appropriately challenging tasks on the other. Support means definition of responsibility in keeping with what a person can do, limiting a person's activity to what he or she is capable of mastering at any given point, and protecting him or her from overwhelming defeat by forces beyond the person's control, like market fluctuations and rivalrous superiors. Because of the shibboleth of freedom, it has become unfashionable to think of appropriate controls and supports, of step-by-step growth. Yet no one can grow otherwise.

As we have already seen, the most significant differences between authoritarianism, paternalism, and that kind of leadership which uses authority and power as devices for enhancing the capacities of people lie in how the leader manages aggressive energies. Every executive who would measure success in terms of the endurance of his or her organization must understand those differences so he can manage, rather than be managed by, his drives. For it is only when people see their leader as most interested in and helpful toward their maturity, only when he or she holds out responsibility and helps them to meet it, that they know they are respected. That respect enhances their self-respect and thereby their identification with both the leader and the organization. There is one condition: that the executive's concern be understood to be based on cold, hard psychoeconomic sense. This means that one cares not out of guilt, nor sentimentality, nor because it is fashionable, but because it is best for oneself, for the subordinate, and the organization.

If business management is to be a profession, then it must be characterized by the hallmark of any profession: dedication to the public good. Said Vannevar Bush, "The central theme of any true profession is ministry to the people. . . . If a man's life is devoted to ministry to people in the best sense, and if his reward is the respect of his peers, then he is a professional man." The executive in an organization ministers by welding people into organizations which serve them and society. The successful executive is a builder of people who are bigger than they know and serve better than they dreamed.

13

SUPERVISING BRIGHT
YOUNG PEOPLE

IN ALL KINDS of organizations, colleges and monasteries as well as businesses, bright young people puzzle, anger, irritate, and frustrate their superiors. Why?

> Just a year out of graduate school, a twenty-five-year-old Kansan manages a three-million-acre Nevada ranching operation. He's the prototype of the hottest commodity in big business—the project manager, firmly grounded in modern management techniques with a "nothing's impossible" philosophy of life.
>
> Twenty of the nation's top corporations tried to hire him from his business school . . . But he didn't want the 9-to-5 work they had to offer.
>
> "I didn't care about the salary," he says. "I don't want to stand still and be stereotyped along with a million others. I wanted to get as close to the pulse of the business world as I could." He wanted a chance to prove himself. He got it in ranching.

So goes a newspaper report on one young business graduate. This man's judgment about what he would find in a corporation may be inaccurate; nevertheless, he chose ranching on the basis of that judgment. People like this—intelligent, able, ambitious—who have elected not to enter corporations dismay contemporary business leaders. Enough of them have opted out of potential executive careers that businesses have started to do something about that loss. But if their recruiting effort is successful, it poses an even more difficult problem for executives: What do you do with them once you get them in the company?

That question will continue to be a pressing one for years to come. Answers to it must evolve from an examination of what it is the executive must deal with. Who are the reluctant ones? Why are they reluctant? Why bother with them at all if they are reluctant?

● *The reluctant ones are the bright young people.*

Responding to a Lou Harris poll, only 12 percent of eight hundred college seniors named business as the career they would choose if they had free choice; 31 percent said they were "seriously considering" business as a vocation. Business ranked fourth as a career choice among one group of Stanford freshmen. When a previous group of freshmen became seniors, 18 percent of them chose business although less than 5 percent had said as freshmen that they would do so. But the rub is that those who chose business careers had lower grades than other Stanford students and they were more conformist in their political and economic conceptions.

Furthermore, according to Professor Donald A. Coombs of Stanford, students headed for corporate careers consider creativity and originality of less importance than do those interested in other fields of graduate study. Calculated risks, financial rewards, leadership, and community respect rank high among the career values of undergraduates who want to become business executives.

At Harvard, too, the lower a man's academic standing the more likely he is to choose a business career. The farther away one gets from the highest-level academic institutions, where proportionately larger numbers of the brightest students are most likely to be found, to colleges of lesser intellectual repute, the higher the interest in a business career. When the Consumer Research Center asked 2,736 male junior, senior, and graduate students how likely they were to consider a career in industry, 28 percent said they would be extremely likely to do so and another 30 percent said they would be fairly likely to do so.

● *The brighter they are, the less they are attracted to business.*

This happens for many reasons. No one asks precocious children what business they will enter. Parents and friends are quick to steer them into scientific and academic challenge. Besides, there are few opportunities, short of delivering newspapers, for children to develop business skills. Much is said about organization men, pyramid climbing, conformity, and the grinding competition in which executives are expendable. Better, then, in the eyes of many, to take advantage of one's skill and talent to be free of such struggle. The young rancher of the newspaper report did just that.

Such reasons by themselves have not been enough in the past to deter significant numbers. A survey by the Council on Financial Aid to Education disclosed that among 471,000 alumni from 83 colleges and universities, 41 percent were in business. A later study of 2,000 graduates by the Yale Development Board showed that 10 years after graduation 53 percent of one class were in business and industry. These statistics appear to be relatively stable. Perhaps those reasons wouldn't be sufficient now if other conditions remained unchanged. But despite recessions and depressions, the brighter students continue to be in demand.

Psychologist Daniel Yankelovich differentiates three groups of students: (1) those who want what society and business have to give and are optimistic about getting it: these agree with their parents' values and emulate the older generation; (2) those who want the same things but do not have the means for getting them: these are the impoverished; (3) those who already have what society and business have to give, but who question the goals of society and business. The last, he contends, are the most affluent and best educated ones, those who will shape the future.

Brighter students increasingly are shifting their interests from the sciences to the humanities. This means that more of them become concerned about understanding the world. Furthermore, as a study by psychologist Richard Flack of the University of Chicago shows, the brighter ones who question contemporary society most vigorously share certain common background characteristics. They come from permissive middle-class homes. They have status and material advantages. They need neither to continue social climbing nor to fear economic deprivation. The usual business incentives which attract students of lesser intelligence—status and money—have little import for them. Furthermore, permissive upbringing, with its emphasis on equality and democratic values, is not conducive to their accepting the authority of hierarchical power. They have little use for status distinctions, little interest in competing for competition's sake, and even less willingness to let someone else control their behavior. Instead, they are more likely to be sensitive to arbitrary use of authority, to question people who don't examine what they believe and why they believe it, and to regard with cynicism the gap between what an organization says it stands for and what it actually does.

From a wide range of other studies and observations, we can infer that these young people are strongly conscience-driven. Their motto might well come from Shakespeare: "To thine own self be true." Often they are dedicated. They demand much of themselves and their society. They want to be identified with social purpose, to make the world better, to solve pressing issues like war and poverty. Large numbers of them were once found in the Peace Corps and as Vista volunteers. A few years ago they were in the forefront of the civil rights movement. They seek rewarding family life, are less willing to sacrifice family relationships and personal identity to careers and organizations. They are committed to competence; they prize expertise as contrasted with seniority. At the same time, they are reluctant to make long-term commitments for they are aware of the rapidity of change.

In short, most of these bright young people do not fit the corporate mold, they don't come with the kind of motivation which business ordinarily wants, they don't value the kinds of rewards business has to offer. As Professor Robert M. Fulmer, of Florida State University, points out, "In business the rewards come at the top of the hierarchy, late in one's career; they aren't going to wait. They don't have to." Dean John S. Fielden, of the Boston University College of Business Administration, notes that even their orientation to behavior is different from that characteristic of executives. The businessman, he says, is more concrete, more action-oriented; the intellectual is more abstract and analytical. There isn't much point in trying to attract the brightest ones, whose values and behavior orientation are less functional in business, he contends.

• *Yet, the bright ones are increasingly necessary to business.*

Survival depends on innovation and flexibility of adaptation. Both are hard to come by in large organizations. They are particularly difficult to achieve with people who become stereotyped in their jobs and views. Some companies try to cope with this problem by buying up small firms which have originated novel products or methods. Others put massive resources behind an innovation whose market worthiness has been demonstrated by someone else.

Both of these avenues have severe limitations. As more people are massed in larger organizations, there are fewer new firms to be picked up and fewer arenas for testing ideas. This means, then, that genuine and continuous innovation must come from within the organization.

Characteristically, innovation comes from strangers, people who can look at a problem, product, or process from an unusual point of view. Michael Faraday, who made important contributions to the theory of electricity, was a bookbinder. August Foppl, a civil engineer, wrote *An Introduction to Maxwell's Theory of Electricity* to make the theory clear to engineers. This was so different from the usual physics textbooks of the time that it stimulated the interest of Albert Einstein. Einstein himself subsequently was a patent examiner, outside the pale of then contemporary physics, when he made his major contribution. There are many similar examples.

Furthermore, businesses have expanded into education, slum rejuvenation, poverty programs, and even the creation of whole new communities. These activities call for a wide range of intellectual skills. Businesses increasingly have become international, thus requiring competence in foreign languages, understanding of culture, history, geography, social structure—those subjects called the liberal arts and the humanities. Businesses must plan farther and farther into the future. The farther one must plan into the future, the more one must be aware of the lessons of the past, of trends and cycles, of the operation of historical, economic, and social forces.

As Roger Blough, former chairman of U.S. Steel, has argued, business needs the intellectual. Various companies have taken steps to demonstrate the need and the possibilities. Robert W. Galvin, then chairman of Motorola, Inc., undertook a series of public correspondences with six outstanding students. The exchanges of letters were published as ads in twenty-nine college newspapers. Joseph M. Bertotti, manager of educational relations for General Electric, did a follow-up study of those who were employed in GE managerial ranks in 1956. The conformists had not moved; the rebels had progressed, he pointed out to the doubting intellectuals. Recruiting efforts will inevitably be stepped up as more companies begin to act in their enlightened self-interest.

More intensified recruiting efforts alone will not attract and keep the young intellectual in the business, nor will public relations image-making efforts, economic education, or persuasion. In fact, those very efforts, which business is so frequently advised to make, are so patently transparent that they drive away the bright people business is trying to attract. The same is true of gimmicky efforts. For example, the Harvard University Graduate School of Business Alumni Association once undertook a project of assigning fifty students to businesses for a summer training program. Only half a dozen returned to their campuses with favorable attitudes about working for companies. Reported the *Wall Street Journal*, "A discouragingly small number is being impressed and many of those lack the blue chip records the recruiters would like for executives-to-be. As far as they are concerned, business cares too little about building a better world, too much for profits; takes too little responsibility for its recruits; imposes a stifling conformity. Too many see business activity as glorified clerical work while they have a hyper-concern for social issues." Furthermore, different studies indicate that from a third to a half of the promising young people change jobs at least once in their first five career years.

There are a number of considerations which may help the executive to counteract these failures. Among them are these:

1. *Reconsider your own attitudes.*

Traditionally companies have hired people for jobs, have assumed that they would want to work their way up and would work hard to achieve their goals. This stance, as we have already seen, has lost much of its validity. Failure to recognize this fact will lead you to resent the younger person for being overpaid, expecting management responsibility before being ready, and being averse to hard work.

As Peter Drucker has pointed out, "You no longer hire a man (or woman) for a job. You hire him for an organization. The job is not permanent but you hope the man is." Much of the effort toward working one's way up is replaced by formal specific training. The young "Whiz Kids" of the Pentagon were able to start close to the top and to do what no amount of military experience and seniority would enable any general at that time to do. Hard work in the classical sense simply is no match for expertise. They know it; do you? This doesn't mean that young people should not and will not work hard. They will—by using their heads instead of their hours.

The matter of pay is a continuously troublesome one. Starting salaries rise year by year. Each rise tends to increase the resentment of older executives who can "remember when" and whose own income increases proportionately less. As a matter of fact, this situation is really not much different from what it has always been. Each generation earns far more than the preceding generation. The only difference is that the pace is now more accelerated.

2. *Beware of your own rivalry.*

Bright, competent younger people stimulate feelings of rivalry, competition, and self-doubt no matter how much one needs and wants them. Most executives try to deny their feelings of rivalry with their subordinates, as if there were something bad about having and admitting such feelings. There is not. They are universal. The problem occurs when they are denied, when one tries to keep oneself ignorant of how one feels. Then, unwittingly, the executive will act on the basis of those feelings and destroy the supervisor-supervisee relationship. If one can accept one's own feelings as legitimate, one can then take them into account and navigate around them.

Despite all of the emphasis on youth, innovation, education, and all of the other things which make older people feel less adequate, age and experience are still important. Education is no substitute for maturity. Facts, skills, even insights, are not wisdom. No person can be a competent executive without good judgment; judgment is wisdom translated into action. The younger person needs you, the organization needs you, for just such qualities, which you, in turn, will underestimate. Like the bright young person, you, too, are your worst critic. Take that into consideration.

3. *Don't press the future on them too hard.*

If it is difficult for younger people today to make long-term commitments because change makes that seemingly less possible, then don't try to attach the bright young people to the distant future in the company. After all, you can't really know what is coming either. Instead, talk over career plans for the next step or two, and review them frequently. Their trust in you and in the possibilities of the next steps will be the critical elements which bind them to the organization.

4. *Understand your basic task to be a grafting process.*

Bringing a stranger into an organization is like grafting a new organ into a living person. The organism will reject the foreign body unless specific efforts are made to counteract the rejection process and additional efforts to support the adaptation of the new organ. This can be done through a combination of methods.

Orientation. Those most wanted young people are nevertheless green and inexperienced. Like all new people, despite their knowledge, they are likely to be anxious and frightened until they can demonstrate their competence.

They usually will have been employed by company recruiters. That in itself is a disadvantage. Most recruiters are far removed from top management. They do not know with any firsthand sophistication what top management plans, what it thinks, and what the possibilities really are. As a result, they are limited to giving the official statement about what the organization says it is and what its policies are. The company will not come alive for the incoming person as something to which to attach oneself unless you take the time to brief him or her on its politics and problems, personalities and possibilities. An honest, straightforward statement of what this organization is like, with subsequent elaboration in the course of dealing with specific problems, conveys a sense of trust and self-confidence. All organizations have politics and problems. So what? Why try to pretend perfection? That kind of confidence game will lead only to cynicism and the feeling of having been taken. Such disillusionment is a major source of turnover.

According to Richard J. Thain, associate dean of students and director of placement at the University of Chicago, when college graduates take their first jobs, they expect a company that would not only teach them, but also would attempt to find out what they know, what they think, and what they have to contribute. They want a chance to work with compatible and inspiring people in a company which has respect for youth and inexperience, and the insights which come with them, as well as experience. Orientation should address itself to these issues, too.

Protection. You must give careful attention to the new

people's colleagues and other superiors who are likely to be the agents of rejection. You must defend them against attack until they are sufficiently integrated to defend themselves. Require new ideas to be examined rather than let them be shot down. You must keep the work group focused on their joint task. What is it that they are to do together and how can this new person help them? How will his or her additional skills and talents serve them? What problems can he or she help solve? If you keep constantly before the group the problems they have to solve and if the new person can be seen as an asset toward their solution, he or she is more likely to be accepted.

New people, in a setting foreign to them, may be reluctant to introduce ideas and conceptions which they know will be strange to their colleagues and therefore likely to be rejected. The bravest of people fear being laughed at. The boss therefore figuratively has to hold their hands, to encourage them to translate their ideas into words no matter how distant they may seem from the issues at hand. This kind of support is an old story to editors and to owners of art galleries. Editors and gallery owners spend much of their time talking with authors and artists, encouraging them, hearing their fantasies, carrying them through periods of depression and lack of productivity. They know it to be necessary to writers and artists.

In doing likewise, the superior must withhold judgment until ideas can be carefully examined. Too early condemnation of an idea not only causes the idea to be withdrawn but, worse, causes others to be suppressed before they are spoken. Let the ideas come through first in meetings with you before being exposed to others. They may not be ready for fulfillment, but they will never be ready if they are not permitted to flower.

Like anybody else, new people cannot do their best if they are made to feel defensive. They then spend too much of their time guarding their flanks, attacking others, arguing points, and trying to prove themselves by attaining status. On the other hand, if you are defensive, then you will block them more than encourage and support them. Sharp criticism from you will only increase the intensity of their internal criticism and inhibit their productivity.

This does not mean that they should be free of judgment and the consequences of error or failure. That kind of permissiveness is impossible and would be of no help if it were possible. Give honest feedback when it is called for. The more clearly you are able to define the nature of the realities that must be dealt with, the more you enable new people to steer an appropriate course with respect to the tasks at hand and the organization.

Another form of protection is to protect young people against themselves. Out of their sense of inadequacy they may be brash, condescending, even hostile. Such behavior should be the subject of supervisory discussion. New people should be aware of how they are making a negative impact on others, and should be helped to examine the possible reasons and alternative, more fruitful, behaviors. They need protection from themselves, too, because they may try too hard to substitute activity for thought. You must require them to take time for thinking, and encourage them to have some privacy to do so. After all, you and they want to capitalize on their intelligence, not their gross muscles. Nothing destroys idea-germinating so much as intrusion and interference, and the impulse to act to appease one's conscience or the expectations of others.

When you support and help people to their creative best, then they see you as a friend and as a partner in their own advancement. Try to be, and to make them, a partner in the organization.

5. *Challenge them.*

To create challenging tasks is the hardest of all supervisory functions for that requires much sensitive thinking about one's own responsibilities as well as the needs of the new people. Yet without challenge, bright people will be lost. Recognizing this, the American Telephone and Telegraph Company, and others as well, have set up programs to accomplish it. Each new managerial candidate is assigned to a specially selected supervisor and given a defined task to accomplish in a limited time. Both they and their supervisors have an immediate opportunity to see what they can do. The supervisor is required to protect them against the tendency to be trapped by the bureaucracy of the organization and to support them as necessary in accomplishing their tasks.

The challenge is important for a number of reasons. Young people want to demonstrate to themselves and the organization what they can do. They must counteract the pressures of strong consciences, which demand of them that they justify themselves. They must also justify the expectations of their professors, their parents, and all of the time and money they have put into their education. They must show themselves that *they* make a difference, that they can have an effect.

Unless there is some kind of challenge, they cannot become immersed in the problems and business of the company. In turn, they cannot contribute to problem solution unless they are immersed. Gutenberg invented the printing press after being deeply preoccupied with the problem of how to print with movable type. Walking through the fields, he observed the peasants pressing wine. The combination of printing and press occurred first because he was immersed in the problem of printing and second because, while immersed in that problem, he came upon a wine press. The two had no fundamental relationship to each other. Only the fact that there was a challenge made the juxtaposition of two unrelated activities conducive to a new solution.

Challenge them to stick their necks out, to think boldly. Teach them to use their power, not to deny it in the interest of getting along and not rocking the boat. "Don't make waves" is an axiom which leads to individual and organizational stagnation. Unfortunately it is a byword in too many companies.

Of course, to be able to do this, the superior must himself be more concerned about getting problems solved than about himself and his own state. He, too, must be willing to stick out his own neck once in a while. Particularly, he must back good ideas and use his power to push them through to fruition.

The success of the whole process of relating a subordinate to an organization hinges on specific supervisory behavior. In essence, in order to supervise new people adequately, the superior must become more like them. He, too, is stimulated to new growth. Thus the process of creating a fertile environment for the stranger inevitably leads to stimulating one's own creative potential.

14

WHAT YOU SHOULD KNOW ABOUT SCIENTISTS

A SPECIAL FORM of the bright young person is the scientist. With increasing pressure in industry for innovation, more scientists are finding their way into the business world as consultants, technical specialists, and researchers. This creates special problems for the executive who must work with or manage scientists and who often has difficulty in his relationships with them. Much of this difficulty stems from at least two major causes: the scientist's public image and the scientist's dual loyalties.

• *The scientist's image.*

Though a scientist is in an occupation highly respected by the public, he or she is also, according to popular image, in a world apart. The public would have him or her nearsighted but farseeing, brilliantly innovative but absent-minded, widely acclaimed but impervious to applause, capable of highly involved abstract thinking but naive and eccentric in everyday reasoning.

Quite unconsciously, the executive often adopts the public image of the scientist and therefore sees him or her as someone strangely mysterious and incomprehensible, in short, a little crazy. Responding to this perception, the executive is certain he cannot possibly understand the scientists nor the scientist understand him. Furthermore, being somewhat frightened at something he cannot understand, he is not certain he wants to try to understand. "Let well enough alone," can quickly become the executive's motto, which in practice means to have as few brief contacts as possible with the scientist.

• *The scientist's dual loyalties.*

A scientist has two obligations: one to his or her employer, and one to scientific colleagues. The latter obligation is no less important than the former. The scientist must therefore always meet two sets of standards: productivity and professional sophistication.

In the course of his own career, the executive has learned that dedication is a major ingredient of managerial ladder climbing. No person moves far in any organization unless he or she identifies wholeheartedly with that company. The executive expects colleagues and subordinates to have the same single-minded dedication. He or she sometimes suspects them of disloyalty when they are not actually disloyal. This is particularly true if the executive sees himself and the company as having to compete with "outsiders" for the scientist's attention, a feeling which becomes intensified when the scientist seems to the executive to be more concerned with the niceties of research than with producing new products on call. Such a feeling also drives a wedge between the executive and the scientist.

If the executive is to work more effectively with scientists he or she must first have a more accurate understanding of scientists and the particular problems they have working in industry. That understanding might well begin with another, closer look at these two causes of difference—the scientist's personality and the frame of reference.

THE SCIENTIST'S PERSONALITY

Generalizing about any group of people is hazardous; generalizing about scientists is no exception. Yet generalizations, used cautiously, can contribute to understanding.

Dr. Bernice T. Eiduson, of Los Angeles' Reiss-Davis Clinic, who studied forty highly creative (male) scientists intensively, points out that scientists are singled out for attention as adults for the same reasons that they were singled out as children: because they seem intellectually gifted. Behind the intellectual gift, she reports, often lies a certain family constellation.

As children the scientists whom she studied had little intimacy with their families. Recognition and approval, first from parents and later by honors, praise, and scholarships, were closely tied to the child's achievement. The child's intellectual abilities made it possible for him to enjoy his own company. He daydreamed, fantasied, worked intellectual problems, read, and followed where his curiosity led him, relatively independent of others. Searching for parent substitutes, he often looked to teachers and other adults who in turn reinforced his intellectual interests. The result of all this was not so much common personality traits among scientists but intensive focus of the scientist's personality on scientific work.

In Dr. Eiduson's study, not only did the scientists have great investment in intellectual things but also they had strong feelings that what they were doing was good and could be done only by them. Their personal life histories led them to be oriented to the new, the different, to the fresh reconception of the old. *Unlike most other people,* who much prefer to accept what they find around them and who therefore are uneasy with people who question the status quo, the scientist built up a tolerance for the anxiety which comes from seeking out the new and unfamiliar. Unafraid of disrupting accepted views and capable of using their own fantasies to try out new ideas, scientists grow up as intellectual rebels. Says Dr. Eiduson, "Once a man takes on a scientific career, he has, in essence, identified himself with a group whose whole rationale is tied up with intellectual rebellion, embodied in the rejection of old knowledge and a courageous search for the new."

Thus the life style of the child becomes the life style of the adult—limited attachments to others, heavy investment in intellectual work and in fellow scientific workers, and creative use of fantasy. Since their work itself arises out of pressing inner needs, other motivations become a poor second stimulus.

"The majority scorn 'impure' motivations such as recognition, exhibitionism, personal aggrandizement, pragmatic reward—unless these are inescapable concomitants of devotion to the search for truth," Dr. Eiduson concludes.

From their study of highly talented graduate students, Professor Eli Ginzberg and his late colleague John Herma, of Columbia University, confirmed Dr. Eiduson's findings on the pressing importance of their work to such people:

"Their search for work satisfaction is more intense than for other people. Not that such people were indifferent to income and status, but they valued other aspects of their work more highly, namely the particular nature of the work and the opportunity for self-expression."

Dr. Anne Roe, formerly a Harvard psychologist, points out that the consequence of being so deeply emotionally involved in his or her work is that the scientist is his own most essential tool. *He* must decide what observations to make, and all his scientific equipment is nothing more than a way of extending his ability to sense and perceive. The equipment neither provides the questions nor the answers. The scientist himself must do that. "Any man who has gone through the emotional process of developing a new idea, of constructing a new hypothesis, in a very real sense it is his baby. It is as much his creation as a painting is the personal creation of the painter. True, in the long run it stands or falls, is accepted or rejected, on its own merits, but its creator has a personal stake in it," Dr. Roe notes.

The scientist's early-developed capacity for fantasy becomes his or her source of creativity. He continues to use a facility that most adults lose as they grow up. In effect, to be creative he must temporarily slip back into childlike ways of thinking, to bring together ideas that ordinarily would not fit together. "What seems to happen," Dr. Roe observes, "in creative efforts in science as well as in every other field, is that the individual enters a state in which logical thinking is submerged and in which thought is prelogical. . . . This stage of the creative process is accompanied by generally confused or vague states of preoccupation of varying degrees of depth; it is well described as 'stewing.' It is this stage which cannot be hurried or controlled. . . . This process requires not only the basic capacity to assimilate experiences but very strong motivation to persist in the effort. Strong motivation is also required if one is to continue with a search which may for a long time be unproductive. Motivation of this kind and strength derives from the needs and structure of the personality."

From these reports, similar to many others, we can infer that scientists are more likely to invest themselves in their work than in other people, that their work itself provides them with both gratification and recognition, and that their work both encourages them and requires of them to think and act independently. To do what they expect of themselves and what society expects of them demands not only that they think differently than others but also that they pursue their own line of thinking with persistent determination.

THE SCIENTIST'S FRAME OF REFERENCE

In the course of graduate training the scientist focuses his or her efforts on learning how to investigate in depth, step by step, building on the work of scientists who have preceded him and hundreds more working concurrently in other settings. He learns how to reason and to investigate methodically so that others, using the same methods, can obtain the same results. His underlying questions are "Why?" and "How do you know?" and his answers must always be based on evidence. As a scientist, his competence lies in how imaginatively he can ask new questions and how thoroughly he can document his answers. This process has a number of implications:

The competence of a scientist, for all practical purposes, can be judged only by other scientists equally knowledgeable in the field. His or her stature and standing *as a scientist* therefore hinge on the judgment of his colleagues in science, not his superiors in management.

Not only must a scientist depend on scientific colleagues for evaluation of his scientific work; his managerial supervisors must also depend on them—unless the latter are themselves competent in his field.

In recent years we have witnessed major criticisms of scientific studies of drug, chemical, and tobacco products. The effects of the thalidomide scare, Rachel Carson's *Silent Spring*, and the cigarette-cancer controversy were not limited to the headlines. These events produced heated debate among scientists, and independent panels of scientists had to be convened to render official judgments, recommend new standards for testing, and weigh the import of the scientific evidence.

There is no alternative but for the scientist *and the executive* to use the profession and its standards as a frame of reference. The executive should therefore welcome the scientist's dual affiliation as being in the company's own long-run interests.

Although the scientist is dependent upon his or her scientific colleagues for evaluating his scientific performance, as an employee of a company he is no less dependent on management for evaluation of his contribution toward organizational goals. He is also dependent on management to make his scientific work in the company possible and for his advancement in the organization. By definition, then, the executive is not an outsider looking in upon the scientific activity in his organization but a participant in the evolution.

THE SCIENTIST'S PRODUCTIVE CLIMATE

The task of the executive is to organize people and processes into increasingly predictable activities. Regularity, control, efficiency are ordinarily his watchwords. But the nature of science is that discovery is unpredictable. Ideas cannot be produced on schedule, and the search for them is anything but regular. The executive, whose task it is to reduce various forms of rebellion, now must facilitate a form of rebellion and encourage those who foment it by creating and maintaining a climate conducive to scientific productivity.

This is the point at which you can begin to apply your understanding of the scientist as a person, and your understanding of the scientist's dual loyalties.

1. *Reject the assumption that the scientist is odd.*

True, the scientist is different in many ways from others, but it is this very difference which makes him or her valuable. And the difference between the behavior of scientists and that of others is not nearly so much as common belief would have it. The executive would have a difficult time picking a scientist out of a crowd.

If, however, you believe that the scientist is odd and radically different, if you expect the scientist to be a problem child, temperamental and erratic, some scientists will live up to that image. They will contrive to be different, whether in dress, appearance, temperamental demands, or in some other fashion.

As Tom Burns and G. M. Stalker point out from their study of scientists in British industry, "Such behavior is sometimes an effort to achieve and maintain a certain status. The cultivation of eccentricities in dress and in leisure pursuits serves the same end. Superficially that end appears to other people involved as the maintenance of a social status superior to that of their 'opposite numbers' in the rest of the concern."

But when you reject the assumption that the scientist is odd, you no longer play into the seemingly irrational behavior of some scientists. You also begin to work toward ending the separation between scientists and others in the organization.

Knowing that most scientists are not likely to be the hail-fellow-well-met kind of people, you will have to initiate personal contacts and facilitate the communication between scientists and nonscientists. You will also begin to assess more realistically how much managerial responsibility a given scientist might assume, rather than rejecting all scientists as unable to take on such responsibilities.

2. *Provide an adequate structure.*

If, for example, the research function is new to the organization, it is likely that there will be some confusion about what the scientist or the research group is to do. And it is also likely that there will be a power struggle to control and contain what to some will seem like a new threat. To cope with this problem, the scientific function should be given equal status with other units of the organization, its head reporting directly to the executive.

Sociologist William Kornhauser, of the University of California at Berkeley, who did a comprehensive study of the role of scientists in industry, concludes that any other reporting system encapsulates the scientist and may well lead to his or her ultimate rejection, for he becomes subordinate to a given unit and subject then to the political struggles in which that unit is involved. As a threat to the way things are presently done, the scientist who is buried in an organizational structure is likely to be suppressed, denied autonomy and facilities to do his work, and not permitted to really be involved in organizational problems.

Having decided to establish the scientific function in an organizational position where it is protected until it can develop enough maturity to hold its own with other units, you can go on to the next step—agreement on goals. Formulating goals for the scientific function will not be easy, for executives typically are not certain what they want from scientists. Some want the scientist to increase the efficiency of present operations. Others want improved products or the development of new processes. Still others want to develop basic research which, though seemingly unrelated to present needs, will ultimately provide the basis for products and processes.

As Professor Kornhauser indicates, these three activities are not compatible with each other in the same research group. Choices will have to be discussed and made. The scientist must know what is expected of him or her, what kind of support he will have in fulfilling these expectations, and what kind of feedback he will have about his work.

Placing the research laboratory on equal footing with other organizational units and establishing agreed-upon goals in itself creates the conditions for a dialogue between scientists and nonscientists. However, given the personality of scientists and their identification with their work and its values, the dialogue may produce conflict. To expect some conflicts is not the same as to be frightened of them because it is out of the examination of differences that the executive and his or her organization hope to profit.

Kornhauser's report indicates that the conflicts between scientists and executives usually turn on differences in values. The scientist values knowledge; the executive profit. The scientist values highly the quality of research; the executive's thinking is usually oriented to lowest possible costs. The scientist is focused on the long term, the executive more frequently on short-term results. These issues will need to be talked out. Only as they are can the scientist invest himself or herself in an organization.

3. *Set up a compensation system which fits the scientist's values.*

Although the scientist is basically interested in the development of knowledge, increasingly he or she has also become a professional. More and more scientists are consultants; many have even established independent laboratories and research firms.

When 82 of the most productive scientists in a 1,200-man laboratory were asked what attracted them to that organization, they replied their interest in the work done there and the technical freedom permitted. Douglas Williams, a management consultant, surveyed scientists to determine the criteria they used for evaluating an organization as a potential employer. He got much the same results. Williams' respondents also valued association with and stimulation from high-caliber colleagues and a creative intellectual atmosphere, technically trained management who did not tell them *how* to do their work, freedom to choose the problem which interested them without too much management control.

Of course, there are qualifications. Mark Abrahamson, a sociologist at Illinois Institute of Technology, reports from his study of 181 scientists in five laboratories, that while the most difficult adjustments for the scientist in industry come from unfulfilled demands for autonomy, this conflict is most acute in the first three years of a scientist's career in industry. The initial three years is therefore one of testing each other—scientist and manager. The conflict diminishes with time. As scientist and executive come to trust and depend on each other, the demands for autonomy decrease and management more willingly grants autonomy. In time this trust, in turn, also makes the scientist less dependent on his or her professional group, for there is now another source of regard which is valued.

Not all laboratories in industry can allow for ideal freedom for the scientist nor for the untrammeled pursuit of basic science. Many have to limit themselves to research leading to marketable products and services. This necessarily limits autonomy. Some companies deal with this problem by inviting scientists to suggest research projects subject to management's approval. Some allow a small amount of free time for research of the scientist's own choosing. Some provide more free choice for senior scientists and those engaged in basic research. Some, like Du Pont, give complete freedom to scientists who have demonstrated their competence to experiment with anything they wish.

Many companies restrict scientific publications in order to maintain the competitive edge for which they invested in research. Yet in order to maintain one's position among one's scientific colleagues, a scientist must publish. Some companies deal with this problem by delaying but not prohibiting publications, or by permitting early publication of papers which do not relate directly to the company's products or processes.

Although a scientist may have considerable status outside the company among his or her colleagues, he can only feel unappreciated if he does not have comparable status inside. According to a study of seventy-five scientists by Albert Chapulsky, of the Philco Corporation, both scientists and research management agreed that merit salary increases, promotions, and increase in complexity and challenge of assignments were highly valued incentives for scientists. Another study revealed that scientists looked for advancement possibilities through two avenues—research activity and administrative channels.

Scientists are often not interested in promotion to administrative positions until they find themselves subordinates to others with less experience and reputation. Then they have status incentives to assume administrative responsibilities. In addition, creativity tends to decline with age. Scientists then need other ways of using their experience and skill, and of retaining their place in the organization. Once in the business world, and either having moved into administrative responsibilities themselves or seeing higher compensation going to managers, scientists will tend to value management positions more highly.

4. *Give careful attention to supervision.*

If the scientist must depend on management for evaluation, promotion, and increasing autonomy, then the supervisory relationship takes on as much meaning as for any other employee.

Two criteria scientists use to judge a prospective laboratory are its reputation for scientific advances and the reputation of the director and the people around him as scientists.

This is partly because of the identification of the scientist with his colleagues and profession; but partly, too, it is because the scientist believes a fellow scientist will understand that bureaucratic controls tend to destroy creativity. A scientist supervisor will more likely depend on control by colleagues than control by hierarchy. Such a control pattern is typical of the university, and the more similar in specialty a group of scientists is, the more colleague control will prevail.

A scientist supervisor, by virtue of his or her own experience, can more easily understand the difficult resocialization process the scientist must experience as he goes from the university to industry. If he can remember his own experience, he will lend his most intensive support during the critical first three years. The nonscientist manager can take a leaf out of this book if he or she must supervise scientists, depending heavily on colleague control and providing especially consistent support during the initial crisis period.

When Albert Chapulsky asked his sample of scientists to

write in their own words the specific nonfinancial incentives which would be the most effective motivators for research scientists, "a surprising 40 percent mentioned appraisal and recognition of performance ... among those scientists scoring above the median on the publication-patent index, this incentive was tied for first place with the incentive of promotion to higher rank." Although this finding might seem to be in conflict with our earlier observation that scientists were unconcerned about public recognition, it is not. Chapulsky adds that the major emphasis in the scientists' comments was not upon public recognition, but instead on the ordinary everyday methods of recognition, such as praise and discussion of performance with the supervisor.

The preference for autonomy together with the need for recognition from superiors for professional accomplishments calls for supervisory practices which run counter to the business practice of close supervision on the one hand and an extreme hands-off policy on the other. Drs. Donald Pelz, of the University of Michigan's Survey Research Center, and Leo Meltzer, of Cornell, found that scientific productivity was highly correlated with the amount of freedom the scientist had, the amount of funds available, and the amount of communication with his or her chief. "We are becoming more and more convinced," they concluded, "that this active interest in ongoing work, combined with a hands-off policy concerning its direction, is one of the most fruitful things a research chief can do." When the scientist finds a lack of support from his superiors, he tends to withdraw from them, and the resulting isolation is detrimental to his productivity.

ALLOWING FOR FAILURE

An important aspect of supervision is allowance for failure. Among one hundred companies recognized for research effectiveness, the median failure rate was 51 percent, where failure is defined as projects instituted or designed for market appearance that was never reached. Support is particularly necessary when failure occurs. When a research unit produces many discoveries and patents but none of them are turned into products because the company is interested in them only to keep them away from competitors, this creates built-in failure which is demoralizing. Even the most ideal supervision cannot undo the effects of that practice.

The question of judging performance, particularly failure, can be a difficult one. Who knows whether another week, a month might make the difference between failure and success? No one of course. Yet a person stands on his performance, and the scientist is no different. Even scientist-managers have a painful time deciding when to stop a given project or to discharge someone. A certain amount of arbitrariness seems to be inevitable. But if the scientist has to be allowed a reasonable rate of failure, so must the executive.

So, in sum, the scientist is no mystery man, and the executive does not have to be a magician to work with him or her. The successful executive's techniques, reduced to their simplest levels, are essentially no different from those applicable to managing others—understanding the way in which personality needs are fulfilled in work and making that fulfillment possible, understanding the meaning of ego ideals among the cultural circles important to the person and making it possible for him or her to fulfill those expectations, understanding the continuing need for growth and facilitating that process through supervision, providing support on the one hand and creating opportunity on the other.

15

HOW TO RETREAD
A BUREAUCRAT

As a BUSINESS ORGANIZATION prospers and grows, it often tries to avoid bureaucracy and stay fast on its feet by pushing authority down so that more decisions are made at the organization level where problems arise. But many firms find that managers at such levels are often reluctant to accept the responsibilities that come with decision-making authority. In contrast to the bright young person and the scientist, bureaucrats present quite another problem for the executive.

Their reluctance poses a dilemma for the senior executive who cannot understand why they don't rise to the challenges and opportunities: Even if they have little concern for the company, why don't they want to do better for themselves? Frustrated when they fail to respond to challenge, he or she turns to cajolery. That failing, he tries to exert pressure. In desperation he may even "cut away the deadwood," but not without some feeling of regret and guilt for sacking people who have given years to the organization.

Why is it the executive fails to retread these bureaucrats despite his or her best intentions?

• *Despite one's intentions, one's doubts and reservations about subordinates may show through.*

These attitudes were prevalent in a survey of 2,800 top and middle managers in fourteen countries made by psychologists Mason Haire, Edwin E. Ghiselli, and Lyman W. Porter. Their study revealed a curious contradiction in management thinking. While the top managers said that

166

they included subordinates in decision making, they doubted the initiative and leadership ability of their subordinates. Professor Raymond E. Miles, of the Harvard Graduate School of Business, reports from his research that managers indicate strongest agreement with policies that advocate sharing information and discussing objectives with subordinates. "However," he adds, "they tend to be somewhat less enamored with policies which suggest increasing subordinate self-direction and self-control."

If the executive has such doubts he or she will express them in many subtle ways. Actions will speak louder than words. The subordinates will respond to the actions; they will confirm his doubts.

● *One's subordinates may not yet view themselves as being the potentially capable people one thinks they are.*

When Ghiselli and Porter asked two groups of top-management and middle-management executives to choose adjectives which best described themselves, there was a striking difference between the choices of the two groups. The top-management men saw themselves as capable, determined, industrious, resourceful, sharp-witted, and enterprising. The middle-management men saw themselves as discreet, courageous, practical, planful, deliberate, and intelligent. There were other differences as well. "Members of top management . . . see themselves filling a role that might best be described as the 'dynamic brains' of the organization. Their role is one of thinking up new things to do, new areas to enter, new ways of doing things. They are action-oriented idea men. Middle-management people, on the other hand, seem to see themselves filling a role that could be called the 'backbone' of the organization. Their chief force is that they provide the careful, thorough investigation of ideas and plans that is necessary before these can be put into extensive use."

In another survey, Professor Hjalmar Rosen, of Wayne State University, reports that the managers he studied defined the future in terms of their present experience; they did not tend to predict change over a period of time. "They literally were saying, 'What is, will be,' " he notes. ". . . The managers indicated by their responses that they see themselves as relatively powerless to effect desired change in their work environment. . . . The organization, in their eyes, seems to call the tune. . . . They must accept the *status quo* or depart in hope of finding a more fulfilling job."

Obviously people holding such views are hardly impatient for great responsibility. Asked to assume it, they can be expected to be cautious about doing so. Furthermore, they are less likely to be creative, innovative, and flexible. If their roles do not reinforce self-confidence, they can hardly be expected to respond positively to pressure for initiative.

The fault may be with the senior executive. According to a national survey conducted by a management magazine, 58 percent of 420 middle and junior executives said their superiors had not told them—even in general terms— what was expected of them to qualify for promotion. Almost half said that their superiors seldom or never commended them or otherwise rewarded them for outstanding work. Forty percent said they did not know whether their worth to the company was recognized, and 22 percent more said that it definitely was not. More than half rated their bosses as only fair or poor in motivating people.

Many middle managers also see a threat in the rapid advances in technology. Asked what is ahead, they often reply that higher-caliber managers than they will be needed to fill the jobs they now hold. Furthermore, that threat is reinforced by their observation that efforts to streamline organizations usually mean cutting out many middle managers who had believed themselves to be relatively secure in their companies.

LOOKING FOR THE GIMMICK

Taken together, then, such generalized experiences reinforce the self-perception of middle management as not particularly dynamic. These self-perceptions, in turn, further inhibit subordinates from responding swiftly to the new climate. Instead, they are likely to be looking for the gimmick behind the invitation to open up.

Sometimes a person is reluctant to accept responsibility because he or she is satisfied where he is. There is not much point in trying to change a satisfying way of life. However, often that is not the case. Many middle managers would like to better themselves.

What species of people are these who, wanting to better their lot, sit unmoved in the face of opportunity? They tend to delay action until problems force themselves forward, or until someone else takes the initiative. They are finely attuned to political power in an organization and tend to yield, even at some cost to themselves, as a tactical device. They are reluctant to make the other person angry or hostile, and to show their anger to others. They shy away from unpleasantness, fixed positions, and firm commitments. They are likely to feel that all problems can be solved if people would but talk to each other considerately. They are frequently held in great affection and sometimes in high esteem. They often make outstanding contributions in administrative positions requiring consummate skill in co-ordination and mediation.

How does the senior executive develop the flexibility and initiative of such men? He or she might begin by asking how and why they developed their particular psychological stance. There are a number of possible reasons, both personal and organizational.

● *They may have been suppressed.*

Some organizations are notorious for inhibiting initiative and independence. This is particularly true if the leader is heavily authoritarian. The more authoritarian leaders punish people so harshly for mistakes ("You're allowed only one mistake around here") that those who stay refuse to take a second chance. A person may already have too much vested in stock and retirement rights to leave when punished. The only alternative, then, is to be passive, to act only in response to someone else's initiative.

To illustrate, in a diversified manufacturing company, a long-planned new product line was introduced on schedule at a time when there was an unforeseeable slump in the market for the product. When the projected sales quota could not be met, the vice-president in charge of the new product line was promptly demoted. Although higher management thinks he could again attain his former level, psychologically he has long since resigned from the organization. His stock options keep him there, but he is marking time until an early retirement.

● *They may have become overly dependent.*

Either in the family or at work, particularly in heavily bureaucratic organizations, some people learn that they are supposed to do only what they are told to do. Someone else will make the decisions, take the risks—and take care of them if they go along. If they learn this in the family, such people gravitate to organizations where they can continue to be dependent. These are the people who suffer most acutely when they are pressured to become more aggressively independent.

For example, a forty-two-year-old man with twenty years of service in his company was second-in-command of a line department where he dealt with a number of personnel problems. Though his record had been highly satisfactory and he was well liked by everyone, he was distressed by the pressure of his job and jumped at the opportunity to become assistant personnel director. He learned quickly and carried out assignments well—as long as his boss took the initiative. He could not be given the next promotion where he would be on his own.

* They may have been hurt.

According to a survey by Dr. John MacIver, former director of psychiatric services for U.S. Steel Corporation, of managers and supervisors in metalworking, many feel they have been done an injustice by their organizations. Says Dr. MacIver, "It is disquieting to me that from this group of basically competent and well-adjusted people, 43 percent say they have been hurt careerwise by organizational changes, and 31 percent expect to be hurt in the future." He reports further that he would have expected more of them to feel that their jobs were fulfilling and rewarding most of the time. Nearly 40 percent did not feel that way.

* They are coping with internal psychological problems.

Everyone is always coping with internal psychological problems. However, those who hold back, who don't rise to challenge, characteristically overcontrol and restrain their own initiative as a *major* device for easing internal conflicts. These are the hardest cases for the senior executive to understand and deal with.

A case in point is a highly educated and socially personable department manager who is reasonably sound in the technical aspects of his sales work. The man is easily capable of meeting and dealing with customers, but he lacks the knack of closing a deal.

Everything develops satisfactorily in the negotiations; he is on excellent terms with the purchaser; yet he inevitably fails to clinch the transaction.

The origins of such repetitive problems can be traced to childhood, and the person who struggles with them is often unaware of the conflict. He or she knows only that too many promotions or sales slip through his grasp. It may be difficult to accept the idea that a person could have residual problems from childhood. Yet, to psychological clinicians, such a phenomenon is commonplace.

WHY THEY ABDICATE

The complicating problem with people who are overly dependent or who must overcontrol their aggressive impulses is that they tend to perceive their supervisory actions as hostile, aggressive acts which will be harmful to subordinates. Such people have difficulty supporting and supervising subordinates adequately. In the extreme, they abdicate the leadership role and turn to group decisions as a substitute for leading. They look upon differences of opinion as attacks. When differences occur, they may become rigidly defensive or too readily concede that the other person is right. They retain the self-image of a "nice guy" and thus avoid the issues, but they also tend to be angry with themselves for this posture.

A variant of this personality style is the person who fawns on superiors but is harsh with subordinates and vents hostility on them. When people like this compete, they tend to do so covertly to avoid possible reprisal.

All executives, as they rise to positions of authority, are caught between the wish to be liked and the wish to be boss or leader. The leader must often live with the anger of subordinates; he or she cannot be preoccupied with being liked. These people, particularly, try to have it both ways and end up having neither. Trying to have both, they suppress conflicts, both their own and those between others. This makes for relationships in which everything seems peaceful and everyone is smiling. There is seething hostility underneath, however, because problems are not solved. People pay a price in anxiety, anger, depression, aggravation, or even physical symptoms. To approach such problems, conflicts must be brought out into the open. People who are overdependent or who must fight too hard to control their hostility simply cannot stand to do it.

The executive who takes over a previously highly controlled or autocratically managed organization, and who now must make it more flexible, will have to devote a significant amount of time to the task of getting people to assume greater responsibility.

First, he or she will have to examine his own attitudes to avoid tripping over his own doubts about subordinates. Second, he will have to deal with the generalized problem of limited perceptions subordinates have of their roles, based on their experiences. Third, he will have to review specific cases to ascertain whether given people are lethargic because they are satisfied, afraid, dependent, or inhibited.

Some questions and observations may help one to differentiate between those who are more capable of assuming initiative and those who are likely to be less capable. One way is to ask a person who his or her models were and what he or she thought about them. A person who admired a father's strengths or a mother's initiative and wanted to emulate that action orientation is more likely to want to assume responsibilities.

Another way is to find out what the subordinate has accomplished by himself or herself, particularly what leadership roles he or she has taken *when there were no other powerful figures around to lean on.* If all of a person's successes have been in the shadow of someone else, there is a strong possibility he or she will continue to need such a figure, or fail. The good No. 2 person who falls in the No. 1 position is the bane of executive selection.

Still another way of differentiating is to ask the subordinate what kinds of problems were most difficult for him or her to deal with in the past, why, and what he or she did about them. He is less likely to be competent with independent responsibility if his difficulties centered on the managing of others, if he too easily attributes the fault of failure to others, and if he was not able to stick out the problem or resolve the issue.

One clue to a person's capacities—and one not sufficiently used in executive selection—is the reaction of that person's subordinates. Subordinates know their bosses all too well.

Another technique is to examine the kinds of ideas a person may have had and his or her fate under previous bosses. Ideas which were left dormant or suppressed suggest greater initiative than none. Is there a difference between what the subordinate undertook in school or when working by himself and what happened to him when he joined the company? Was the difference because the company suppressed his activity, because it provided inadequate support, or because there was no powerful authority figure under whose wing he could operate? Was his previous work experience in a company where conformity was the first rule of survival? Such questions begin to provide some clues to a person's life style and the reasons—temporary or permanent—why he or she maintains it.

Remember, however, we are dealing with clues and cues, not established facts. These are merely points to be followed up and examined more closely when there is a need to differentiate among individual potentialities.

If a subordinate's constrained behavior pattern is not a lifelong posture of strong dependency, the following suggestions may be helpful in fostering the continued growth of previously suppressed or dependent people.

1. *Provide careful guidance.*

Regular appraisals against mutually predetermined goals, in relatively frequent supportive meetings, can be the basis for step-by-step growth. Inadequacies of performance need not be glossed over but are better used as a basis for learning than an occasion for fixing blame. Tell the person precisely what his or her responsibilities are.

2. *Encourage such people to speak up in staff meetings by briefing them in advance.*

Invite their criticism and judgment. Try to minimize attacks on them or by them by requiring that the discussion be directed to problem solving. Show them by your actions that they will not be hurt if they speak up, even if you must control the manipulative or hostile efforts of others.

3. *Support them in the appropriate and constructive expression of aggression.*

If their experience has been limited, show them how to define problems and the step-by-step process of problem resolution. Recognize their successes and point out their growth—honestly.

4. *Do not expect them to lead by themselves before their own capacities and successes are self-evident.*

Until they are self-confident, they may do very well as

long as you are behind them, but fail if they feel they are standing alone.

THE RESENTFUL SUBORDINATE

Here is one example of how such a process was carried out.

A new department head encountered a subordinate who had held the No. 2-spot in the department for many years and who had been passed over for promotion. The subordinate resented his new boss, although he himself did not have sufficient leadership ability for the job. The new boss went out of his way to keep fully informed on what the subordinate's staff group was doing. He actively supported the subordinate on some of his *good* pet projects. He quietly checked into and corrected some minor irritants which had irked the subordinate. He assigned the subordinate a major project, and in the process the subordinate saw the need for other than an authoritarian approach. The boss then saw that some of the subordinate's more successful projects got company-wide attention, which led to the subordinate's being consulted by other departments. The result was a noticeable improvement in attitude, not only toward the boss by the subordinate, but also toward the subordinate and his group by other management groups.

5. *Be prepared to be distrusted and tested; also be prepared for some turbulence.*

After having been in a more passive role for a long period, people will find it hard to believe that someone wants them to be more active. Quite unwittingly, they will test the boss. They may at first be reluctant to speak up, and then seem to do so too much in a quarrelsome way. They have many pent-up feelings to discharge, and the superior will have to allow time for such feelings to be expressed. As they are expressed, the subordinates will come to feel disillusioned, and somewhat overwhelmed by the problems they are now asked to tackle. This is the point at which they need the greatest support; it is a psychological dip before the upward climb begins.

The disillusionment and disappointment occur because, before, they at least had a familiar position, they knew what to expect and could lean on someone else. It is therefore hard to give up, just as it is hard for the adolescent to give up the pleasure of being dependent on his parents. The adolescent has to fight his way out of his adolescence, often using the parents as foils. The people we are discussing also have to fight their way out of their passive position, using the superior as a foil.

WORTH THE EFFORT?

By this time, the executive may well wonder if it is worth all the effort. That he or she will have to decide for himself. In varying degrees he will have to follow the same principles with most subordinates if he is to foster their growth. His only other alternatives are to try to manipulate them, which won't get him very far, or to abandon them to their passive roles, or to fire them.

Nevertheless, his success will be limited. Not everyone can become a self-starter, or assume independent responsibility. Those who cannot still have talents.

They often do very well in staff roles. Many can be particularly successful as compromisers, mediators, or bridges between people. If they do not displace their hostility on those of lower status, they can act in an interested, supportive role toward others. They do better, too, in roles where they do not have to promote themselves. Often, because of their tendency to be self-sacrificing, they will go to inordinate lengths to help others.

Some people are often good salesmen (if they don't have difficulty closing the sale) in situations where they have to please the customer, rather than overwhelm him, or where they must absorb considerable hostility from customers. They can handle positions in which they are exposed to the public if they can be helped to understand that people who meet customers inevitably serve as easy targets for displaced hostility. Much of the criticism they are likely to get is not meant for them personally, but unloaded on them because they cannot fight back.

In sum, many people who seem reluctant to assume initiative can be helped to do so. Many others cannot change significantly. The wise superior will be extremely cautious about labeling people and judging them on the basis of labels. He or she will first examine his own assumptions about them, then theirs about themselves. Then he will try to differentiate those who might assume larger responsibilities from those who cannot. He will not persist in trying to remake the latter if reasonable support efforts fail to help them blossom. There is room in every organization for the person who holds things together; sometimes those who have no power aspirations for themselves are the only ones who can be trusted by their more competitive colleagues.

16

THE MANAGEMENT OF WOMEN

LIKE MEN, women come to an organization with a variety of motives, preparation, and expectations. Some will come with little more than potential; others will come with proven skills and talents. Some will come primarily for social relationships, others for money, still others to build a professional career. The needs of some will change as they remain in the company over a period of years; others will move and transfer at a rapid pace, and *their* needs will also change. Whatever the needs, demands, and expectations that the growing number of working women bring to their organizations, they will have to be met.

Most of what we know about women at work derives from research studies on unskilled or semi-skilled workers in large factories. These studies are frequently too circumscribed in their scope to be able to tell us much about the motivations of women other than the fact that most in those situations have needed to work for economic reasons. In general, however, the motivations of women at work are very much like those of men at work. At lower socioeconomic levels where monetary needs are primary, money will be a very powerful motivator for most, and working conditions frequently will be quite secondary.

Beyond motivation, there are special managerial problems to be faced both by the growing numbers of women workers and managers and by the organizations as they incorporate these women into their ranks. Many of these will be subtle problems of attitude, climate, and prejudices. In addition, there will be more concrete problems, such as

177

balancing a working mother's family obligations against her organizational responsibilities.

It is often said women are more emotional than men. However, what this really means is that women are freer to express their feelings because the culture permits it. Men are frequently restrained by the culture from such expression because they are expected to be stoic, to overcontrol themselves, and to take whatever pain and anguish may come their way without venting their despair and anger. In fact, women's social freedom to express emotions sometimes threatens their male supervisors and leads them to describe women as "too emotional."

With the advent of greater social freedom for women, this traditional emotional expression is now frequently punctuated by the use of coarser language and expletives which only a few short years ago were rare in ordinary conversation. While there may be ethnic and local differences in the freedom to use four-letter words, there is no question that the general trend is for women's language to approach that of their male counterparts. This may be even more frightening to male supervisors.

One of the earliest studies on participatory management, reported by Dr. Alfred Marrow in the Harwood Company,* was done with women employees in Virginia. That study indicated that when women employees were given the opportunity to participate in the decisions which affected them, productivity, absenteeism, grievances, and turnover were all influenced positively. The study also showed that—like men—women emphasize heavily the expectation that their bosses be near to them. This is a difficult issue. Closeness between women employees and male supervisors is frequently seen as a product of a sexual liaison. Partiality is difficult enough because of the unfairness and resentment it creates, but it is all the more difficult when compounded by sexual rivalry, jealousy, envy, and maybe hostility on the part of those who either want the same attention or resent the fact that such attention intrudes on the work experience.

This issue of managing psychological distance from male supervisors is more pressing for women at work. Women must always be on guard lest a friendly smile or a casual

* Alfred J. Marrow, David G. Bowers, and Stanley E. Seashore. *Management by Participation.* New York, Harper & Row, 1967.

interest be taken by males to mean more than was intended. Often they must walk a tightrope between the extremes of aloofness and informality. Frequently they do so in work groups by using one of their number to deal with male supervisors and managers. Where there are large numbers of women, male supervisors may act through a foreman or some other person whom management designates as the contact with women.

There is another reason that working women must learn to manage psychological distance. If a woman becomes too close to her job, comes to depend too heavily on her organization and especially her boss, she runs the risk of emotional turmoil when her connection with the organization is severed. For example, a secretary to a top-level manager may find herself "widowed" when he dies or is transferred and she cannot go with him. Often there is really no other place for such a woman in the organization. The manager's replacement most often will want to bring his own secretary with him or hire a new one. Without her former boss, the woman has lost her primary attachment to the organization through him, and, in addition, her source of power in the organization. Emotionally, she cannot easily transfer her allegiance to another boss, nor will she be likely to find one with whom she can work as comfortably and efficiently. She will be widowed in a very real sense.

Many women prefer to work for a male supervisor rather than a female supervisor. Why they want to do so is sometimes not altogether clear either to themselves or to those who must work with them. Most often there are two reasons. The first is unconscious: women usually are or have been more tightly controlled by their mothers than boys are by their fathers. This is especially true in adolescence. As a result, women do not want to be "mothered" by controlling and directing women bosses. The second problem is more conscious. Women who move quickly into supervisory ranks tend to be the more aggressive women by definition. They are the ones who are considered able to take charge of others, to supervise and direct work. Sometimes, these women identify with male styles of managing and tend to act like male supervisory models. When women act as they think men would in a given situation, then they incur the resentment of both women and men who resent the fact that they are not acting within the gender stereotype, as they should. In fact, one of the major problems that males have with females, particularly aggressive women who compete with them for positions or who are upwardly mobile in managerial ranks, is their reaction to that kind of aggressive behavior, which they think is not feminine. They resent the woman for not being feminine. Adjectives like "uppity," "pushy," and phrases like "she doesn't know her place" recall the same kinds of automatic reactions to blacks and other minority group members who in years gone by were supposed to play a passive, nonassertive social role.

Women at work carry heavier responsibilities than men do, in the sense that they most frequently continue to have responsibilities for home and children. This is especially true of lower socioeconomic levels, where people cannot afford maids, babysitters, nurses, and others to care for their children. They usually do not have adequate family care services or support services and therefore need both the understanding and the help of the work organization to make it possible for them to meet both their home and work responsibilities. Their supervisors should recognize that they are likely to be more immediately worried about family problems than their male counterparts because of the heavy dependency of their children. The wise manager will therefore have ready sources of information from the personnel department for educational, medical, and other forms of organized social help. The Community Services Committee of the AFL-CIO has set an excellent example by making such information available through union channels.

Generally speaking, women may be in a more vulnerable position than men because on the whole they tend to be less mobile because of their family obligations. Often they have a more limited range of work experience. Despite equal opportunity efforts, no large numbers of women are pouring into work roles, especially in the skilled trades, which historically have been the province of men. As a rule, women have had little everyday training, in the course of growing up, in doing some of the things that men do, ranging from auto mechanics to climbing utility poles. While this may be changing, some of the problems of preparation, acceptance, and congeniality limit their participation and make them feel, rightly or wrongly, inadequate for undertaking such roles. There are few role models for women in these activities, and those role models which do exist tend to be either so rare or such outstanding examples that most women feel that they cannot possibly emulate them.

Older women who are returning to work after raising a family are the most vulnerable group. After several years outside of the work environment, they have lost touch with the experience of working. Reorienting themselves to the office or the shop or factory can be unsettling, and they may tend to lose confidence in themselves and become anxious or concerned about their competence.

All this means that women who want to take advantage of new opportunities will need a good deal more encouragement from their superiors. They need apprenticeship programs, and encouragement to talk about their anxieties and concerns about undertaking these new roles; opportunities should be provided for groups of women who are entering new roles to sit together and talk about these anxieties and concerns.

Those who may experience frustration because of their vulnerability or inexperience will find it helpful to discuss those frustrations and to learn that their managements are interested in helping them make the best of the opportunities that are available.

For some women, there will be another problem: fear of advancement. This fear has a number of different dimensions. First, it has to do with underlying feelings, still strong among many women, that they should not compete with men for the same jobs. Second, those who are married frequently fear getting ahead of their husbands. This is especially true at lower socioeconomic levels, where upward occupational mobility also means for many a change in style of dress, language, and business associates which may make the spouse feel inadequate. Third, some women may fear that as they advance they may have to take away from their families to give to their jobs. They may hesitate to take on more responsibilities at work to prevent having to compromise their obligations to their families. There needs to be an opportunity for women to talk about these kinds of problems too with their bosses.

Until recently women in managerial ranks were rare. Most women found their careers in motherhood or homemaking or in jobs traditionally defined as "women's work"—nursing, teaching, clerical or secretarial work. Exccutive careers only opened up to women in general after World War II. Prior to that only family wealth or exceptional talent and ambition could open the executive suite to an occasional woman. Things have changed in our lifetimes, and organizations now accept and train women to take positions at every level of the hierarchy. As more and more women join managerial ranks, organizations have passed the stage of treating each female newcomer as a special case. But even today there are many difficulties and conflicts associated with supervising women managers which must be understood and discussed before they can be acted on.

ROLE MODELS

The first and most obvious problem in managing women is the very novelty of the issue. Without guidance and discussion, it can be very confusing to sort out the general problems of managing women from the problems of managing a specific woman or group of women.

Because women in general are relatively new arrivals in executive ranks, their experience with managing and being managed is brief and ambiguous. There are few role models, few examples of women who have built a managerial career. Although some have made it to the top of the organizational ladder, there are comparatively few examples yet of women who have worked their way up during a career lifetime or who have leveled out in middle-management ranks.

The lack of role models poses problems for young female managers and for their supervisors. For women, the lack of role models means that there is no "normal" pattern of success. In essence, there are no standards. With no women mentors, seasoned by experience, to coach newcomers through the difficult stages of their careers, women will have to meet each crisis in their personal and professional lives as a unique case, without precedent.

The bright young woman is left with three choices: she can play by her own rules, or she can take as role models either the superwomen who have been successful in the past or her male supervisors. If she chooses the first path, she will forfeit the kind of positive guidance that role models provide and will wind up paying a heavy cost for her choice in terms of frustration, confusion, and anger. By identifying closely with the superwomen, she is setting unrealistic standards for herself. Such superwomen's careers are the exception, not the rule. The singular personal characteristics—exceptional talent and ambition or charismatic leadership—that have enabled these women to succeed in a hostile organizational climate are beyond the reach of most executives, male or female. By trying to live up to unrealistic standards, women doom themselves to failure and disappointment.

If the woman chooses to identify with her male superiors, she will have to pay equally heavy costs in terms of conflict of expectations. Sex role expectations will tend to "jam" the process of identification. Especially on the part of the older male supervisor, stereotyped ideas and feelings about "women's work" vs. "men's work" will stand in the way of forming an alliance between male supervisor and female subordinate against the problems that confront them both.

SEX ROLE STEREOTYPING

Although more and more women are moving into management ranks, there is still no denying that there is strong resistance from both sexes to this violation of the traditional male/female division of labor. Many men feel that a woman's place is in the home, rearing children. These men feel that women cannot and should not do men's work and consider it a slight to their masculinity if their wives work or if their own jobs can be or are being done by women.

Women not only face these feelings in their male colleagues but also within themselves. Research into the problem of the psychology of sex differentiation has found that as women reach college age, they begin to have a real fear of competing with men—the natural fear of losing and the fear of winning too.

This stereotyping actually breaks down communication between female managers and their male colleagues, subordinates, and superiors. For example, some men feel that the normal organizational climate will be broken down by the growing numbers of emotional women. There is a real fear that women will cry when they are denied promotion or face other similar setbacks, or that they will not play by male rules.

Likewise, male managers fear that women are not tough

enough to compete in the aggressive business world. But when women demonstrate that they are sufficiently tough and aggressive to compete, then many male managers become frightened of them, for they no longer seem like women to such men. Like it or not, most people like to think of their mothers as warm, affectionate, kind, and loving, whether they were so in reality or not. This leads to expectations that all "good women" will act as the ideal mother, real or fantasied, should and did.

The problem of managing aggression will be more difficult for many women than it is for men. Despite the greater openness in young women fostered by contemporary child-rearing practices, many women, particularly those who go into managerial ranks, have been taught to please others. In a managerial situation, they are often likely to be kinder than men, which then increases the amount of testing they will get from subordinates and increases their frustration as they find that they must cope with this testing process by taking active charge of a situation. Some may need warning of such situations from their superiors and coaching on how to handle them. Reassurance that their superiors are allied with them and ready to help them learn to cope with some of the most difficult managerial problems will relieve considerable anxiety and mitigate self-doubt. Without such coaching, they may react to testing by going to the extreme of checking their subordinates too carefully and recapitulating the nagging-mother syndrome.

For some, the open horizons to management success may be frightening, and anxiety may increase with promotions. This is not a problem limited to women. However, many will fear that to move up may inhibit their chances for marriage, and such feelings may increase in intensity if there's no opportunity to talk about them either with groups of women in similar situations or with understanding superiors. Some may be reluctant to have their whole lives totally involved with their jobs, as many men must in order to become successful in certain organizations. Others report feeling more comfortable because they have an understanding with themselves that they are going to stop working someday and by marrying will have someone else to support them. Confusing and contradictory feelings about these matters are more likely to come to the fore at times when opportunities for marriage, for having children, for moving higher in the organization, begin to wane.

Travel is one of the inevitable aspects of most managerial jobs. Conventions, sales meetings, and other previously all-male activities may sometimes pose problems. The wise boss who is familiar with these events in his organization will give prior thought to the needs and requirements of his female subordinates—which he might ascertain more closely by talking with them. For example, it is not unusual for company management meetings to be held at hotels where colleagues may play golf together. Men and women do not often play golf together except as couples; more often there are separate tournaments for men and women. A special arrangement may have to be made for women managers, especially at those meetings where wives are present: single men will usually manage more easily than single women, who will more likely be involved with management activities than with those activities scheduled for the wives. The husband of a woman manager in such a situation may be in an uneasy position. Thoughtful managers will consider such situations in advance.

Although it is wise to consult with women managers about their special needs and requirements, some are hypersensitive about their femininity and may reject overtures to give them special consideration. Only out of experience with any given woman manager will her male superior learn the ground rules for working with her.

SUPERVISION

Now that larger numbers of women have gained entry into organizations, they still find the going rough inside. They have to learn to play by the rules, many of which are unwritten. For instance, it is an unwritten rule that people in organizations succeed to the extent to which others help them. Older supervisors—guides or mentors—ease the way for younger managers by eliminating obstacles, showing them the political ropes, teaching them the shortcuts, and sharing the wisdom of experience. These mentor friendships develop casually both at work and outside—at the country club, at football games, and in men's rooms.

In the last decade, as women and minority group members made their entrance into managerial ranks, we have discovered how important the mentor relationship is. Because the mentor relationship is informal, newcomers have often ignored its importance and been puzzled later that they did not advance as quickly or as steadily as they had expected.

Even if women acknowledge the need for a mentor, they are faced with an additional problem. As discussed above, they are unlikely to find female mentors, and if they turn to male supervisors for this kind of help they are just as likely to be frustrated. The mentor will most probably shy away from this close relationship with a young woman, and if he does not, it may lead to rumors within the organization that she is repaying his organizational favors with sexual favors. This rumor could cripple both their careers.

Although these pitfalls are present most intensely in the mentor relationship, they are present to some degree in every supervisory relationship. Both mentor and manager will have to discuss and deal with these problems.

FAMILY OBLIGATIONS

The executive mother will have even further problems: motherhood will interrupt the normal career pattern. Early in his career, the average manager has an intensive training period with rotations, transfers, and assignments which require a great deal of overtime. It is the unfortunate fact that this demanding period coincides with a woman's childbearing years. If she is going to take time out of her career to have children, she will have to make some sacrifices. In addition, she will have to discuss and arrange with her supervisor a program of reading or observation to keep her abreast of developments in her field. In individual cases, she may be able to work out a part-time schedule or be able to work freelance or on a consultative basis.

Usually when a male manager is ill or has an accident, provision is made for him to catch up or make up his lost time in such a way that his "progress" is not impeded. His peers or those who substitute for him close ranks behind him in dealing with the emergency. However, this is less likely to be the case with pregnancy. There is no emergency to respond to, and some may feel that the woman's choice to have a child puts an unfair burden on them while she is away from the job. If the boss has such feelings, these will subtly infect the others in the organization and make the woman's return to work difficult. While no one wants to be without the good employee on whom he or she is counting, nevertheless times of absence will occur, and managers will have to learn to plan for them and accept them with equanimity.

RIVALRY

Rivalry of course occurs among women just as it does among men, and pecking orders are established in organizational structures. Pecking orders among women are most evident in such places as company towns and military bases, but with larger numbers of women moving into managerial ranks they will become evident in management.

Experiences in business schools indicate that women can be just as rivalrous as men, an experience already borne out in those work situations where women have long had successful roles, such as in advertising agencies, teaching, and journalism. The behavior of the superior is a key factor in rivalry. The more intense the downward pressure he creates, the greater the rivalry there will be, and the less people will be able to cooperate with each other, whether they are men or women. If, in addition, the supervisor wittingly or unwittingly plays favorites, then the rivalry will increase in intensity and be disruptive to his organization. If the superior is also a woman, she may experience considerable rivalry with herself, as mothers often do when their daughters vie for the approval of their fathers. Only after the boss looks at his or her own behavior is it possible to affect the behavior of the subordinate. Merely talking about it will be of little help as long as the superior's behavior fans the flames of rivalry.

As more women work in business organizations and move into a greater variety of jobs and into managerial ranks, there will be less and less need for special considerations having to do with the management of women. However, the problems and concerns outlined here will be with us for some time and a few guidelines may therefore be helpful in dealing with them.

1. *Try to learn if there are special problems for the woman in this organization and in the role she is about to take on.*

No one can fault a manager for trying to be helpful. He or she can ask what experience she has had which may have been difficult for her or interfered with her task accomplishment. He might describe what situations in his own unit or in his component part of the organization there might be which might create difficulties or which might need to be dealt with. In doing so, he makes himself available for continued discussion or for whatever counsel may be asked of him, and he can therefore be experienced by the woman as an ally in her work and work adaptation.

2. *In a mentor role, arrange for women subordinates in managerial ranks to be able to talk together about their experiences and to be briefed in groups about organizational politics, advancement patterns, pressures, opportunities, and resources.*

The use of groups of women for this purpose will alleviate some of the pressures which otherwise might make a close mentor relationship difficult both for male superiors and women subordinates. Since there are plenty of male models of mentors around, that problem is less difficult for a man unless he happens to be from a minority group, in which case the same thing should be done.

3. *Become familiar with resources available in the community and through the organization to help with family problems.*

The ability of the boss or the personnel department to mobilize such resources, to make it possible for women who have families to work more comfortably and to deal more readily with family problems when they arise, is most important. Knowing where to find a trustworthy babysitter at a moment's notice can be a tremendous relief for a mother.

4. *Talk and rehearse.*

If you find yourself concerned about potential emotional expressions on the part of women subordinates, or if you are uneasy about expressions of aggression which seem unwomanly to you as a male manager, then it would be wise to talk over these feelings with your own peers in the organization, preferably in seminars or group discussions under the sponsorship of a personnel or human resources department. Through the process of rehearsal and anticipation of such events, or in being able to talk out such feelings, the pressures often decrease, and it is easier to act in a rational way in relationship with the women.

5. *Women will present the same problems as men.*

Just like men, women have a great variety of character

types and personality structures. The problems they run into, particularly as managers, will be the same problems they would experience as men of the same personality style. It is important to differentiate between the things that occur because of one's personality and those that are precipitated or brought about because the person involved is a woman. Most of the time the supervisor will find that the problems a subordinate has with others are more often a product of personality or organizational pressures than of womanhood. That perspective should enable him to act with greater wisdom and judgment and less preoccupation with male/female differences.

I believe that it will be three generations before women feel themselves to be at home in organizations and before organizations adapt fully to accommodate them. That means that those who manage women may have to cope with the pressures of that experience, both within themselves and within the organization as well as within the woman, for some time to come. They will, however, decrease with time, just as they have in the area of coeducation. Both employees and organizations will be the better for it.

17

DO YOU LOOK
FOR CULPRITS—
OR CAUSES?

A MAJOR PART of all supervisory and reporting relationships is the exercise of responsibility and control. As a result, the good executive is a master detective. He or she spends much time ferreting out errors and searching for culprits. He often finds both, whereupon he usually proceeds to "lay down the law" and to punish the guilty.

Like most efforts to stamp out crime by punishment, this process does not work very well. The reason is that many errors and violations of rules, along with much sickness, absenteeism, and accidents, are symptoms that something is wrong in the managerial house. Take one symptom away and, as long as hidden tensions remain, another will appear.

Does this mean that the executive must stop looking for errors and searching for culprits? Yes and no. Obviously he or she cannot permit waste, poor quality control, and duplication of effort. But he would do far better not to limit his detective work to finding error, and to think differently about culprits and blame.

If errors, accidents, and similar events are symptoms, then the important question for the executive is, "*Why* did they occur?" Only by understanding the "why" can he or she effectively prevent their recurrence. Rarely is there a single cause for a single event. Most of the time behavior occurs because of the force of many factors acting at once. The executive's first task is to look for *causes* and how they fit together to produce the undesirable behavior.

HIDDEN ANGER

The job is not easy. The main point of this book is that the most important causes of human behavior are people's feelings, some so subtle that the individuals themselves are unaware of them. Of our myriad feelings, those which make for the most trouble, as I have already noted, are fear, doubt, and anger. And the angry feelings which are hardest to deal with are those which people hide from themselves as well as from others. To make things more complicated, sometimes people have so much difficulty in dealing with their unconscious feelings of anger that, as I have previously pointed out, the only way they can get rid of them is to hurt themselves in some manner.

To the psychologist, the policeman, and the physician, self-inflicted injury is an old story. But the executive in many instances is quite oblivious to this phenomenon and acts as if it did not exist. He or she keeps searching for culprits, acting on the assumption that if he weeds them out or punishes them sufficiently, his troubles will disappear. To a certain but extremely limited extent, that assumption is valid. If it were as valid as we like to believe, our prisons would be empty of repeaters.

When an executive finds a situation in which people are hurting themselves, either physically as in accidents or psychologically as in ways which cost them money or status—and hurting the organization—that is a strong indication that there is a need to look further. His or her next two questions should be:

"What's making this person or these people angry?"

"Why do they have to express their anger this way?"

The answers may not be readily apparent, but they will not be apparent at all unless he or she looks for them.

Take this example. In an engineering design organization of some three hundred men there were three levels of operation: a five-man management group, the engineers, and the supporting technicians. The management group had a suite of offices in the front of the building. Management went to great lengths to retain engineers, paying them well and offering many perquisites. The supporting technicians were paid prevailing salaries. Management was aware that the organization was sluggish, that there was considerable conflict, and that turnover among the technicians was high. Management attributed the conflict to the temperamental engineers, conflict which it thought it might solve by weeding out a few. A few short hours of looking around and asking questions produced quite a different perspective:

• *The engineers and technicians knew the company's executive suite as "Peacock Alley."*

By this designation they said, in effect, that management was "putting on airs," "strutting," "self-centered," "oblivious to what was going on outside its circle," and "uninterested in other employees."

• *The technicians did not mix with the engineers as the engineers did not mix with management.*

The technicians saw no future for themselves in the organization except as flunkies for the engineers, and spoke frequently of their search for other jobs. Among the technicians, the biggest hero was the man who could most successfully foul up the engineers, and the more massive the foul-up, the greater a hero he was.

• *The work of the engineers was done in sequence.*

Each did a part of the design and passed his special work on to someone else who added his specialty. The engineers did not like this work process. Each would have preferred to do a whole design. Although many of the engineers expressed a wish to leave, they stayed because the salary and perquisites were so good.

WHY THEY LEAVE

Nor was this a unique situation. A similar one was reflected in research by psychologist Frank Friedlander, of Case-Western Reserve University, and his colleague, Eugene Walton. Friedlander and Walton interviewed a sample of 82 out of a laboratory of 1,200 scientists and engineers. "When asked what factors might cause him to leave, the scientist's reasons are concerned almost entirely with elements in his work context or in his community environment, rather than in the work process itself," they conclude. That is, although the scientist or engineer might have been attracted to this job in the first place because of his interest in the work and his technical freedom, he would not necessarily leave it if these diminished. He would be more likely to leave if he were dissatisfied with pay, supervision, management, housing, living costs, and similar factors.

In our example, the engineers stayed. None of the factors around the work situation itself was sufficiently distressing that they would leave. But it was obvious to management that they were not producing as they could.

A diffident management was buying off the engineers. The engineers were angry with management's lack of genuine interest in them and with the mechanical way in which the designs were handled. Yet they could not afford to leave nor could they be consciously angry with a management that "treats them so nicely." It is extremely difficult for people to admit that they are angry with someone who is kind to them because it seems so inappropriate to be angry at kindness. The anger is therefore repressed. The engineers themselves were not clearly aware that they were angry, but the fact that they were was only poorly disguised in their humorous references to "Peacock Alley."

The engineers' anger was further evident in their treatment of the technicians. They treated the technicians as management treated them: with contemptuous tolerance. The technicians were angry in turn, but they had no way of getting back at either engineers or management without hurting the organization or themselves. Whether in sabotage of the engineers' efforts or in leaving the organization, they hurt both themselves and the company. Anger must out one way or another, even at this price.

What could management do when it realized what was going on?

Lectures and exhortation would be useless. Firing an engineer or two or a half dozen technicians would only have increased the anger and solved nothing.

The most important action management could take would be to talk with its people, without anger or implied criticism, about their mutual problems. Out of their discussion in small groups might well come some constructive ways of dealing with their problems.

For example, a shift to a project-type operation in which management representatives, engineers, and technicians were involved as a group on a single task probably would eliminate much of the hostility between the groups and make it possible to direct more of their joint energies into the work and less against each other. This is not to say that project-type management is a panacea, but rather that, if management could see the underlying aspects of the problem, it could work out more appropriate solutions, among which this is an alternative.

Better than waiting for "crimes" to occur, the executive might turn to discovering clues to potential difficulty. Many are fairly obvious. Here are some typical managerial situations which are likely to produce or reflect destructive manifestations of angry feelings:

The happy family. No family in the world lives without some friction, pain, turbulence, or difficulty. Neither does any business or other social institution. An executive who says blithely, "We're all one big happy family here," is either a fool or a liar. Whichever the case, it is usually apparent from the executive's Pollyanna-ish attitude that he or she does not like to recognize manifestations of anger. He is likely to try too quickly to smooth over or suppress anger as if by doing so he could make it go away. Instead, it is only thinly disguised by fixed smiles through gritted teeth.

The happy family, exaggerated though its happiness may be, is often nevertheless something of a family. When a merger occurs, the people in the company whose identity is lost often feel they are like stepchildren and even many years later still speak fondly of the old organization. The same may happen in mergers of divisions.

The tight ship. This is the corporate equivalent of *The Caine Mutiny.* A place for everything and everything in its place. When an executive says, "I run a tight ship," he or she usually means every job is described, every task assigned, every motion is timed and measured, and everybody feels like a machine. This rigid style of management may be the industrial engineer's version of heaven, but it is hell on earth for those who must live with it. Its underlying purpose is to exercise such detailed and rigid control over people that their feelings will never get in the way.

While order and system are necessary, too much is self-defeating. Not only do people lose their flexibility, but also, being overcontrolled, they feel like animals in a cage and their anger reverberates throughout the system.

Much of the time such anger is reflected in passive resistance. The lowly soldier knows that the best way to beat his officers at their own game is to do exactly as they tell him, no more. This failure to take responsibility, make decisions, or expedite action is a chronic middle-management disease in all organizations. Where conformity is the first rule of survival, initiative is likely to be found only in dictionaries on the secretaries' desks.

The tight ship is sometimes a hollow mockery of an organization. The names and faces are a kaleidoscope of comings and goings. Only the rules remain the same, constituting the image of an organization.

The rudderless ship. Some businesses are not managed; they simply exist. Executives may fail to assume their leadership role, or having done so, may abandon it. This happens for several reasons. The executive may be afraid of his or her role, fearful of exercising authority over others. Or he may perceive directing others as being aggressive and feel guilty. Or he may be unable to supervise others adequately, and, overwhelmed by his continuous pile of work, try to do it all himself to the exclusion of others.

Another way of coping with feelings of inadequacy as a leader is to go to one training course after another. In any of these instances the subordinates are abandoned, for all practical purposes, abdicated.

The consequences usually include some form of panic and rebellion. Sometimes, sensing weakness on the part of the leader, the subordinates become openly hostile to him or her and dare him to take charge. Sometimes they fight with each other because they cannot fight with the boss. If the work group is loyal to the leader, despite his abdication, they tend to split into two parts one part wants to go ahead and do what needs to be done while the other feels that the first group is trying to usurp the leader's role and resists its efforts. Whichever happens, the usual outcome is increasing anger of the work group members toward each other and to the executive. There are also withdrawal of interest from the job and subtle gestures of hostility toward it. The latter range from readiness to leave the job promptly at quitting time, regardless of what extra effort might be needed, to bypassing the boss and dealing directly with his or her superiors.

In addition, the group flounders; without a firm hand at the helm the organization drifts hither and yon, acquiring the barnacles of inefficiency and the scales of corroded reputation. Businesses, too, can become derelicts. We even speak of those who take over such businesses for manipulative purposes as "pirates."

The rudderless ship phenomenon is widespread in large organizations which rotate executives every two years or so. Though the executives rotate, most of the employees remain behind permanently. As we noted earlier, they establish their own ways of doing things and learn to bow their backs when another transient boss tries to take hold of the organization. The employees know full well that they will still remain when the boss is gone.

The sacrificial altar. Ancient peoples used to place their sins symbolically on a goat and then sacrifice it or drive it away, presumably getting rid of their sins with the goat. These days scapegoating is done in more unconscious fashion. We can see it readily in various forms of prejudice. It is more difficult to discern in managerial practice, yet it occurs frequently, as we saw in earlier discussions of displacement.

Sometimes an executive consistently picks on a subordinate, or a group of executives focus their anger on one of their number rather than express their anger at each other, or one person in the group is viewed as a hapless, helpless fellow and treated as such.

And sometimes the victim is one of a kind, as for example when a series of sales managers is hired and fired with the phrase, "Salesmen are all like that." Sometimes a particular division or unit is the victim. Scapegoating is a frequent consequence of the previous three styles of management.

The sacrificial altar goes by many other names: "cleaning out the deadwood"; "bringing in a new team"; "trimming off the fat"; and so on. Much of the time, however, such activities are necessary because executives failed to manage adequately in the first place and subordinates are victimized as a result.

When an executive, following symptomatic clues to their source, discovers such situations he or she is still left with the problem of what to do about them. His actions should be directed to correcting the underlying problems rather than fixing blame and administering punishment. These actions can be taken in three steps:

1. *Feed back factual findings to the responsible subordinates.*

The executive can then discuss them, check them against his or her own obervations and experience. While preserving his self-respect he can recognize the effects of anger and take steps to alleviate the tensions.

2. *Support the subordinates in their efforts to correct the situation.*

Support takes many forms. Examining with them their alternative courses of action is one mode of support. Reassuring them that they will lose neither face nor power if they let people express their feelings about their work situation is another. Standing behind subordinates through the turbulence of change or the exercise of authority is a third. These three are usually required at minimum.

3. *If a subordinate cannot do the managerial job, after having been given reasonable support, then both he or she and the organization would be better off if assigned to another task.*

But the qualification is important. Despite extensive managerial training in business, industry, and government, too many executives still do not know the need for and the meaning of support of subordinates. As a result, too many promising executives fall from the managerial vine at an early age.

Most important of all, the executive should look at his or her own style of management. Professor Edwin Fleishman once did a series of studies on supervisory behavior at International Harvester. He concluded that the single most important influence on the leadership behavior of the supervisor is the behavior of his own supervisor. Uncomfortable though that finding may be, all executives must live with it.

18

HOW TO UNDERMINE
AN ORGANIZATION

LOYALTY, as we have observed, grows out of identification. One identifies, in turn, with an image, a "picture." Image, therefore, is a critical organizational issue.

A New Jersey barber once suggested that barbers upgrade their image by adopting the name "hairtician." "After all" said the barber, "a hospital has a dietician, the beauty parlor has a beautician, and undertakers are known as morticians."

The notion was good for a ripple of amusement in the newspapers. Yet we live in an image-conscious age, and organizations, as well as individuals, are in deadly earnest about the image they project. For reasons I have considered, they should be.

Most people tend to organize their thinking in broad categories and attach sweeping value judgments to these categories—social groups, business firms, religious and racial groups, even nations, tend to be thought of as good, bad, or indifferent. When, as individuals, we find ourselves dealing with another individual or an organization that falls into one of our categories, there is a strong tendency to apply the pre-existing value judgment to it.

All this, of course, is now a part of the popular psychological lore, and along with popularization has come the conviction that while images are important they are also rather superficial things that can be altered pretty much at will. Not so. A barber's status does not suddenly soar when he announces that he is a hairtician, nor does that of a business if it switches from Athena Storm Windows to Athena Aerospace and Electronic Corporation.

Such changes, in fact, can be damaging. While the public may be fooled for a time, neither management nor the employee is. Business firms as well as individuals have self-images, and a name is certainly a part of one. Like individuals, firms also have *ego ideals*. The ego ideal and the *self-image* are closely related. An organization's ego ideal is what it thinks it should be; its self-image is what it thinks it is. The distance between the two is an index of self-esteem.

A business, as well as an individual, is asking for trouble when its self-image and ego ideal are allowed to stray too far from each other or—what is far worse—when they are cynically manipulated.

COLLECTIVE ASPIRATIONS

Freud pointed out that individuals in a cohesive organization identify with the ego ideal of their leader. As an organization expands and matures, this ego ideal tends to become the collective aspiration of its people. Diffuse as this may sound, it is real. Industrial psychologists have long known that people, if they have any choice in the matter, will not work for an organization when they disapprove of its image. Though they won't express it in psychological terms, employees have intense and often quite accurate conceptions about these factors. If they are merely indifferent to the company's ego ideal they may continue as employees but will do nothing beyond the minimum demanded of them.

Businesses have come to recognize this, too, and companies have become quite explicit about what they are, or at least about what they believe the best in themselves to be. A major oil company states its platform this way:

". . . Oil Company believes that a company can in the long run operate successfully only if it has public understanding and approval, because these are necessary to maintain the confidence of shareholders, loyalty of employees, acceptability of products, and freedom from unduly restrictive regulation.

"We believe further that this understanding and good will must be earned through the application of sound and ethical principles in the conduct of every phase of our business."

Of course, the difficulty is not so much in articulating the ideal; it is in acting consistently according to it. Consider, for example, the customer who thinks he is doing business with a company which stands for trustworthiness and finds it to be otherwise. He is much angrier and more disillusioned than he would have been with a fly-by-night outfit.

Disillusionment on the part of the customer has relatively simple consequences: he or she goes elsewhere if he can. But the problem of employee disillusionment is much more severe, particularly if employees cannot readily leave a company. They may then have feelings of depression, apathy, alienation, or outright anger toward the organization. Such feelings can occur under these conditions:

• *If the company does not strive to live up to its stated ideal.*

Many companies advertise that people are their most important asset. Suppose that one of these companies were actually insensitive to its people and high-handed in its personnel practices. When employees saw advertising proclaiming their importance while recalling their own experiences to the contrary in the organization, they could only feel that their leaders were hypocrites. As a result the employees would become hostile to the company. Quality control would be difficult to maintain, and the company's reputation would suffer.

In a public utility company the employees have long identified with the ideal of good service. They take pride in their service and in maintaining it even under adverse weather conditions. They become extremely angry, therefore, when they are not allowed to live up to that ideal. If, for example, a community manager wants to do a special favor for a friend or a politician and places that person at the head of the service list, employee anger will reverberate in the group for months. If the employees feel that the manager is not being fair and honest with everyone, then they become angry not only with him or her, but also with higher management for letting him stay in that position. They also become irritable and angry with themselves for staying in that company. No one knows how many accidents result from such feelings. I am sure some do.

• *If the employees cannot act positively toward attaining the ideal.*

The employees of a company which makes a certain kind of steel panel are justly proud of the products they make. They believe theirs to be the best products in the field. That is, all the employees but those in the paint department. The painters chafe because the paint they spray on the panels is not baked on, and therefore will wear off faster. They have been told that the company does not have the capital to construct baking facilities, but that statement does not ease their consciences because no one has given them the evidence and they don't really believe it. As a result, they are cynical about what they are doing. Turnover is high.

There are, of course, many causes for employee cynicism. As another example, one company indoctrinated its new young managers by sending them into the field to study practices and problems. They were then rotated through various departments for several years to gain experience. Far from appreciating this extensive training, the young men felt that they were not working toward the goals for which they were educated, and felt themselves demeaned by petty assignments. They did not see themselves moving toward their own aspirations, meeting the demands of their ego ideals, let alone those of the organization. As a group they were disappointed, irritable, and hostile to the company. Many left as soon as they could.

• *If the company does not have a clearly enunciated ideal.*

Where there is no consistently identifiable ideal in a company there is no psychological device for binding people together. They may work together as long as they are threatened from the outside, or if they have no possible job alternatives, or if they can make a quick dollar, but that will be a transitory alliance of desperation or opportunism. If people cannot share an ideal, they cannot be psychologically close to each other and cannot sustain a relationship. This is true even in families. Many families live together physically in the same homes for years, but the members form no close attachments to each other because they have few common goals or aspirations. They merely tolerate each other for the sake of convenience.

Many businesses are just like such families, some quite obviously. They may be transient manipulative businesses, out to make a quick killing with inferior merchandise. They may be organizations built around exploiting a fad or gimmick. They may be companies which believe that loyalty is something that can be bought.

Whatever the case, no organization can long survive by its own momentum without developing internal ties among its people, at least among those who are its core group. If money is all that holds them to a company, they will demand increasingly more and turn to the next company which offers them more. In some industries there are floating populations of just such people, and university administrators are beginning to complain of the same problem.

INEVITABLE CONFLICTS

These considerations offer the executive an avenue to think about his organization's ideals, the image it projects based on such ideals (or their absence), and the resulting impact on employees, customers, and the public alike.

An organization in many respects is much like a human being. If you want to understand a person, you examine him or her. You may do so systematically, as a physician does, or you may get to know much about him over a long period of time, as a friend does. First, you try to learn who and what he is. Second, you try to learn how he behaves under various circumstances. Third, you want to know what he believes and how he sees the world, how he presents himself to the world and why he does so that way. If there is a wide gap between the image one projects and the person he or she really is, emotional conflicts are inevitable. The same is true of a business organization: the greater the gap between what an organization pretends to be and what it really is, the more internal conflict there is likely to be. When public posture and reality divide, difficulties will arise.

The executive may focus on these issues by examining in his or her own organization the three elements of an image: (1) what an organization says, (2) what it does, and (3) what people believe it to be.

What a company says is reflected in its advertisements and public statements. They may be noisy, raucous, deceptive, dignified, pretentious. They may be pious—"We're for the good of the people"—yet hostile, opposing what protects people. Its annual report may be honest, detailed, easy to understand, or it may be obscure, pedantic, or self-promoting. It may offer a concept for its existence: "Service," "Better ways of living through chemistry." Whatever the case, it is trying to say, or not to say, something to someone. What? And why?

What a company does is evident in its products and services: whether they are of good quality or shoddy, well organized or sloppy. What it does is also evident in the way it regards its employees. Are they tacitly assumed to be economic units to be purchased and directed? Or does the management really think of them as capable, mature people? Does it conceive of communication as exhortation and persuasion or mutal definition of common problems? Does it make employees feel defensive or worthy? And what about the customers? Is the customer somebody to be conned by promising more than can be delivered, or duped by clever packaging? Does the company spend endless energy and money manipulating government agencies and regulatory bodies? Does it blame others for its failures and misfortunes, or does it look first at its own practices? Does it hear new ideas and take them seriously, or does it already have the answers? Is its motto, "You can't quarrel with success"?

What people believe an organization to be can be readily learned by asking them. This can be done informally in direct discussion with customers, the public, and employees. It can be done more formally with opinion polls or attitude surveys. One major company conducted a contest among its employees for the best-written statement about an employee's job. They received many entries and awarded numerous prizes. But the company was not really interested in the positive comments employees made about their jobs. By noting what they omitted, management could identify trouble spots.

The questions to be asked can be made quite concrete:
1. *If you have a company image, do you live up to it?*
Do you say one thing and do another? If so, the experiences of employees will probably be much like that of the vacationer who is enticed by a lavish brochure to visit a hotel, only to find when he gets there that the hotel is shabby and second-rate. If you convey to your own employees

that you are a specialist in hypocrisy by the way you think or act, you can expect them to be cynical in their relationships with management and cavalier about the product or service.

2. *If you have a company image, can employees live up to it?*

If people cannot act in keeping with the organizational ideal, usually something is keeping them from doing so. Exhortation and persuasion will be of little permanent value. Examine the work situation with them to discover the blocks.

Perhaps there simply is not enough capital to get the equipment to make the best possible product. Maybe there are other things which have higher priority. Defining reality—how much money there is, and what are the limitations of the market and production—will make it possible for people to adjust their ideals in keeping with what is realistic for them. Facing reality directly will also make it possible for them to evolve substitute actions—better ways of solving problems. Do not simply explain to them, although that will help, but invite their questions and discussion so that together you and they can evolve joint action which will deal with both your consciences.

You know employees are having difficulty living up to the image which you are publicly holding forth, if you have to force them to do so. Often this occurs because of conflicting demands. In manufacturing it is not unusual for people to be asked on the one hand to produce quality products, and on the other to be pressed by intense work schedules or disruptive demands. Nor is it unusual to indoctrinate people with the concept that they are to see themselves as professionals, offering a professional service, and then to pay them on a commission basis for selling a single product. In marketing, it is commonplace for companies to expect their salesmen to "con" customers with various kinds of gimmicks, and then expect them to respect the company and the customer. These are only a few of the possible conflicts. The inquisitive executive will find many more in every company.

3. *If you have to change the company image, have you helped the employees make the change, too?*

If a change must be made, as indicated earlier, the only way to help employees make the change is to talk it through with them. What are the problems which have to be dealt with, requiring the change? What does it mean in terms of the organization's survival? What kinds of conflicts will they have in this changeabout? Some people, of course, will not be able to stay with a change in values and ideals. Others will have to be brought in who fit the new image. It is an interesting fact that in re-organizing state hospitals it often becomes necessary to employ a completely new group of psychiatric aides. If the old ones have been chosen because they could operate in an autocratic atmosphere, they cannot readily adapt themselves to a patient-centered program. The same is true with supervision in previously autocratic companies when participative management is adopted.

4. *If you have no recognizable organizational image, is that the way you want it?*

Without a clear-cut image how do people know what you and the organization stand for and where they are going with your company? Do you want the confusion, the limited identification, and disparate values? Is it really expedient to have the resulting turnover? What other means, except for these clearly stated goals, do you have of developing loyalty, quality, product identification, and customer endorsement? The absence of a definable company image, assuming that the company is to survive, is cause for considerable thought about where this organization is going and what its management wants to do.

To be without a clearly recognized company image is not the same as having no image at all. Every organization has an image. The only question is whether it has the image it wants to have—in fact as well as in fantasy.

19

WHERE DID LOYALTY GO?

As EVERY EXECUTIVE KNOWS, organizations are held together by loyalty. A leader depends on the loyalty of his subordinates for his effectiveness. But whatever happened to good old-fashioned loyalty?

Company presidents complain that managers no longer identify with their companies. Despite promotion-from-within policies, management development programs, and generous salaries, managers increasingly leave one company for another. Executives in turn complain that employees no longer seem to care as much as they used to about maintaining the company's reputation. Again and again they have to be "sold." Craftsmanship, cost control, the profit requirement—don't they understand the need for these? Often, in the executive's eyes, the ultimate act of disloyalty is to form a union or to elect more militant union leaders.

Union leaders voice a similar cry. Why don't members come to union meetings anymore? Why does the membership of one large union reject a long-term leader who has "done so much for them," and the staff of another form a union within their union to represent them in dealings with their leadership?

A noted college president complains that faculty members flit from one college to another with little feeling for any one of them. Many, he complains, are preoccupied with the wooing of grants from foundations and government sources. They seem much more concerned with research that interests them and a congenial environment, than with their obligations to the institution.

Recent newspaper stories report the protests of priests

here and there, both in this country and abroad, about certain church policies. Yet these men have insisted that they continue to be loyal to the church. "How can they be and act that way?" some ask.

QUID PRO QUO

Loyalty is an ancient concept which goes hand in hand with honor. In feudal times a man gave his king or lord his fealty in return for the lord's beneficence or protection. To be loyal was to have a place in a formal social structure and to live according to a code of fixed relationships and mutual obligations. In return for loyalty, the more powerful took care of the less powerful. Though there were restraints of mutual obligations, the lord could give and the lord could take away. He controlled the lives of his subjects. To question the lord or to act against his wishes was to be disloyal. Put another way, it was to threaten his power.

The British scholar, W. N. Evans, pointed out the unconscious meaning of the political concepts of "left" and "right" in the struggle of men over power. "The word 'left,'" he noted, "derives from a Dutch base *lub* from which we get the Dutch, *lubben*, meaning 'to castrate,' and the word 'right' from the root *reg* ('to rule'—with an accompanying moral flavor). Thus we can begin to understand how the ruling elites responded to those who would question their authority as subversive, threatening, and morally reprehensible, i.e., 'not right.'" To the less powerful, greater freedom, by definition, means taking some power from the more powerful who control them; and it is necessarily seen by the latter as not right, or disloyal.

The same ancient concept of loyalty was carried down to other social institutions—the business, the university, the union, the church. All are organized in a hierarchical pattern in which the underlying assumption is that each level has command control of all below it. Those below are expected to be loyal to those above and to respond willingly to their power.

When they are not "loyal," the common reaction is that people are not behaving as they *should*, because they are ungrateful, unappreciative, and selfish. The protestors share a common feeling of *righteous* indignation. As they experi-

ence the actions of their subordinates, they feel that they
have been treated unfairly, rejected, or even betrayed.

THE "NICE" BOSS

Indeed, there remains much of the tradition in management circles that if the employee is paid reasonably, if the
workplace is adequately comfortable, and if the boss is
"nice," the employee should do as told, and do it cheer-
fully. Above all, the employee should stand behind and for
the person who provides his bread and butter. If he or she
does not do so, and does not appreciate what he is getting,
he is not a loyal employee.

This view is implicitly paternalistic and, in fact, much of
the human relations movement in business during the last
four decades has been an effort to disguise such paternalism. The manager, from foreman to executive, has been
advised to be kinder, warmer, friendlier, more considerate
so that subordinates would accept his or her control and
direction more readily. That thesis could not and does not
work, disillusioning many who tried to be "nicer." It did
not work because changing circumstances made traditional, paternalistic conceptions of loyalty obsolete for
many individuals and many organizations. Among the
many circumstances which produced this result, three
stand out:

• *There is a drastic change in the ability required to rise
in the ranks and hence in the rewards which loyalty alone
can confer.*

Paul B. Wishart, a leading industrialist, put it succinctly.
"There was a time within the memory of many of us," he
said, "when a reasonably intelligent, reasonably personable
individual with the self-discipline to learn the business, the
drive to work a little harder than the other fellow and the
courage to assume leadership responsibility could usually
work his way to the top. . . . This type of manager is having increasing difficulty; today's business complexities call
for a different type. . . . The rate of development in the
myriads of technical specialties has been so rapid we refer
to it as a technological explosion. It would obviously now
be impossible in the span of one lifetime for a top business
manager to be able to have actual, meaningful, experience
in each of these activities. The modern manager, therefore,
requires a broad-based education and experience that en-

ables him to exercise effective managerial leadership of professionals, engineers and scientists, even though he does not have, by education or direct experience, as much knowledge of their technical specialties as they have."

Mr. Wishart's comparison between past and present emphasizes that becoming a top executive is no longer a matter of rising on a fixed ladder in a stable organization to a *command* position. Today's emphasis is on the *leadership* of highly diverse specialists toward ever-changing goals.

Furthermore, such leadership ability is relatively rare, and when the choice must be made between unquestioned loyalty and unquestioned competence, today's organizations usually opt for competence. (This fact of modern life has not been lost on the ambitious. Since blind obedience is no longer a liberally rewarded virtue, it is no longer an assiduously cultivated one.)

Interestingly enough, the transfer of loyalty from the institution to the goal is also occurring in the military. Professor Allen Guttmann, of Amherst, points out that, ". . . compared to the European soldier, the American is as deficient in reverence for the past as in a sense of military honor." Professor Guttmann is not deprecating the American soldier. His point, however, is that "honor" has become less significant in the military as "heroic leaders" have been replaced by "military managers" and that, rather than revere the past, the professional American military manager uses its lessons for innovation.

Dr. Robert J. Lifton, professor of psychiatry at Yale, observes that in the samurai code, as also in Western feudal tradition, a heroic form of death in battle on behalf of one's lord was the ultimate expression of the meaning of life. Men no longer die for this purpose; they don't work for it either. Women never have.

• *There is a drastic change in people's expectations.*

The late Abraham Maslow pointed out that man's needs are arranged in a hierarchy. There are, first, basic biological needs; then needs for safety, protection, and care followed by needs for gregariousness, affection, and love relationships; and beyond these are needs for respect, standing and status, consequent self-respect; and the need for self-actualization or the fulfillment of one's potentialities. When the more elementary of these is satisfied, the next higher-level needs become the more powerful motives. Although I believe the ego ideal–self-image conception is more valid, the general thesis is useful.

The very success of American enterprise has changed the relative pressure of the psychological needs. Many people and particularly those in the managerial and professional groups found it relatively easy to meet their basic needs. To a lesser degree working-class people also found these basic needs fulfilled and became relatively secure about them.

As a result, those in industrialized societies usually have turned to their organizations for fulfillment of higher-level needs—their need for safety, protection, and care. The organizations responded with seniority provisions, health insurance, pensions, and the like. Needs in turn moved to a higher level. Respect, status, self-fulfillment—psychological rather than material needs—have become paramount.

This is what Mr. Wishart means when he says, speaking of the employee, "He now requires of his work experience a much broader, deeper and more satisfying return than was generally true in the past." People expect more, psychologically speaking, from the organizations in which they work. They must because of the overriding importance of work as a means of establishing their identity as adults and as a basis for establishing their self-respect.

This does not mean that people are unappreciative of those things which help fulfill the more basic needs. It means that they can readily fulfill these basic needs in almost any organization. They are therefore motivated to fulfill higher-level needs. They are more likely to want to work toward goals which will meet those needs.

As Professor Frederick Herzberg, of the University of Utah, and his former colleagues Drs. Barbara Snyderman and Bernard Mausner, have shown, when people have good wages, hours, and working conditions—these are hygienic or environmental factors of work—they will return a fair day's work but have little incentive to go beyond that. When, in addition, they feel they are being recognized, that they are achieving their goals and making good use of their capacities, they give more of themselves in the form of innovation, creativity, and investment of energy.

A simple analogy may make the issue clear. Some parents work so hard to give their children the material things of life that they have little time to spend with their children. When, as it usually turns out, the children do not seem to appreciate what the parents have done for them, the parents become angry and accuse the children of ingratitude. In effect, the parents have expected to earn the love and loyalty of the children with gifts, rather than with that love and respect which helps the children to become mature adults. Like the feudal lord, the parent in such a situation wants loyalty for past favors.

The same situation prevails with companies which try to buy the loyalty of employees with good fringe benefits while at the same time acting on the paternalistic assumption that the employees will then enthusiastically do what they are told to do. In such situations, and this is true of most business organizations, management keeps trying to fulfill needs which are no longer paramount. Executives then become angry when this "buying off" process not only requires that they constantly raise the ante but also fails to inspire loyalty.

• *There is a drastic change in the way families live.*

Extended family units live together far less frequently than they used to. Grown children are often separated from their parents by many miles, and in some cases by vast social gulfs as the children attain education and status that the parents could not dream of. These days many sons are employed by large organizations, and, if they are moving upward in executive ranks, they move about geographically. Their orienting point is no longer the family, the neighborhood, or the community as much as it is the company, the military, the governmental agency, or other employer with which they are affiliated over a period of years. People seek out such affiliations and employers encourage this identification by promotion from within, pensions, and other forms of reward for long service. Company insignia on tie clasp and cuff links has replaced the fraternity pin, the college ring, and the lodge emblem as the symbol of identification of the rising executive. This means that the relationship between a person and the organization in which he or she works has become an increasingly important one and must be cultivated continuously.

At the same time, successive younger generations have become increasingly independent. They have more money, more automobiles, are better educated, and have higher aspirations. (In fact, we have returned to the earlier independence of an agricultural era.) Any of them, with a reasonably good education, is confident of his or her ability to find employment. The result is that young people grow up feeling that they are more on their own, and often they are.

When they come into organizations as employees, they have greater expectations of being able to act relatively independently, to take a task and accomplish it, and to be heard. Contemporary social change activities, no less than wars, are primarily the working, fighting, and dying goals of young people. Regardless of anyone's value judgments about these efforts, *they are realities*. And they demonstrate what young people will do for goals which they feel are worth the doing.

It is often difficult to identify with an organization when a person brings a wish for increasing independence to an organization which operates on the paternalistic assumption that he or she will simply do as he is told and wait his turn. The relationship with an organization becomes even more trying to both parties when it takes place in an environment in which *everything* is subject to question, and the younger person is likely to be asking the questions.

Everything means just that—scientific facts, business practices, and "truths" that many have held unquestioningly for centuries. Nothing could be more astonishing to traditional Catholics, who thought their religious forms were what always was and what always would be, than the contemporary changes in the church following the Ecumenical Council. Newly documented translations of the Bible tell us many of the things we took for granted were simply not true. Religious dogma, racial prejudices, political theories—the very biases by which men live—turn out to be obsolete. The word "revolution" characterizes all sides of our society—church, school, industry, government. Nothing is as it was ten years ago. It is already an old story among professional people that their professional knowledge has a half life of ten years and that new graduates have conceptions that old pros can't begin to understand.

So it is that the axioms passed down from father to son lose their meaning, and the pronouncements from authority no longer carry weight. Authority doesn't count; expertise does. The test is in the doing. More and more, everyone has a batting average. Peter Drucker has pointed out that the next political power group will not be management or labor or rural or urban or minority, but bright, young, highly educated adults who are upwardly mobile in society as well as in their organizations.

THE NEW LOYALTY

All this does not mean that loyalty has gone or will go. It means, rather, that paternalism, however disguised, is going, and the kind of loyalty which was characteristic of paternalism must necessarily go with it. The old ways of achieving loyalty—preaching it, inducing guilt, reinforcing it by tight controls and severe penalties, buying it by keeping people dependent and grateful—no longer work.

And what will be in its place? Speaking of what has happened within the Roman Catholic church, editor Robert Hoyt, of the *National Catholic Reporter*, says that Catholicism is being transformed from a religion of paternalism to a religion of personal responsibility. In such a transformation, freedom of language and thought by the laity is not just a by-product of loosening controls but is required, for it becomes part of the responsibility of the laity to express their opinions on those things which concern the good of the church.

The same trends which are at work in the church are also at work in business and other social institutions. Mr. Wishart noted this in observing changing styles of leadership in industry. Instead of trying to compel loyalty by the forces of guilt or outside social pressure, the new-style leader creates conditions under which it evolves naturally.

He or she begins by recognizing that loyalty is a feeling of living according to values which have special importance. People these days want to live with themselves and with others as mature adults. They want to behave in those ways which are most effective in helping them not only master their world but also to live in it with reasonable psychological comfort.

The new kind of loyalty—really, it is quite old—comes about in several ways, the most important of which is by identification and assimilation. People identify with others and want to emulate them, to make the values of the others a part of themselves, if they experience positive relationships with others. Bonds of affection are the true bonds of loyalty. Affection and respect arise when people feel that others care about them. We feel that others care about us when they teach us fruitful ways to live and how to solve our problems better. Most of us remember teachers, ministers, scoutmasters, who at one time or another were like parents to us. We frequently wish we could be like them in their helpful ways. The values of these people are enduring ones because they are built on love and consideration: they help young people grow to independence and maturity. The same considerations govern loyalty in the workaday world.

THE NEW LEADER

To create the conditions for loyalty, the executive may find these suggestions helpful:

1. *Be open with subordinates.*

The omnipotent boss is going fast. Nobody knows enough these days to pose all the problems or to have all the solutions at hand. Bosses pretend they are omnipotent when they play it close to the vest. Such pseudo-omnipotence is merely a form of manipulation, and those who are subject to it are rightfully contemptuous when the same boss talks about loyalty.

2. *Make it possible for people to meet together as responsible adults to solve mutual and common problems.*

Where the lives and livelihoods of many people are involved, they have a right to help solve their own problems. Rather than threatening them, driving them, comparing them unfavorably with one another, or trying to buy them off, let them see the problems to be solved in making the business profitable. If the problems are worthy of their effort, and if the leader provides guidance and support, he or she will not have to worry about loyalty.

3. *Offer people both the opportunity and the challenge to be responsible both for their work and the fate of the organization. But do not try to con them by equating opportunity with money, and responsibility with doing what you want them to do.*

What can they do with their lives in the organization that makes life worth living? The work itself often doesn't do that; not much of the work people do is worth the expenditure of their lives. But no matter what the work, by sharing in the responsibility for planning and executing the work, a person can feel like an adult—and that is worth living for.

4. Recognize that loyalty is no longer to be equated with blind obedience.

The most loyal person may well be the most fervid member of the loyal opposition. The person who raises questions about how things are done, what assumptions are made, and what changes have to take place, what is coming in the future, what things anger and discourage people, is the person who helps the organization survive. Provisions should be made for hearing his or her voice. Yes-sayers are agreeable, nay-sayers the yeast of growth.

Most progress comes from questioners, dissidents, minority opinion. (Today's minority is tomorrow's majority.) Jazz arose from the lowest forms of entertainment in the most deprived social groups. Women's fashions and cosmetics, too, have their beginnings among the most unsavory elements of society. Political credos come from the oppressed (e.g., the American Revolution and the British Magna Carta). Scientific progress comes from those visionaries who are often ostracized by fellow scientists, the church, and politicians. We may not like what we hear from such people because they challenge our beliefs and values. However, no greater loyalty hath any person than the one who contributes to the advancement and wellbeing of his fellows.

The fundamental conditions for loyalty, then, are simple: freedom for ideas to be examined, freedom to define the problems to be solved, and freedom for all in the enterprise to direct their energy into solving them. When those conditions are met, an executive will never need to ask where loyalty went.

PART FIVE

Family Life

The process of leading, despite its gratifications,
is a lonely, sometimes burdensome task. However, it is not the executive's only task, for most
are husbands and fathers, wives and mothers, too.
These roles have their own gratifications and
burdens. They are nodes of happiness or the
pressure points of pain; no career is free of their
influence. Like all other roles, they profit from
active management based on understanding. We
turn now to an examination of the executive's
relationship with spouse and children.

20

MARRIAGE

ALMOST EVERY EXECUTIVE has obligations and gratifications in two areas: family and business. The positive and negative experiences in each can profoundly affect the other. For executives, two aspects of family life are of primary interest: relationships with the spouse and the critical and sometimes painful issues of dealing with adolescents. We'll take up those of marriage first.

When either husband or wife or both are in executive roles, there are essentially five different kinds of problems they must resolve. The problems discussed in this chapter illustrate these five central themes inherent in the marriage relationship:

1. Sustaining the loving relationship
2. Maintaining the concept of family
3. Coping with career compromises
4. Managing competition
5. Handling loneliness, anger, and disappointment

THE LOVING RELATIONSHIP

Once the family was geared to having and rearing children. Today, the primary function is mutual gratification and support. The contemporary family is a crucial sociological and psychological unit, concerned with its role beyond the merely biological process of reproduction.

We know from considerable research that people engaged in a mutually supportive relationship cope better with the stresses and problems of life. They are able to adapt better when they are supported by others who care about them. For adults, that primary support ideally comes from the spouse or spouse surrogate. The marital relationship serves to meet sexual, dependency, and love needs and to counteract and relieve feelings of inadequacy, failure, and guilt.

When one or the other spouse is the mainstay of the family's economy, decisions about the family must necessarily give priority to that person's work role, needs, and aspirations. The dependency of the other is increased, which may in turn affect the self-image. Until recent years the male in our culture was most often responsible for the economic support of the family. In the conventional case of male economic responsibility, the wife usually must conform to the requirements of the man's job. She, in turn, is primarily responsible for psychological support. When woman's single role was that of wife and mother, a significant part of her job was to enhance her husband's career through support and nurturing, by serving as a sounding board, and by counteracting feelings of failure or pressure with faith, love, and confidence. "At her best," said sociologists W. Lloyd Warner and James C. Abegglen, "she provides her husband a base of operations that gives the kind of support essential to advance his career."

The support of the wife materially enhances the possibility of success in tasks and in the capacity to direct one's energies to meeting the requirements of work and the organization. One management consultant estimated that a good wife could increase her husband's lifetime earnings by as much as $250,000. As Dr. Fausto Tanzi of the University of Chicago Medical School put it, "If the family is happy and the wife can put the greatest percentage of her efforts on this relationship, making the family pleasant for the husband and children, I think this would probably increase the life and productivity of the individual more than anything else."

Today sex role stereotypes have broken down. More and more women are pursuing independent executive careers over their entire working lifetime. Although this is a long overdue use of womanpower—a previously undeveloped resource—like any significant change, it will present considerable problems.

People bring to every relationship a history of needs and expectations—both personal and cultural, overt and unspoken. In each relationship those involved must negotiate an emotional settlement to insure mutual gratification of needs and wishes. For the most part, this settlement, or the psychological contract, is unwritten or unspoken. Much of it is unconscious. Its terms are fluid, changing with time and with context, but because people expect their wishes and needs to be fulfilled, the contract as a whole is binding. In marriage, the most intense and intimate of relationships, the psychological contract is crucial; violations of the contract can have alarming effects on the marriage.

For example, when the wife of a male executive returns to work, the latter no longer counts as much on the former for gratification of affection and dependency needs, simply because she is no longer so readily available. She is not always at home, and when and if she is, she may no longer recognize the daily caring and serving function as something she wants to or should fulfill. In addition to her traditional obligations to her husband and family, she now has obligations to her own ambitions. Others in the family may more often have to fend for themselves, not only in the simple functional tasks of homemaking but more importantly in dealing with their own emotions and feelings. The daily triumphs and setbacks of both her children and her executive husband may be overshadowed by her own set of problems. Where before there might have been only the problems of the children and the home for both husband and wife to deal with, there may well be an additional set of problems which demand their own psychological time and preempt support time.

There may also be limitations to the support a wife can provide for her husband's career if, out of obligations to herself, she is less willing to move and take up a new job in another community to enhance his career. Here we see the ego ideal–self-image problem for the husband. It could occur equally with a wife who is an executive. Companies which rotate executives are already confronting this problem and discovering that many people on whom they had counted to be mobile are unwilling to move because of the disruption of the career of their spouses.

Just as the husband cannot count as much on the many personal attentions which presumably were available to him at an earlier era, now the executive wife for somewhat different reasons is less able to count on the support of her husband when she in her new role encounters some of the problems that he himself has to deal with. If both partners are working and particularly if both are in managerial roles where they also must travel, they may not be available to each other to provide the reaffirmation that they need to cope with personal and professional problems. This becomes an ever more pressing issue for the person in the executive role who at work must support many people, sometimes a whole organization, and who therefore requires greater support when turning to the spouse at home.

From the beginning, the relationship between husband and executive wife must be built around the fact that the executive who is also a wife has already had to violate certain social conventions to compete with men, to surpass them, and to climb the organizational hierarchy. She has likely been discriminated against, envied, and often viewed as an illegitimate competitor. Some may still believe she attained her position because of sexual favors rather than competence. These are issues that she must deal with, and so must her husband because she will bring them home. She requires more self-image support from her husband in this sense than would be the case if their situations were reversed. She is fighting on two fronts simultaneously: coping with social pressures which historically have defined the woman's role as mother and homemaker, and combatting pressure in her organization as she moves into responsible executive positions.

Even if the husband is available, he may not be skilled in listening, empathizing, and relieving the pain of defeat and anger. Women still have greater experience in the comforting and supporting role than men characteristically have. Historically men have been the warriors, not the nestbuilders. Few have had to counsel and console others who feel defeated, inadequate, and worthless.

CONCEPT OF FAMILY

The basis of any marriage or continuing relationship is the bond of affection, esteem, regard—essentially love—between two people. A mutual exchange of affection is the crucial element to be sustained in a relationship. When the affectionate bond is impaired or severed, the relationship, for all practical purposes, is merely an expedient accommodation. In order for that relationship to be sustained, people need time to be together, to exchange affection, to hear and touch each other—in short, to work on the mutual psychological obligations of the relationship. The relationship must be cultivated like any other living organism. Thus husband and wife, when either or both are in occupations which make many demands on them, must arrange for appropriate time to sustain and work on the relationship.

One of the most important ways they can help each other is to enhance the sense of worth which necessarily is continuously threatened by the experiences of defeat and frustration which are a part of being in competitive organizations. Theirs is the task of supporting and enhancing each others' self-images. They owe it to themselves to set up the necessary time and place to do this marital work.

The crucial element in building an affectionate bond is the capacity to tell and listen. Many people tell each other a great deal—sometimes too much—about the wrong things. They complain, harangue, nag, and criticize. Few tell each other their innermost feelings and concerns and wishes. As a result, their partners are on guard against the threatening comments and cannot hear the more subtle expression of psychological need. Yet, without hearing such feelings, one can respond only to the superficial aspects of behavior. Thus, frequently people live a lifetime together without working on their relationship, without responding to powerful and deeply held needs and feelings. Each must learn to express his or her personal feelings, fears, anxieties, and wishes when they arise. In so doing, one enables the other to respond and gives the other permission to do likewise.

The increasing freedom of women in many ranges of human activity includes increased sexual flexibility and freedom. This in turn has proved to be something of a threat to many men. In fact, it has been reported that the single most frequent reason that young men come to college mental health clinics is that they become impotent in the face of sexual expectations and demands on the part of women. They frequently have the feeling that they cannot live up to those explicit expectations and demands. Such feelings are likely to be exacerbated among executive couples when husbands for one reason or another are defeated in their upward climb or in other ways have their self-images depreciated.

From time to time there have been reports to the effect that the work of executives is so demanding that it has interfered with their sex lives. There is some reason to think that there is an element of truth to that assertion. If it has validity, then it is likely to have equal validity for female executives. That in turn poses a problem for them if their work then interferes with their relationship to their husbands. Some sensitive executives, male and female, are already making it clear to their superiors that they do not expect to sacrifice their family life for their work. Others may be less sensitive to the possible consequences of being preoccupied with their careers. Some may become even more impatient with what they experience as the inappropriate demands of their partners, particularly in the face of managerial burdens.

The greater freedom and activity of the wife should not blind her to the fact that her husband's potency is much more tied to his feelings of self-esteem than her own. The wife of an executive as a result has to be more sensitive to the kinds of requirements and demands she may make in her natural exuberance and freedom—demands for her own gratification which may at inopportune times have negative effects on her spouse. The fact that he is an executive, if that is the case, should not blind her to the additional fact that he is also subject to the role definition of a man and to what is required of him in that role. This issue becomes most clear when male executives lose their jobs and their wives become the major supports of the family. Frequently, husbands see themselves as less manly and therefore less able to perform adequately in the sexual roles. When women executives lose their jobs, there may also be reverberations—either greater demands on their husbands for comfort and gratification or withdrawal in depression and anger. In their day-to-day activities, the pains and misfortunes of the day already reverberate to the bedroom, but they are likely to be more intense when the self-image is more severely threatened.

Of course, the wife becomes more dependent when she requires the more active support of her husband during pregnancy and the early days of family responsibilities. This magnified dependency requires more thoughtfulness on the part of the husband. In most cases, the female executive who has one or more children may, at least temporarily, sacrifice career progression. She will need special reassurance and help from her husband, particularly in efforts to stay in touch with her career, to keep up with information that she needs to have, and to maintain a continuing relationship with the organization which employed her. This may pose added family management burdens for the husband and require him to assume responsibilities that might otherwise be uncongenial or for which he has little or no preparation.

The fact that there are now others—children—to come between husband and wife and interfere with intimacy tends to pull the parents apart. The couple's concern is focused on the children rather than solely on themselves. This increased distance between the partners must be acknowledged or it will divide the couple. In such cases, they may stay together "for the sake of the children" and feel disappointed in each other and in the marriage. They may then resort to heroic efforts to maintain the integrity of the family and to salvage some of their dreams. The late Dr. Nathan Ackerman, one of the pioneers of family therapy, noted that such efforts ran the gamut of extremes: from togetherness to self-indulgence, from overcontrol to permissiveness. Some concentrated on one or two activities in the hope that intensive investment in music, athletics, or child care would keep the family from falling apart. Others scapegoated one of the family members as if all of the conflict were his fault and there would be no problem if only he would behave. None of those efforts accomplished what either party in the marriage wanted: genuine intimacy.

Underlying the difficult decisions of family planning—whether to have children, how many to have, when to have them, how to provide for adequate child care—is the larger emotional issue of men's and women's intense desire to procreate. In one crucial sense, the wish to build a career and to have and rear a child are the same: both are an attempt to leave a legacy, to insure that one's life has a meaning that will survive one's death.

Just as some women have found that they deeply regretted not having pursued a career, others will find as they approach middle age and have passed the child-bearing years that they regret acutely not having had children. Couples may discover only when it is too late that their decision not to have and rear children has violated fundamental unconscious expectations of marriage. By then the couple, both man and wife, will have to deal with the anger and disappointment resulting from their choice. That loss may be even more severe in later life for the woman or man left alone through death or divorce with no family to turn to.

Intimacy is a mixed blessing, and the wish for intimacy is simultaneously a threat. The more intimate one becomes with another, the more one expresses one's deepest feelings to the other, the more one asserts one's need for the other and becomes dependent on the other. A person becomes increasingly vulnerable to having the psychological rug pulled out from under him or her by even trivial slights, which seem to suggest that the other person does not love him. This is an especially difficult problem if one partner is unduly rivalrous with the other. The more one learns to respond to another person's needs, the more one must change oneself, and nothing is so frightening as the prospect of changing oneself.

Wanting to come closer emotionally, but fearful of doing so and subtly angry about becoming more dependent, each party may react by withdrawing even further from the other or by testing the other person. Hostility serves both purposes. Hate creates distance between people and is therefore, paradoxically, more tolerable than love if one is afraid of intimacy. Being angry is also a method for testing how much the other person is willing to tolerate and thereby how strong the marital bond is.

Keeping busy is another way of coping with intimacy. The busier a person is, the less time he or she has to reflect on his own feelings, the less time for intimacy with himself or his partner. He never discusses how fearful he is of feeling helplessly dependent on the other person. Only his speed and intensity suggest that he is running from something.

COMPROMISES

Once a woman is no longer limited to her homemaking role and chooses other alternatives, compromises will have to be made with respect to her wishes and those of her husband. If she chooses to take formal courses or undertake significant work in the community or in other ways meet her internal demands for making a contribution, the husband's economic and business role may have to yield some or he may have to compromise the kinds of demands he makes for the nesting activity. It is this frustration of husbands which often produces great conflict between spouses. One way or another the nesting activity must be carried on in such a way that the relationship and the home will continue to provide surcease from the business world. If both people are involved in demanding careers, they will both have greater need for this refuge and be less likely to be able to provide it for each other. If the need is not met, there is little purpose for marriage.

If the wife chooses to work, there will be many compromises, ranging from such simple things as compatible hours and vacation time to which career gets priority at certain stages of its development. Each person must seize advantages when the time is right or that person's career is stalled. Sometimes if one or another is unwilling to yield, the other feels abandoned or neglected, if not downright defeated or betrayed. When both spouses work, particularly if one or both are in managerial or executive ranks, they must actively negotiate their common priorities, evaluating the phases and stages of career development and the kinds of experiences which seem to be needed in each stage.

The question of transfer from one place to another can raise difficult issues. There are yet too few examples of husbands moving to accommodate executive wives to be able to spell out the specific problems for male spouses of female executives. Whatever they may be, they will rest on the same psychological issues. However, one of the difficult problems for the female executive who must move to accommodate her career is the implications of that move for her husband's career. In the past, when wives have moved to accommodate their husbands' careers, it has been assumed that the wives' careers were less important or that they could simply pick up relatively unskilled jobs or specialized work wherever they were going. With male spouses, however, there may be additional problems of self-image and career mobility that may pose complications for the female executive—complications that the male executive did not previously experience in the same degree. For example, the nonexecutive male may be unwilling to take whatever limited or part-time jobs are available. Although now male executives may frequently decide not to move in order to accommodate the wife's job or the children's schooling, the mobility problems for male executives seem to have not yet approached the potential psychological importance that they may come to have for female executives. Women executives probably will have more difficulty getting their husbands to move.

Prior discussion of priorities can help both parties articulate their psychological contract and make it possible for them to make a decision based on that agreement. However, no prior agreement can take into account all the factors likely to arise, and such agreements must continuously be revised and reevaluated in the light of whatever opportunities develop and their impact on the psychological needs of both parties. As a basis for negotiation and decision making, couples would do well to define their values and value systems, the things that are important to them and in what priority.

Sometimes careers do not advance. One or another partner may be demoted or lose his or her job or be put under great pressure to take an assignment which may not be to his or her advantage. These experiences precipitate considerable strain. It would be helpful therefore for couples to talk together about such potentialities and to establish reserve positions for themselves. Wise executives always evolve contingency plans for unanticipated circumstances. The same kind of practice should be followed by executive couples. They cannot cover all contingencies, but a well-prepared position makes it possible to act without panic or great pressure in the same way that rehearsing accident-prevention procedures makes it possible to cope with an emergency when it arises.

People with intense ambition have much more difficulty effecting compromises. Each partner should weigh honestly for himself or herself and for his or her spouse the degree of intensity of the wish to achieve. There's not much point in deluding oneself or one's partner. When the time for compromise arises, the one with the more intense pressure will be less willing to compromise. The other is then going to feel the contract has been violated. The relationship is thereafter impaired. When there are likely to be such differences, it is helpful to have a confidant who knows both parties and can be reasonably objective with respect to both to help them talk through their alternatives and the possible consequences.

The resistance to compromise is likely to increase when one or the other achieves officer rank or a similar high-level position. The greater the responsibilities, the less the role itself will allow him or her to compromise. Therefore, significant steps in promotion require prior renegotiation in considerable detail. Usually the higher the position one attains, the more the partner has to compromise his or her wishes to complement the work of the higher-level person. Many people deny such issues, but they are indeed fact.

Women in executive roles will have a more acute need to talk with their husbands because they will be less able to discuss some of their managerial problems on the job, inasmuch as they cannot do so with their subordinates and frequently may need to consider issues before taking them up with their superiors. Thus, a female executive, perhaps even more than a female in other roles, will need a sympathetic and understanding husband. If either spouse is unable to find that kind of empathic consideration in the other which he or she would normally require, it might be helpful to have an external source of professional counsel who can be seen on a regular basis. That will tend to reduce some of the anger of unmet dependency needs in the relationship.

COMPETITION

Like it or not, spouses are frequently in competition with each other even when one is the homemaker. That competition may increase when both are in executive ranks and is compounded when the dependency of one on the other is increased, but particularly when the dependency of the male on the female is increased.

Dependency problems are frequently difficult to handle. Some men deny their dependency needs by not talking to their wives, not bringing home their feelings about solving their business problems. If an executive completely denies his or her spouse access to his relationship with his work, if he or she cannot accept the spouse as a partner or refuses the spouse a complementary role, he or she makes it impossible for the partner to help. Sometimes a spouse does not want to accept the responsibilities of supporting the other's dependency. Both positions deny the dependency needs of the other partner and therefore make for conflict between them.

Historically, the female has been the more dependent. In middle-class American culture many have rejected that dependency because of what they sensed to be their vulnerability, particularly in middle age when widowed or divorced women frequently found themselves unable to sustain their previous standard of living. This rejection has threatened some males, and many of them still protest against it. Many men are willing to accept an interdependent relationship, but have greater difficulty when the wife becomes the more adequate, more powerful breadwinner. One of the difficult problems to be dealt with is what happens when the wife does indeed surpass the husband. That experience often leads to feelings of resentment and hostility about being Mr. Jane Doe. It happens very frequently when women at lower socioeconomic levels, whose husbands are unskilled or semi-skilled, attain positions which are economically and socially above those of their husbands. It takes a sensitive and thoughtful couple to handle such a relationship with compassion and consideration rather than bitterness.

At whatever managerial level husband and wife find themselves, the reversal of traditional roles requires a good deal of talking together, of assessing with each other the psychological costs. Female executives will have to give careful attention to preserving the self-image of their spouses in the sense of not allowing their success to simultaneously signal their husband's defeat. It is easy to fall automatically into one of two extremes: on the one hand, the wife avoiding promotion in order not to put her husband down, on the other, taking a promotion regardless of the consequences. Neither husband nor wife should deny their competition, however subtle it may be. Only when both are willing to recognize it can they deal with it. This is a critical point for the renegotiation of the psychological contract.

LONELINESS, ANGER, DISAPPOINTMENT

Feelings about intimacy can be avoided, or masked by hostility or activity, until middle age. When, however, the children begin to leave home, when one's career path has already been established and a certain degree of financial security is assured, there is less external demand for the same intensity of activity. Middle age is a time of crisis, reorganization, and consolidation. It is also a time of accelerating physical change. For the middle-aged woman, there is the reality of menopause. If there are children, both parents, especially the mother, feel that the nest is empty. And there is the compelling issue of having to take stock and reevaluate one's own requirements and choices. This is exacerbated by the crisis of middle-aged executives of both sexes—the need for most to come to terms with having reached their occupational peak and try to integrate their life's efforts and experiences.

Both partners may then find themselves ready to return to giving more attention to each other. This is difficult to do unless they have consistently worked at sustaining their relationship as they have gone through the process of achievement, attainment, and family development. In addition, as one executive put it, "You discover that there are only so many weekends left in life." This is brought home when parents die, when one becomes aware that he or she is the elder now, that there is no longer another generation between himself or herself and death. One perceives, sometimes not so dimly in the distance, that there is an end. With each passing year that perception becomes more painfully vivid.

The threat of death magnifies the feelings of loneliness which have already been increased by the problems with intimacy. It stimulates fantasies of being deserted and lost, feelings which seem so childlike that adults are quick to push them from consciousness. They remain behind the scenes, like a Green Monster ready to pop out if there is a respite from busyness. The psychological contract has changed.

Now both parties have to struggle with the fear of love on the one hand and the fear of loneliness and ultimate death on the other. Both would like to cry out their pain and their fear, but to admit that they hurt makes each even more vulnerable to deflation by the other. Renegotiation is thus difficult if not impossible. Instead, they clutch at each other with nonnegotiable demands, each trying to motivate the other to meet his need by making him feel guilty.

These frustrations (contractual violations) result in mutual anger and disappointment. Each person is also disappointed and angry with himself or herself and regards himself as a fool for ever having trusted the other or believed that the other would meet his needs. Neither believes in the loyalty of the other, giving rise to further mistrust, fear, and doubt.

Often couples are angry with each other for these

reasons without ever knowing why. The anger increases in intensity as the children leave home, depriving both parents of other sources of psychological nourishment. This loss is particularly painful for the mother, who also loses the feedback on her maternal performance. Those who are more rivalrous with their husbands, especially if they are not pursuing gratifying careers, are now without a home-based task of their own. They become fearful of their increasing dependence on their men and begin to compete more actively. They seem to need to fight for control, to win so that they may be in charge of themselves.

Some can accept the responsibility of caring for their children, but never that of caring for their men. When the children are grown and gone, they are faced with that issue more starkly. Some women at this point say they want to become independent and do not want to have responsibility for someone else. This is often a rationalization to mask the fact that they simply cannot care.

Thus, the needs of either or both parties go unmet as they flee from prospective increased intimacy with each other. The home becomes a battleground. As in all wars, the issues are obscured in the noise of the fighting and shrill cries of justification.

Anger undoes people. It impairs their judgment, makes them fearful of what they will do, or immobilizes them with fuming turbulence. As it rises, it becomes harder to hide. People become ashamed of their anger and feel guilty for it, especially if it seems to outweigh the circumstances which precipitated it. They cast about for reasons to justify the "burn" they have built up. Sometimes they find them, but most people know, somewhere in the recesses of their minds, that they have created the reasons, which adds to their feelings of guilt. If the marriage partners turn to other partners to obtain the love they seek, or in revenge, all these feelings are even further intensified.

Anger increases subtly in the very process of aging. Some friends fall away; interests tend to become more narrow, and physical capabilities are no longer what they were. The bifocal lens is incontrovertible evidence of the loss of physical flexibility. All these are losses of psychological gratification, and the loss is never without accompanying anger.

In the absence of continuous renegotiation there is a cycle of wish – dependency – hostility – withdrawal – wish

— clutching — guardedness — hostility — withdrawal — desperation. It is at this point that the second peak in the divorce rate is reached.

RE-CREATION

Aging, bringing a person closer to the inevitable, stimulates questioning about the significance of life and the meaning of immortality. It also increases the wish to experience life to the fullest before it slips unnoticed through one's fingers. Some respond to these feelings by becoming increasingly philosophical, rethinking their life purposes and goals. Some take to mystical cults. Others begin racing against time and loneliness, afraid to slow their social activity for fear that to do so is the same as surrendering to death. But socialization is not the same as intimacy. When the evening is over, the void remains.

The sense of being diminished, rejected, and passed by is a psychological eddy, and almost anything can become a straw to grasp. People seek even the smallest gratification as a way to avoid facing the underlying sense of helplessness about their fate and the threat of nothingness and annihilation. Earlier in life, these fears were avoided by assuming that one day one would be master of oneself. As an adolescent girl so beautifully put it, "When you are a little girl you are full of fears. You feel when you grow up and become an adult, it will be the difference between black and white. You will move into the white area and understand everything. Everything will be all right and you will do it all right. You will no longer be afraid." The fundamental psychological discovery of middle age is the illusion of that belief. It shatters on the hard promontories of time.

For many couples, this is the time of the second honeymoon. Still wishing intimacy, but still fearful of self-exposure; afraid of introspection, dependency, and the need to change oneself, but even more afraid of loneliness, they desperately seek an avenue to each other. They try to retread the original path to each other in an effort to rekindle old flames. Some even build new houses. Building a new house becomes, as one executive's wife put it, the physical manifestation of a psychic rebuilding. It provides one with a sense of continuing to grow and with a device for the husband and wife to work together on a common task. Couples look upon it as if it were *the* magic wand. Unfortunately, most of the time it is a clutching because the three problems we have just been discussing (disappointment, loneliness, and anger) have changed in meaning between the first and second honeymoons. Once the new house is built, with nothing further to discuss and the unseen psychological barriers still between them, the couple begins to drift apart again with deeper disillusionment. What is supposed to be a reincarnation turns out to be the construction of an altar to a fictional idol. Husband and wife fall back into their old psychological ruts with even greater distance between them.

While these are the painful experiences most couples face, they are not insurmountable. They can be worked on and worked out if executive and spouse can become more psychologically comfortable with each other and more accepting of each other.

The following steps may be helpful as guides for dealing with problems of the husband and wife relationship:

1. *Recognize the importance of continued loving between men and women.*

The best way to do this is for husband and wife to continue to talk with each other and express their feelings about each other. They have to assure each other that they will make the appropriate time and undertake the appropriate activities to support their loving experience. Each needs to know what the other person wishes and what is in turn wished for from the other person. They must make their differences a legitimate subject of discussion. These are the unwritten details of the marriage contract, which is after all only a one-paragraph verbal agreement.

2. *Create opportunities to talk to each other, openly and seriously, about your deepest feelings.*

Unless you can trust each other with such feelings, you are doomed to clutching and desperation. You will continue to claw at the invisible walls between you. There is nothing wrong with feeling lonely or frightened; the wrong lies only in trying to hide those feelings from the partner whom you have tacitly asked to help you combat them. It is difficult to create such opportunities. A starting point may be a discussion of this chapter. Sometimes, it is easier to talk about such feelings in groups—a church-couples group, a group discussion of family problems. However, men are often reluctant to bare their feelings publicly. Sometimes discussion among men with a professional leader can open avenues for subsequent discussion in mixed groups. A caution should be observed here: many quacks hold themselves out as marriage counselors, and many people conduct group discussions. Couples should be careful to undertake such public examination of their feelings only with qualified and reputable professionals, or they may well find themselves farther apart than when they started.

3. *Anticipate fear and anger when you begin to talk to each other.*

There is always fear of discovering areas of communication, because if there are such areas, people will begin to open up. Then they expose themselves to the possibility of being let down and of having to change their behavior. Both possibilities threaten their deeply held images of themselves. Men, particularly, are afraid of losing their aggressiveness by devoting themselves to a contemplation of their psychological navels. There is also always anger as old wounds are reopened, long-held resentments come to the surface, and ancient disappointments are illuminated. The initial stages of any important communication of feelings among people are the most difficult for these reasons. That is why discussion most often is closed off. A couple needs time to get these feelings on the table and out of the psychological way. Each partner needs to be able to let the other express them without anger and retaliation in return, or there can be neither acceptance nor trust. Once that shock wave passes, the conditions are conducive to further talk.

4. *Create a climate in which feelings can come to the surface.*

Feelings are like bubbles. When they can come to the surface they can be seen, acted upon, and dissipated. If they cannot come to the surface, they create a sense of pressure. Furthermore, like carbonation in soda water, they may pop out embarrassingly at the wrong moments. One must always be on guard against them. Far better to understand that there is nothing wrong with having and expressing feelings, just as there is nothing wrong with any other human process. There is no need either to keep them buried or to store them for later explosion. Nor is one blameworthy or inadequate for still struggling with feelings which have their roots in childhood. Human beings think they can shed their feelings as they grow up just as a snake sheds its skin when it grows out of it. They cannot and do not. A snake's skin is outside his body; feelings are inside. You can deal with feelings only if you can bring them to the surface of consciousness and make them a subject for consideration and a basis for action.

5. *Understanding and helping each other with the expression of feelings is the most viable basis for sustaining a marriage.*

That experience is the chrysalis of growth, the bridge for affection and the basis for trust. How do you know that is what you are doing? You can differ without fear of disaster. You share common goals for which you need each other and you expect the marriage to be the vehicle for attaining them. You take pride in each other, not just the children or the home.

Only such a relationship replaces clutching with intimacy, biting with kissing, competition with co-operation, loneliness with love, and self-doubt with a sense of personal worth.

21

FAMILY

THE CHOICE of whether to have a family and how large it should be is increasingly one that husbands and wives must balance against their single or mutual career aspirations. Recent studies indicate that today's college-age women expect to have considerably fewer children than did their parents. Many couples are already choosing not to have children, and there is already an organization of nonparents.

In contemporary society, family planning requires a good deal of thought and discussion. The values of the couple, the pressures from family and friends, contemporary economic circumstances, are all crucial factors, and all raise intense emotional reactions. Those who have not faced such a dilemma may not appreciate the intensity of feelings they arouse; those for whom such questions are automatically answered by certain religious values or other orientations to life may be equally puzzled.

If both husband and wife have strong career aspirations, the couple has to also arrange adequate child-care. The child-bearing years coincide with those in which people in managerial and professional careers establish themselves, develop reputations, demonstrate their competence, and become visible to their superiors. A woman who decides to have one or more children necessarily does so at some expense to her career. At a minimum, she will be absent for one or more periods of three months. Her absences may coincide with the crucial initiation or conclusion of projects or major campaigns. In three months, the organizational environment may change rapidly. Furthermore, being responsible for an infant is a handicap in itself in the sense that to have a child is to incur additional obligations and responsibilities. The longer a woman stays home with her child, the more she risks losing momentum in the organization.

Among the things which one may miss out on in this period of time are certain training and rotations which are easier to handle when one is single. Some managerial roles call for a good deal of travel. This may be more difficult to manage in later stages of pregnancy and in the early months of the life of the new child. If a woman chooses to nurse her child, the absence will be prolonged, and she will have to compensate actively in order to stay in the competitive swim.

In organizations that can manage such breaks and are willing to do so, there may be an advantage in the sense that such companies may be placing their bets on the later, more mature years at higher levels of responsibility. Nevertheless this is a period of concern for everyone who aspires to an executive position and one which requires a great deal of thinking and planning. The woman must know especially from her organizational superiors what special problems there will be, if any, and what organizational risks she is taking so that she can weigh her choices realistically.

The decision to have children is not only a question of timing or number. The couple must also discuss what roles they are prepared to play in child-rearing. A woman's dependency on her husband increases during pregnancy and for some time after delivery. If she has difficulty accepting her dependency needs, she may become resentful. If she is intensely rivalrous with her husband, she may also resent the fact that he is in a more competitively advantageous position. In this case, she is likely to become angry with herself and with him, which may have significant effects for each of them as well as for the child.

The arrival of one or more children may pose new kinds of questions about whether the wife should work part-time, full-time, as a consultant, in freelance work, or in some other way balance work and family obligations. How she deals with this problem will relate significantly to her own ego ideal and her aspirations both in motherhood and in executive achievement. Some of her alternatives will hinge specifically on the kinds of arrangements she can make at

home in order to support her role in management and the
degree to which her husband can cover for her in family
emergencies.

There are decisions which have to do with whether the
family should move in the interest of one or another
career. When both partners are working, it may be easier
to debate the financial and psychological cost of moving
than when all of the income responsibility is carried by one
family member because there are conflicting economic
forces to be balanced.

As the dependency of the wife and children on the male
decreases with the increased independence of the wife,
there is the greater need for continuous negotiation of
plans and activities. Both parents and sometimes the child
are called upon to negotiate between themselves and often
with their children the significance and implications of
whatever requests, requirements, and demands are made
by the employing organization. When both parents work,
these negotiations must necessarily increase. The discussions center not only on the achievement of the given individual, whether husband or wife, but on the impact of such
potentials as advancement and transfer on the family as a
system. Many organizations report that men are now less
willing to be transferred around the country, indeed
around the world, because of the impact of such moves on
their families. Some men decline transfers because they are
already located where they want to live, and the work or
achievement in the organization is secondary to that desire.
Some decline because their wives do not want to give up
their jobs. Families should discuss issues like these and
define their positions before they are faced with the problems in the form of a request for transfer or the opportunity for promotion.

There are sometimes special problems which specifically
limit the alternatives a couple may have. If a child is hand-
icapped in some way or requires special education or treatment available only in certain places, then much will have
to be sacrificed for the needs of that child. Sacrifice by
definition always involves giving something up, a feeling of
loss, which in turn produces anger. Those who feel themselves to be giving up a great deal, like executive aspirations, should be especially prepared to talk over their
feelings with a psychologist or psychiatrist in their own interests and that of the child.

Many of these problems need discussion beyond the two spouses involved. Often the wife needs social permission and support from her peers as well as a safe place to vent her frustrations among others who will understand her feelings from firsthand experience. It is easier to make choices when one can do so in the context of weighing experiences of other people. It is also easier when one feels supported by others.

The fact that women now are more frequently in the role of partner and co-breadwinner does not mitigate the pressures that many women may feel to achieve motherhood. Those pressures become particularly acute for both single and married women in the period roughly between 27 and 30 years of age. At that point, many women come to the realization that if they are going to have children they had better do so quickly or the optimum time for doing so will be past. The choice point creates a dilemma which is often difficult to resolve. The woman needs ample opportunity to examine her feelings and make her choice in group and individual discussions with others in similar positions and with counselors. Her efforts to resolve that dilemma require great understanding and support on the part of the husband. It also requires great understanding and support on the part of male managers and executives in organizations where women work.

Now let's turn to the adolescent.

More often than not, executives are all too keenly aware of how much time they take from their families to give to their jobs. Many live with guilt feelings for having slighted their children while striving for success. They, like most parents, do not understand the adolescent—his moods, his fads, his rejection of parents. They are troubled by the teen-ager's unpredictability. They feel as if they are on the outside of the child's life looking in. Yet they are still responsible for him, and they are almost desperate in their desire to help him do well.

There was a time when, after a boy or girl reached puberty, marriage was not far off. Children learned the work and duties of adults by performing them with adults, and then they went right to being adults. Not so anymore. Today's adolescent has a big job on his hands—bigger than his father had, and a lot harder. As a result, the parents' job is harder.

Take the matter of education. In a highly innovative and competitive industrial culture, education has become the ticket to social and job advancement. "It's pencil or pick now," a laborer told me to explain why he wanted his son to go to college.

In three generations the scholastic price of admission to opportunity as an adult has increased by eight years and two sheepskins. Today's great-grandparents were doing well to get through the eighth grade before they went to work. Today's children often know—even before they reach the eighth grade—more about the sciences than their parents do. Those who have acquired such knowledge often feel they cannot afford to stop short of the college degree, and if they want a running start, they had better have an advanced degree too.

Even the sheepskins cost more now. College-selection officials are reputed to favor high school students who have taken part in a wide range of extracurricular activities in addition to having high scores on national competitive exams. Students are working harder and ranging farther in their activities. When they get to college they are aware, even if their parents are not, that the pace has increased. In a major university, known for its high academic standards, the registrar reported to the faculty that 1961 freshmen who made the same grades as the middle third of the 1956 freshmen found themselves in the bottom third of their class. That pace has continued to accelerate, especially because of increased competition for admission to graduate and professional schools and the reduced numbers of graduate school places since 1970.

As each generation becomes more broadly educated than its predecessor, the adolescents of that generation tend to become correspondingly more separated from their parents. This is one of the reasons why executives feel isolated from their teen-age children. Unless the parents can somehow manage to keep up with their children, they simply have to accept the fact that there will be fewer matters to share as the children grow older. Adolescents in such circumstances abruptly recognize the fact that their parents aren't as all-knowing and all-powerful as they once thought. This awareness tends to make them look to others for guidance and to increase the distance between them and their parents. They also come face to face with their own inadequacies.

Furthermore, they often cannot model themselves closely on their parents because they themselves, knowing how short they have fallen of their own aspirations, have indicated their children should do better. Parents frequently encourage their children to aspire to higher social status. Often they tell their children they want the children to earn more money than they did, and to enjoy life more. They point out their own mistakes and what they believe to be their social and occupational failures. The distance between the generations is an extremely painful experience for both.

THE STYLE OF GROWING

The executive parent, preoccupied with the pursuit of success, is often unaware that the whole style of growing has changed. Grandfather was the boss of his family and part of his job was to transmit a set of standards and values. His son or daughter, today's executive, was to be like him: to stand for something and to shape the world according to his or her values.

An outstanding example of this tradition is the independent, taciturn Maine farmer who is reputed to care not a whit what anyone else thinks. That attitude was fine as long as grandfather (and the Maine farmer) worked by himself. Father and mother, however, discovered that they had to work in organizations with other people. That meant they had to take into account how others thought and felt. Father and mother also became parents at the time when authoritarian parenthood was no longer in fashion. Today's adolescent has heard much about "getting along" from relatively nonauthoritarian parents.

"Getting along" has a special meaning for those executive parents who knew times when there were no jobs to be had and the only way to hold a job was by getting along. Such parents also say they have worked hard and they urge their children to work equally hard. "Choose a path and stick to it," they say. But the adolescent is skeptical of such advice and his skepticism enrages the executive parent who has achieved success by following this adage. More emotional fuel is added to the family fire by the executive's feeling that his or her adolescent must succeed in some socially acceptable fashion or they themselves have failed.

In fact both children and parents may be caught in a

double bind. A heavy emphasis on getting along usually means a lesser emphasis on grades and, indeed, steers the child to a socially oriented peer group. If the parent is then dismayed that the child is not achieving up to capacity and therefore may not be admitted to better colleges and advanced degree work, the child sees the resulting pressure as unfair and irrational. He or she cannot now become part of an intellectual social peer group without losing social face. To do so may well mean that the social orientation may have to be given up—which will displease the parents further. The parents then fume in frustration without recognizing the priority in values they have inculcated.

While the children *are* working hard, their paths are already considerably different from those of their parents. This has come between children and their parents, though they live in the same household and speak the same language. Executive parents sought to find secure places in an organization. Within that structure they could compete, but if they chose the right organization, they could remain even if they did not get very far in the competition. The adolescent is more likely to seek challenge, which becomes an almost open criticism of the parent.

THREE VITAL ISSUES

Children of executives have three issues to deal with which for most of their parents were much less pressing:

• *They do not have to work as hard as their parents in the same way.*

Professional know-how is today's salable commodity; the hard physical work of the world is done by those who do not have other skills to offer. In addition, the adolescent has only to read the newspapers to know that he or she really cannot expect to "stick to it." He is not compelled to stay in a field once he enters it, either because of an economic depression or from frozen occupational lines. His field may, in fact, become obsolete in his lifetime. Seniority is no longer the automatic gateway to success. In our technological age some careers in specialized areas start, flower, and die in a fifteen-year period. The keynote, therefore, is not rigidity of direction but broad grounding and flexibility. Today's parents have difficulty grasping this concept. It is as if not only the rules but also the game has changed. It has.

• *The very success of their parents has made it possible for today's adolescents to live the good life as it has never been lived before by such large numbers of children.*

They have learned multiple uses for leisure. Many parents complain about the burden of extracurricular activities, and the nagging demands from the teen-ager for the family automobile. Furthermore, less pressure for economic survival has also made it possible to live more closely in families than urban families had in the last two generations, and today's adolescents think of enjoying their own families when they become adult. Several years ago *Time* reported that a study of a group of Princeton men disclosed that they were more concerned with having the good life of family and leisure than competing in the business world. This finding provoked some consternation in business circles. As a matter of fact, the Princeton men could not live at the level they were talking about on the salaries they expected to get, but still the emphasis on family living and leisure tells us something about how today's adolescents expect to live.

• *The adolescent has a harder time picking and choosing what he or she ought to be.*

Most adolescents cannot have had sufficiently varied work experience out of which to make career decisions. Few are even vaguely familiar with their parents' work, for most of that goes on in a workplace distant from the home. In addition, if the parents have discouraged their children from adopting them as occupational models, and there are relatively few other models handy, the adolescents must decide for themselves who they are and what they are going to do with themselves as adults.

This is the crux of the struggle for identity, the task of becoming some unique *one* as an adult with inadequate knowledge of both himself and the hazy, changing outside world. As a result, the adolescent has a certain reserve about committing himself or herself to a direction.

"PLAYING IT COOL"

This is particularly hard for executive parents to accept, for they had to make commitments to their careers in order to compete for their places on the executive ladder. But as Dr. Kenneth Keniston of Yale's Department of Psychiatry has observed, the word "cool" has an important

meaning for the adolescent. "Playing it cool" is being carefully judgmental. You pick and choose, try this attitude
and that experience, live it up as you can. So the adolescent may become temporarily enamored of this person or
that possibility, or even terribly defeated by some minor
failure. But he or she tries withal to keep a certain distance from a fixed position because he is not yet sure. This
is not to say he does not have ideals and values. Probably
adolescents live more by their ideals than do their parents.
It is to say that adolescence is a period of experiment, experience, and examination, in short a conflict-filled period
of practice for adulthood.

Of course, adolescence has always been a period of
struggle: between the desire to grow up and be free, and
the wish to be a child; between sexual stimulation and social controls; between the demands of fellow adolescents
and the rules of the parents; between the wish to be attractive and accepted and the wish to be independent. These
are adult-size problems. They appear with harsh impact in
adolescence, and they continue to exist for a lifetime. They
are the continuing, often painful, undercurrent of every
adolescence, molded, shaped, and given special meaning by
the pressing social currents of each generation. It is with
these underlying problems, essentially, that every parent
must deal, despite the distance between himself and his
children and the latter's skeptical view of the former's perspectives.

The executive parent who has to deal with the adolescent comes to this task with no mean handicaps. We have
already noted some having to do with education, occupation, and the changing social scene. In addition, there are
psychological   handicaps.   The   parents   have   already
repressed many of their own adolescent conflicts. They no
longer remember the details of their own struggles. It is
difficult for them, therefore, to identify with adolescent
problems. Even if they have not forgotten, much of their
experience, anywhere from fifteen to twenty-five years old,
is often outdated. Times have changed. They cannot even
dance the same steps as their children, let alone enjoy their
cacophonous music. They are chagrined at how little they
understand contemporary life. It is interesting that when
the young speak of the "old days" they mean twenty years
before.

The behavior of the adolescent often reawakens in the

parents some of their old conflicts about sexuality and adolescence. The parents, well aware of their own adolescent experimentation and their own mistakes, desperately want their children to avoid both. Yet they accept the current social theme which holds that their children have a right to make their own mistakes. At least they give uneasy lip service to it.

A number of social trends make the parents uncertain about what they ought to do and how they ought to do it. For example, the executive parent is confused about controlling adolescent behavior. Both parents would like to exert stronger controls, but they find it difficult to be as authoritative as their own parents were. They frequently are afraid that if they are, they will lose the love of their children. Furthermore, they live with the fad of freedom. Today's social controls are less rigid than they were a generation ago.

The contemporary conceptions that children should be given greater freedom than their parents had occurs in a context of greater mobility of families. The families of executives, particularly, move often. It is not unusual for executives to report that they have moved annually, or nearly so, for up to fifteen years. Executives and their spouses, as parents, have less support against pressures from outside the family as they live shorter periods in neighborhoods and are therefore less known. Furthermore, today's families live more in the backyard than on the front porch, and they see less of what goes on in the street. With weaker community ties, and less informal community and neighborhood control (though more readiness to call the police), more responsibility falls on the parent for knowing where his child is and what he is doing.

The adolescents, however, are harder to control. For those adolescents who work, jobs pay more than those their parents had, and those who do not work get comparably large allowances. Both make for greater personal freedom and, at the same time, threaten parental controls. In addition, today's adolescents have at their disposal that uniquely American instrument for isolation and experimentation, troublemaking and self-destruction, the automobile. Coupled with the lowered voting age and the rising level of alcohol consumption among adolescents, the automobile has become an ever more destructive instrument.

Parental control is further threatened by the adolescent's

manipulation of the parents with the phrase, "But everyone is doing it," and by the pressures which parents feel to be agreeable members of the parental herd who "don't rock the boat." No parent wants his children to look upon him as a "square," nor does he want them to be "squares." This is a particularly difficult pressure on executives for two reasons. First, as people who hold a prominent place in the community, they and their families are expected to be examples of ideal behavior. Second, as executives move from one community to another, preoccupied with their business problems, they do not know firsthand the varying styles of adolescent behavior which may be expected of their children. They are therefore more likely to give in to the adolescent's demands even if they themselves do not really feel they should.

Another problem is much harder for executives to discuss. Parents live with their own feelings about the prospective separation from their adolescents. No matter how much they want the child to become an adult, they still do not want to lose him, as they must. Some cannot let go, and thereby handicap their children with unsevered ties and demands. Others withdraw into indifference, and a few are glad to be rid of what for them has always been a burden. Mothers cry at weddings with good psychological reason: They do lose their sons and daughters in a deep psychological sense.

A FAMILY AFFAIR

Adolescence, then, is a family affair. Often it seems as if the adolescent is testing his or her parents by his demands, his rejections of them, and his resentment of their controls. As a matter of fact, usually he is. Sometimes he is asking with near desperation for the parents to set the limits and to reaffirm the rules. His or her sometimes aggressive, angry behavior is often a way of trying to get the parents to define what is acceptable behavior, and to demonstrate whether the parents care enough about him to help him maintain his controls.

Parental reaction to the adolescent's unpredictability and hostility is often vacillating. For example, when the adolescent makes a mistake, the parents may hold themselves responsible, or they may go to the other extreme and place all the blame on the adolescent's shoulders, rejecting any responsibility themselves. When their own doubt and anger are aroused, it is difficult for them to take a considered view of whatever problem stirs them. In the quiet few moments some parents still have together, a good many ask themselves, "Are we doing what we should be doing? Is this crazy behavior our fault?" When the adolescent's behavior has been exceptionally good, there are parents who cannot enjoy such an experience for fear that some dire event will come their way. If the adolescent is following his varied course, these same parents will worry uselessly about the terrible future such behavior portends. None of this obsessive questioning or self-blame will relieve the anxiety of the parents or solve any problems.

There are, however, some specific things the executive and spouse, as parents, can do, no matter what the business pressures. Essentially, they should maintain a strong role as parents. They should continually strengthen the external supports for the personality of the adolescent. Strengthening takes these forms:

1. *Make it possible for the adolescent to speak his or her piece and express his hostility without being angry because he is angry.*

This does not mean that they should permit the adolescent to spew forth his or her venom on his every impulse to do so. Rather, recognizing good manners and the appropriateness of any situation, he can still say how he feels with the knowledge that he will be heard.

The parents need not push for intimacy with the adolescent to make the adolescent confide in them, nor should they keep themselves aloof if he or she has rejected their interest. If the adolescent has learned to trust the parents, he will come to them when he is ready. If he has not so far taken them into his confidence, they will have to learn to earn his trust. That requires that the parents listen to what the adolescent has to say; there is little point in his saying anything if he knows what the answers will be before the questions have been heard. It requires also that the parents regard whatever they hear with the same seriousness with which it is spoken; too many take the words of their children too lightly. Finally, it requires respect for privacy; what goes in one ear should stop there. Adolescents will repeatedly try to turn to their parents in subtle ways. Parents must be careful not to reject these efforts unwittingly. Their task is to remain readily available until needed.

This simple principle can be distorted by the parent who is merely giving lip service to it. An executive who was telling me with considerable aggravation of his recent problems with his son emphasized how willing he was to talk with the boy. He had given him an appointment in his office for the next afternoon, pushing aside business to do so. There it was, duly noted in the appointment book. I did not ask the executive what went on at home.

2. *Parents should try to understand what the adolescent is attempting to say between the lines of his or her argument or report.*

This is hard for the executive to do because so often he or she thinks in factual rather than emotional terms. Ordinarily he tries to disregard feelings; here he cannot. What conflict is the adolescent trying to deal with, what pressures are being brought to bear on him? How does it look to him? What are the realities he has to live with? Is he diffident because he is afraid he cannot compete? Does his temporary withdrawal from an activity mean he is afraid he might fail? Does the request for a nose job tell us about a fad, or, more ominously, is it an indication that the adolescent is thoroughly dissatisfied with himself or herself? To understand requires listening, and listening in turn requires silence. Parents, like all others, cannot hear when they are talking. Furthermore, unless they can retain whatever confidences they may be given, they will not hear very much.

In trying to understand, the parents provide reassurance and support. These are particularly important for the adolescent in periods of self-doubt, mistakes, even failures and difficult new experiences.

3. *Help the adolescent recognize that his or her struggle for identity as an adult human being is one in which all the family shares.*

The adolescent's ups and downs are almost as hard on the parents as they are on him or her. This is not to criticize him, but to recognize the effects of the behavior of one family member on the others. Sometimes his anger with others, particularly his parents, will reflect his anger with himself. His criticism of parental imperfections frequently are displacements from his dissatisfactions with himself.

4. Teach the adolescent ways of coping with problems he or she is likely to meet.

This is less a matter of telling him or her specifically what to do than of examining with him the possible alternatives. To do so wisely, the parent must know the company the adolescent keeps and must establish the rules by which he may keep it. The adolescent must assume the responsibility for his behavior to the extent that he wants the privileges of freedom. He should not have freedom beyond his powers of self-control.

Particularly, the parents must teach children they do not have to buy their way through life with their bodies. Physical attractiveness, though esthetically admirable, is not the end-all and the be-all of existence, nor must one pay for social favors with sexual favors, despite an ethos of greater sexual freedom.

5. Parents should stand like rocks.

Whatever rules and values are important to them, they must continue to hold forth consistently. The adolescent, like anyone else, can adapt to consistency. Inconsistency is like psychological quicksand—it provides no stable basis for behavior.

Parents' reaffirmation of their values and rules gives the adolescent something to test himself against, and a continuing guide to acceptable behavior. To advocate a strong parental position is not to offer an excuse for inflexibility. Stability is not the same as rigidity. Even the Empire State Building swings a little in the wind; if it did not, it would be destroyed. But the parents who stick with what they believe take the position that each person in a democratic society is entitled to his or her own beliefs. This is an important lesson in itself. Such parents say further that they are not going to make believe that they are something other than what they really are and what is comfortable for them to be.

6. Parents should explain the reasons for their decisions so that the adolescent can understand that decisions are not usually arbitrary.

It is extremely important for him or her to learn that the best decisions about behavior are made in terms of long-run consequences. The parents must ask of themselves and of the adolescent, "What is the price of this particular piece of behavior, this activity for which you are requesting permission?" If the price is too high, then good judgment dictates a negative answer.

If, for example, a fifteen-year-old boy wants the car for the evening, rather than giving him an arbitrary "no," his parents might better point out to him that he cannot have the car because he has only a learner's permit which forbids him to drive other than to and from school. He would be in violation of the law. Furthermore, if he should have even the slightest accident, his parents would be responsible even if the fault lay with the other person. Such a risk is too high for the parents to take. The decision becomes rational in terms of personal and social cost, and the adolescent has the opportunity to learn to make decisions on the same basis.

Such a position assumes, of course, that the decision is based on rational judgment and is not merely an arbitary decision which is later rationalized. The hypocrisy of that kind of ploy will be readily apparent and strongly resented. The adolescent will then feel, as he or she should, that he is being manipulated. Of course, some decisions must be made arbitrarily, based on the intuition of the parents and on parental values. All of us must learn to live with a certain proportion of arbitrary decisions; the adolescent is no exception. If he has confidence in his parents, he can accept the occasional arbitrariness.

7. *Finally, the parents should recognize that there is love and hate in every act and every relationship.*

As a result, a fundamental psychological task for every parent is to help each child channel his or her potentially destructive energy into constructive channels. Love neutralizes hate, as religious sages pointed out long before Freud, but love is more than a word or gesture. Ideally, it is consistent parental action which helps the adolescent master a small part of his world, to have his creative effect on it. Some adolescents will do so through service to others; others in athletics, science, writing, building, and so on. However they do it, they need their parents to help. And in that they also learn the living meaning of love—a demonstration which requires no book learning.

WILL THEY MAKE IT?

This discussion might well make it seem that the teenager has nothing but tribulations. Adolescence, however, is not all frustration. Necessarily, it is a period of achievement, recognition, and growing sophistication. It offers a wonderful variety of pleasures. But, given all its psychological crosscurrents, it is, to say the least, turbulent. Some parents are amazed and relieved to discover that so many children get through adolescence so well as they do. Many parents at one time or another are not sure they will make it through their children's adolescence. To the best of our scientific knowledge, they will.

PART SIX

Social Responsibility

In contrast to most other professions, that of the business executive requires one to also assume community responsibilities. Too often this is seen as "going through the chairs" or taking one's turn at community chairmanships. This is more likely to be the case if the executive does not pick and choose, if one does not manage community leadership obligations and personal giving to meet one's own needs as well as those of others. In this section I will examine how the executive might better do just that.

22

CHOOSING
COMMUNITY
ACTIVITIES

RELATIONSHIP TO and responsibility for one's community have always competed with home and family for executive time. They press even harder now. Today's executive is keenly sensitive to his or her social responsibility. Executives—business leaders—revitalized St. Louis. They gave impetus to rejuvenating downtown Philadelphia. They brought new vigor and culture to Minneapolis. National, state, and local boards of all kinds of service and charitable agencies are replete with executive members.

Many an executive harbors a dream of a responsible governmental post. Some make it a reality. A mayor of Dallas was the former head of Texas Instruments, a governor of Michigan used to lead American Motors, a senator from Illinois guided Bell & Howell. Others have been in cabinet posts.

For many executives, doing good community deeds starts early and officially. When one major corporate leader became national chairman of the United Fund appeal, he assigned half a dozen of his bright young junior executives to help him. The contribution of executive time and corporate resources is made everywhere. Corporations supply many executives for government panels, and chief executives themselves go back and forth between business, government, and voluntary service.

The male executive—and his wife—for years have been

the backbone of community service. Where, then, is the rub? Why is it that probably no activity is more frustrating to them than just that very service? There are three rubs:

• *One is the compulsory quality of and the insatiable demand of the community for leadership and service.*

Both the compulsory quality and insatiable demand arise from the executive's position. The fact that a person is an executive in a corporation automatically gives him or her a place in the community power structure, country club membership, and similar prerogatives. In return for the stature accorded, the community demands commensurate leadership. For purposes of goodwill and community citizenship, the corporation, too, wants the executive to assume that function. Both the demand and the social responsibility accompany the executive and, if a male, his wife wherever they move for the company. Company and community alike expect a person in a given position to serve in certain ways, regardless of who the specific person may be. The executive and spouse therefore are under severe continuous pressure to take part. Service seems to be the price of upward social and economic mobility.

It is one thing for one to undertake community service as an assignment during working hours, another to feel required to do so on one's own time, at the expense of pleasure and family. Being compelled to take community leadership is vastly different from seeking political position voluntarily. The activity a male executive's wife undertakes for her own enjoyment is hers by choice; she can stop when she wants to. That which is demanded, even at the cost of one's preferences, is burdensome. Said one community experienced executive wife, "You feel badly when you don't contribute by volunteer services. Everyone expects it of you, even if you have to give up things that really interest you. And if you don't do it, if you do what interests you, then you become isolated from the others who are active, and pretty soon you're afraid you will be forgotten. You also feel you are selfish, particularly when you feel you have so much. But you're visible, you have a name and a position. So the problem is how to have a personal life, some privacy, to satisfy society without robbing oneself of private life." We do not yet have sufficient experience for male spouses to know of the pressures on them.

● *A second problem is the comparatively slow pace of service activity.*

Executives tend to be an impatient lot. They seek out executive positions because they aspire to power and achievement. A major psychological difference between those who enter competitive business and those who pursue government or agency careers is reflected in the respective kinds of schools such men attend: schools of business *management* for one, schools of public, hospital, or social service *administration* for the other. One avowedly pursues leadership, the other more often denies his own wish for power. The latter tends to see himself as bringing conflicting interests together and carrying out policy.

The business executive who is asked to serve in government or on agency boards often feels himself or herself to be in a political morass. Without the leverage of the delegated power he or she has in his company, he must devote endless hours to clearing channels and obtaining consent. Consent, in turn, hinges on how deeply people will trust him, and building trust takes even more time. "I've just finished working on a five-year project," reported one executive. "It took me four years to persuade the community they needed a new hospital and one year to build it. By the time it was done, even though they admitted they needed it, they couldn't accept any other ideas I might have because to do that was tantamount to admitting I was right and they were wrong."

Another kind of morass is that of time. Between meetings and various kinds of negotiations, background reading, and just touching bases, an inordinate amount of time, let alone energy, is consumed. Most executives underestimate the time demands, both on themselves and their spouses.

The executive quickly discovers the bowed backs of civil servants and agency staff who have learned to survive one political master after another by simply doing nothing. The psychologist speaks of this as "passive aggression," the military of the "old army game." The structure in which one is asked to work, without a source of power in property ownership, is intended to inhibit direct action, to avoid autocracy. The checks and balances of political relationships are often the stumbling blocks to solving problems effectively. As one State Department official once told me, "We have to work on twenty-year problems with five-year plans, two-year appointees, and one-year appropriations."

Coupled with these problems are the political tactics—sometimes name-calling, attack, distortion, misquotation, accusation. This can happen whether a person is on the board of a girls' club seeking a new location or being consulted about one's area of competence. Those who feel themselves to be threatened will attack. One of the most conspicuous examples in recent American political history was Henry Wallace. A successful farmer-businessman, he was villified for programs which rescued the farmer and for daring to imagine that the federal government should aim toward creating sixty-six million jobs (about eighty million are working today). When he died in 1966 his contributions were publicly praised by the same newspapers which had ridiculed his farm and economic programs, now made tame by time. "Don't ever run for public office," a prominent executive once advised me, "you'll never live down the lies people will fabricate about you."

Most executives, particularly those who render public service, have strong consciences. They judge themselves harshly. It is difficult for them to take public criticism, particularly unwarranted attack, and even more difficult to attack publicly in return. The same is true of their spouses.

Because of their own hazards of conscience they must be more careful than others when they are involved in public affairs about conflict of interest issues, seeking or giving special favors, and contradictory community demands. Their only protection is to become more expert than anyone else in their voluntary responsibility, and then to stand on the position at which they have logically arrived. Often, however, that will not endear them to anyone. Conscientious service has its own burden of loneliness.

The executive is no stranger to empire building and political infighting. With the unique rules and problems of private or governmental agencies, one is in a different psychological world. One's spouse, too, finds public service an arena in which he or she must be sensitive to myriad political and social nuances.

• *A third rub is the feeling of being exploited.*

In many instances an appointment is intended to be mere window dressing. The executive and spouse are asked, sometimes in so many words, to lend their names, prestige, or resources to either a board or a political position. When such requests are obvious they pose no problem. The executive can say yes or no. Problems arise either out of manipulation or misconception.

More than one executive has been on a blue-ribbon panel which made a detailed report to a public official —which was then quickly filed and forgotten. Even something like that one can anticipate; one can make participation conditional. It is much more difficult when one is trapped like this:

> An executive is asked to serve on a Boy Scout council. Having considerable respect for the Boy Scouts, he agrees. He is assigned to the budget committee and there reviews the seemingly reasonable proposals of the executive. Subsequently he is asked to present and defend the budget he has worked on before a budget committee of the United Fund. This he does willingly; they, too, are his friends. To his chagrin and embarrassment, he discovers that he does not have all of the facts and figures the United Fund committee needs, that for several years a clandestine battle has been going on between the two organizations because the Boy Scout executive does not want the United Fund executive to have power over him. Each has mobilized a powerful committee of leading community citizens, obtained their commitment to his agency, and, now armed with the respective biases, pitted them against each other.

A more subtle form of manipulation occurs with the agency executive who claims to want his or her board members to be active but who manages to keep them away from all policy and programing matters except those he or she presents to them. This is becoming an increasingly difficult problem because of the growing practice of national agencies of having local advisory committees for public relations purposes. It is further complicated by the growth of comprehensive fund-raising agencies like United Fund and practices like payroll deduction. No longer faced with the need to justify themselves directly, individual agencies can operate obsolete programs for years with impunity. One local USO, for example, prided itself on serving 350 different soldiers in the course of a year when the nearby base had 5,500 men. A YMCA did its local job so poorly that a Boys' Club had to be organized to make up for the deficiency. Both inadequate agencies continued to operate, protected by not having to raise their own funds.

Sooner or later, the executive (or spouse) becomes aware of the manipulation and withdraws. He or she may be angry, but is at least aware of why. Such is not the case with misconception. Dr. Ralph Crawshaw, a psychiatrist in Portland, Oregon, points out how this can occur.

"Our exemplary man," says Dr. Crawshaw, ". . . is highly qualified in meeting the ever present problems in business, and, as he sees his contribution, it will be drawn from his fund of experience in business." In the agency, however, he is expected to act as a money raiser. The individual he has to deal with is what Crawshaw calls "the middleman for charity," who is known for his professional ability. The agency executive has his own set of purposes and values. He seeks room and money with which to operate. The executive is likely to think of what can be done with available resources; the technician wants to solve a given social problem. The executive, from his citizen role, may see the broader social context; the specialist is zeroed in on his specialized target. However justified either position, both talk past each other in endlessly repetitive board meetings. Each complains that the other does not understand. The result is frustration. The executive ultimately withdraws in angry disappointment.

To help cope with this problem there are a number of ways which simultaneously meet one's sense of social responsibility and self-respect. I would put them in this order:

1. *Recognize the inevitability of the demand and expectation.*

Every executive knows the axiom that there can be no responsibility without authority. It is equally true that there can be no authority without responsibility. One cannot claim a social power role in a community without assuming the leadership responsibility which goes with it. The spouse who would be a partner with the executive must do the same.

2. *Allocate your time and resources.*

Ultimately the highest gratifications in life come from one's own personal relationships, particularly those in the family. Plan first for family time. That, too, is an obligation. Asked to become president of a chapter of the

League of Woman Voters, a wise woman set the conditions: providing that she would not have to take more than one out-of-town trip during the year; that she could delegate required trips to others; that she could be home at 4 P.M. each day when her children returned from school; that those who had asked her would also assume specific obligations. Men are less likely to set conditions of this kind; in their own self-interest they should.

3. *Choose your activity.*

The executive and spouse must not be content with simply lending their names to any agency, however worthy, and going to its meetings. That is burden without gratification and permits others to exploit their names without responsibility. Rather they must choose agencies whose purposes are important to them and whose way of carrying out these purposes is congenial to them.

Given a limited amount of time, they must limit themselves to those activities which either give them pleasure or require their specific power for the public good. The latter is sometimes a difficult issue to decide, but is largely a political and economic matter. If a person has an important place in the top power structure of a community, he or she will make better use of his resources on those activities which require the support of the power structure, rather than to dissipate them at lower levels. For example, an executive may want to support an agency for retarded children because he or she has a retarded child. Fine. However, if he happens to be the manager of the community's leading plant, he might make a more effective contribution by working for a statewide program. Similarly, he would do better on a committee mobilizing the resources of the entire community for a hospital than on the board of an adoption agency.

4. *Define your "contract."*

What does serving this agency mean? What will you be permitted to do or not do? How far does the influence of the board extend? Why have people left the board? What responsibility does the agency or its executive assume toward you if you assume one toward them? What channels are there for insuring that those mutual responsibilities are fulfilled? Why do they want *you?* Can you provide what they want? What do you want in return? In what way will this agency change because of your presence? If it will not, should you be there? Obviously your company has to change frequently to keep vital. So do you. Will the agency? Lest such questions seem cold-blooded, remember that you are bartering irreplaceable time and your own feelings about yourself. The more realistic both parties are, the greater the opportunities for gratifying success. Furthermore, as an executive you have considerable influence to bring to bear. Do you serve yourself or the community if you do not make constructive use of it?

5. *Make your service human.*

Dr. Crawshaw distinguishes between charity and welfare. Charity, he says, is supplying understanding and initiative. It is marked by compassion. Welfare, by contrast, is providing, supplying money and institutional followthrough. He argues that charity is becoming welfare at an accelerated rate, and that institutional help in communities is a process that is ". . . depersonalized, dehumanized, cost-accounted, and computerized" to the point where an individual has difficulty sharing his well-being with a fellow man. He calls for a way to give in which the giver "can experience compassion while the acceptor experiences gratitude, and both of them experience love." To have such feelings, in addition to giving money and service, the donor must give values.

Giving values means more than lip service to the brotherhood of man or similar virtues. In practice it means that the executive must continually examine the process by which the agency carries out its work with the question, "How does this affect the people we serve?" To do this constructively one must know the problems of the recipients of the agency's service and in what ways the agency both compounds their problems and increases their dependency at the cost of their dignity.

For example, is housing assured for those to be displaced by urban renewal before the work begins? Does the charity medical patient in the emergency room have to humble himself by orally answering a personal questionnaire in public? Is the Cub Scout derided for not having a full uniform when he already has enough of a problem scraping up money for his dues? Is the organization run for the professionals and the professional volunteers? Does the agency exploit its clients? The last is an interesting question which few agencies face and of which many are guilty. I am always pained at Christmastime to see newspaper pictures of smiling service club members leading impoverished children through department stores to buy their toys. How must the children feel when publicly identified that way? How must their fathers feel, or if they are without fathers, how much more they must resent that fact? Or even when the same agency provides lists of poor families on whom guilt-ridden middle-class people once a year unload baskets of food?

6. *Pace yourself*.

Only you can control what happens to you. The more you and your spouse talk over such problems and make your choices, the more you will live your own lives. Service, like charity, also begins at home. There is an especially pressing reason why even these choices should be talked over, apart from the fact that the obligations of one become constraints on the other. You need to support and protect each other from interference in your family relationships. "I've done my duty," said one middle-aged matron through gritted teeth, "now I'm working for myself." How long she will be able to hold out without the support of her husband is debatable because, as another wife put it, "At times you need somebody to say, 'Chuck it,' to give you permission to quit. Your husband must; no one else can."

7. *Build trust*.

The most significant contribution one can make to one's community is to build trust among people. This does not mean the suppression of differences. Rather, it means the respectful airing of differences in an atmosphere where people care to hear what troubles someone else. There is a difference between deliberation and debate; the former is thoughtful consideration before action, the latter a war of words. There is no trust without caring and no care without hearing. Finally, there can be no trust unless one can take a firm stand when that is required. Here is one way it was taught in one brief moment by Mrs. Alf Landon, the wife of a one-time presidential candidate.

A local committee had been formed in Topeka, Kansas, to help pass a school bond issue which had once failed. To establish trust, the committee was made up of representatives of every segment of the community. The bond issue went well. However, when the successful campaign was over, to the startled amazement of the committee, the school board fired the superintendent. The committee was deluged with calls, designated a subcommitee to undertake an investigation and make a report. When the report was brought before the whole committee, those who were frightened and those who were partisan began to back off. The committee began to crumble before the eyes of its members. Then the diminutive, elderly lady spoke up: "If those are the findings of the subcommitee, then those are its findings. We will stand on them." The committee stood with pride and self-respect. Years later, the members of that committee still have great affection and esteem for each other and what they did together. The psychological reward of their achievement would have been lost if one wise woman had not stood firm.

23

THE HIGH RETURN ON ENLIGHTENED GIVING

In ADDITION to serving the community, an executive has unique opportunities to capitalize psychologically on his or her material advantages. "No matter what your age or job in life, you are more mature if you have found a 'cause' in which to invest your time and money for some social good," wrote Dr. William C. Menninger. "Through it you can achieve an outstanding characteristic of emotional maturity—the ability to find satisfaction in giving."

When it comes to giving, many successful business executives are not notably successful. Not that they do not make personal contributions to various causes and charitable organizations—most do. Not that they give too much away. Few of us give as much as we can. But many executives do not know *how* to give in a way that will bring them emotional rewards.

Because they don't know what else to do with their money, they buy more clothes than they need, spend too much time playing golf or bridge, and travel widely in luxurious accommodations that keep them away from the very people they have gone to observe. The way they make use of their money rarely seems to bring them pleasure in and satisfaction with themselves as people.

The fact of the matter is that money need not be something a person spends for the sheer sake of spending. It can be a medium of genuine and continuing satisfaction if one gives some of it away with enlightened self-interest. To do so the business executive might apply the same consideration to personal giving as he or she does to corporate giving. As a representative of a company, one is besieged with requests for contributions to various causes and for leadership in fund-raising drives. Such requests have become so time-consuming that many companies have had to establish official quotas and policies. Some justification, in terms of the corporation's interests, must be established for corporate giving. The executive is therefore careful in giving away the corporation's money. But rarely does one give away one's own money in such a way that one gets the utmost emotional satisfaction from giving. Why?

PATTERNS OF GIVING

To find continuing satisfaction with himself in any aspect of living, a person must be involved with it. A happy marriage, a successful career, a growing business—all require consistent intensive effort. So it is with giving. A person who expects his or her giving to yield emotional dividends must work at it.

Most of us, of course, are willing to give—$5 here, $50 or $100 there—to an institution or cause if we really believe we are furthering something we care about. But much of this is a way of fulfilling an obligation, or getting rid of solicitors, or appeasing the pangs of conscience. Many important causes need to be supported even though one has no major interest in them, and it is probably just as therapeutic to spend a few dollars to relieve guilt pangs as it is to buy new hobby equipment when a person is feeling low. However, the satisfaction in most giving of this kind is either temporary or lies in the avoidance of more negative feelings.

Many executives do, on the other hand, plan to make a major contribution or bequest to a favorite charity or institution. There is personal involvement in this kind of giving, and anticipating the positive effects of the donation may give them many years of psychological satisfaction. But there are still two questions:

• Will the giver obtain as much continuing gratification in his or her daily living from this method of giving as contrasted with another?

• Will he or she accomplish with this gift what he intended to accomplish, or will his "cause" turn out to be of no practical use to anyone and even a white elephant for the very people he wanted to help?

There is, in fact, an axiom in fund-raising circles that a

bequest to an offbeat cause is likely to become obsolete in twenty-five years. Consider a few examples. Even the enlightened Benjamin Franklin made such a mistake when he set up a fund for indentured apprentices in Boston and New York, a class of deserving young men who no longer existed once the indenture system disappeared. Funds for Veterans of World War I have increasingly fewer beneficiaries. Bequests for orphanages and children's homes have become obsolete as more children are placed in foster homes or given for adoption. The fund for the relief from Barbary pirates and a $350,000 bequest "for the establishment of horse troughs throughout the world" now serve no more useful purpose than to stimulate a smile. In Great Britain, more than two thousand endowments for primary education and many endowments for hospital beds became useless when both primary education and health care were taken over by the government.

In this country millions of dollars are tied up in college scholarships whose conditions are so narrowly circumscribed that there are no takers. More millions of dollars are tied up in institutions and causes so obsolete that the fact that they have financial backing is the only reason why they continue to exist. Furthermore, and particularly with posthumous gifts, the givers had all too little psychological reward for their giving.

Typical of how a person may cause his or her resources to be dissipated and lose out on the pleasure of giving is this case. A wealthy Midwestern man lived all his life in his community. Though there were many needs in the city in which he had earned his wealth, and many people sought his help, he gave away little while he was alive. Using his money, as contrasted with acquiring it, was never a medium of pleasure for him. He saw no clinics rise, no children educated, no slums cleared, no jobs created—which he had made possible. Instead, he left a will which instructed that a trust be formed, to be governed by his heirs. The heirs knew nothing about giving money away, so they employed an executive. But the real power remained in the hands of the board, the several children of the wealthy benefactor. Each of the children soon had his favorite charity and when the grandchildren came of age they, too, had their favorite ways to spend the money. The only way to compromise the resulting conflict was to seek the lowest common denominator: they agreed to build a much too elaborate old-folks' home one thousand miles away from their own community. The bulk of the fortune remains unspent, and a cause of continuous argument within the family.

Not all bequests, of course, are failures. Just a few of the more conspicuous successes are Carnegie grants for libraries, Rockefeller grants for health research, and Rosenwald grants for the advancement of colored people. One bequest that might have become obsolete—but hasn't—was established in 1851 by Byran Mullanphy, a former mayor of St. Louis. Mullanphy set aside in his will a fund of $200,000 to help poor emigrants and travelers en route to the West through St. Louis. When the westward emigration declined, and heirs sought to break the trust (by then worth $1½ million) the court held that "while the Sante Fe and the Oregon trails may be paved with concrete and poor travelers may be outfitted in Model T Fords rather than Prairie Schooners, there still must be poor travelers who need assistance." There are, and they are still aided today by the "Mullanphy Traveler's Aid" in the St. Louis train and bus stations.

THE NEED TO REFUEL

What difference does it make? What does all this have to do with the executive of more modest means? In Chapter 2 I pointed out that in order to have good mental health, a person needs many sources of gratification. That is, a mentally healthy person finds pleasure in many things, people, and experiences. One important source of gratification lies in the giving of love to others. As a person grows from child to adult, ideally he gives up the self-centeredness of childhood and takes greater pleasure in what he can do for others. No one can be a good parent, for example, without making this psychological shift.

At the same time, one must, as Dr. William Menninger once pointed out, continue to refuel one's giving capacity. To do this one must receive for giving some psychological gratification which makes it possible to give more. Sometimes this gratification is direct appreciation for what one has done. Sometimes it lies in seeing what good has come of one's efforts. Whatever the reward, it is important to receive it.

There is nothing wrong with wanting to be appreciated

or in wanting to see the fruits of one's efforts. Something important in life is missed, however, if one deprives oneself of that pleasure—either because one thinks it is wrong or because one does not know how to give in one's own self-interest.

A prerequisite to getting more pleasure from giving is to understand some of the reasons why a person finds it difficult to give. There are many psychological reasons. Among them are these:

● *An infant's first struggles with authority and power usually occur during the period when its mother is beginning to teach it to control its bodily functions.*

At this time children discover that they have something the mother wants. That which they hold within themselves must be valuable because so much attention is paid to it. They discover that they, too, have a certain kind of power—they can give or withhold that possession at will. When battles become severe, the child may learn that stubbornness or holding on is an effective way of maintaining a position of power. Subsequently, it may gather and hold on to money or other possessions as a style of life.

Echoes of this struggle are found in the many ways in which money is equated with dirt—"filthy lucre," "filthy rich." Those who hold onto money are described as tight, or misers. A miser is defined as one who *lives miserably* in order to hoard his wealth.

● *In many Western cultures, the motive to achieve is a prominent one.*

From the studies of Harvard psychologist David McClelland, it appears that this motive stems from a certain family constellation. The motive is highly developed in boys where the parents have high standards of achievement, where they provide warmth and encouragement, and where the father is not dominating and authoritarian. Achievement in a competitive industrial society is most easily pursued through the medium of money. Power in such a society is equated with getting and often holding on to money.

● *People who have suffered psychologically from being impoverished and who have either the education or talent to overcome their obstacles, see their poverty as oppressive and fight it.*

This is particularly true if, for example, a son wants to please his parents by lifting them out of their economic mire. Such men are determined not only to overcome their poverty, but also never to be poor—and therefore helpless—again.

The common thread running through these reasons is that the same motivation which drives people to acquire money also impels them to hold on to it. The same reasons which made them successful keep them from enjoying the fruits of their success. They need to *have* the money. Good enough. There is nothing wrong with acquiring money, having it, and not giving it away. There is the problem, of course, that everyone who has money faces: one must give much of it away or lose it in taxes. But more important, and our concern here, is the cost, in terms of mental health, of not making good *psychological* use of it.

The process of acquiring wealth often has a high psychological price. People who are intensely involved in a continuous competitive struggle tend to limit their gratifications to that struggle, and to imagine some distant happiness their achievement will bring them. Too often they find that the achievement itself does not bring them the gratification they had wished for, and they have missed developing other sources of gratification along the way. People must build—and maintain—satisfying relations with others or they will have no *human* relations, whether friends or family.

Many people who acquire wealth and position, unsure of their relationships, fear that they are liked only for their money. They may therefore distrust the motives of others who then come close to them and are never quite certain how others would regard them if they did not have money. Sometimes they feel they have to buy their way through life, as if they thought themselves unworthy to be liked for themselves. If their pursuit of money has been at the cost of broader experiences, it is more difficult for them to judge which causes are deserving. The fact that they have money attracts a wide range of sycophants, each trying to manipulate them, and an even wider range of causes, each seeking their support.

WHEN GIVING HURTS

And then there are people who have fought their way to success and who often believe that they have "made it" by hard work alone, and that everyone else could make it the same way. They tend to view those who need help of whatever kind as being weak or losers. Worse yet, some tend to view themselves as suckers if they give. As a result, some have great difficulty giving money away. Although few people have become successful without hard work, no one has ever "made it" by himself. Whether one is willing to recognize it or not, someone else has always been in the picture with a helping hand. Even Horatio Alger heroes had such a helping hand. To hold a distorted image of one's own success and others' failure is merely a rationalization for the underlying contempt such a person has for other people. Such contempt can only be a barrier to warm relationships with others.

People who are on guard cannot enjoy spontaneous relationships with others. People who are afraid have to keep their distance. People who are constantly competitive drive others away from them. People who feel they are likely to be manipulated become hardened. Taken together, such experiences make for loneliness and consequent loss of gratification in giving. There is enough painful loneliness in aging without building more into the process. There are enough avenues for gratification in giving that no one need be deprived of such psychological rewards.

This does not mean that the alternative is to give all of one's money away. I suggest rather that one plan and direct giving systematically for *one's* own intended purposes—among them psychological purposes. One's giving then will be a specific part of some relationships but clearly not of others. The choices will be one's own. The fact that one has made plans for giving tends to clarify one's relationships both for oneself and others and thereby to lower one's psychological barriers. When people learn that giving plans have been made, those who want only a person's money will drop away. That person will then be more certain of his or her relationships with those who remain.

A person does not have to be a millionaire to give amounts of money which are significant to the recipients. Gifts of $1,000, $500, even $100 to colleges, charities, political parties, and similar beneficiaries are not so frequent that they go unnoticed. A person who gives as much as $500 a year to even big-name organizations is looked upon as an important giver. More than a few executives fritter away such sums.

What do you get when you give even $100 regularly? You buy a stake in the work your beneficiary is doing. You have the opportunity for a consistent relationship with the people whom you are supporting, particularly if you go to see their work and talk with them. You can share directly the excitement of pioneering research, of helping sick children to recover, of building a much-needed institution. You help make possible the smiles, the new leases on life, the scientific papers. You are a welcome partner in the collective effort and treated as such. You get directly the psychological gratifications of giving.

TIME AND TALENT

Money, as we are considering it here, is merely another resource which can be used toward greater, more solid satisfaction. If a person has no money to give, there is still nevertheless the opportunity of giving time and service. Many people give time and talent that otherwise would have to be paid for. Some who cannot themselves give money raise thousands of dollars for worthy causes. Still others give counsel, encouragement, and hope. Whatever the way, they acquire important purposes in life and make significant contributions.

Some people have to learn to give. This is an important reason why patients in psychiatric or psychological treatment are often urged to undertake volunteer activities in the community. Such activities are a form of personal philanthropy. When a person uses his individual talents to make something for others or to serve others without charge, he or she not only gives, but equally important, also receives. He learns that someone else needs and wants something he has to give. Such an experience counteracts feelings of personal failure ("I'm not much, it's just my money"). As a person becomes more proficient at making something for others (like furniture for children in a day nursery) or at helping someone (like drawing out a reserved, inhibited child or teaching another to read), that experience also produces a sense of growth.

When a person uses himself or herself in these ways he can see his own improvement in the more positive responses of others to him. Furthermore, his volunteer activity provides him with experiences to share with those who are doing the same. True affection and esteem among people grows out of their doing something constructive together.

There are other good reasons for personal philanthropy. The pleasure of eating a good meal is lost as quickly as the meal is eaten. A delightful vacation fades all too quickly from memory. But when people have rewarding relations with others, they acquire a kaleidoscope of images and never-to-be-forgotten memories. Such a psychological treasure chest is the unique property of those who have lived while they have aged.

The difference between living and existing is that in living one imparts something of one's own character to others. Professor Loren Eiseley, the noted University of Pennsylvania anthropologist, has observed that the ability to impart of himself in this manner was characteristic of a good teacher and one of his rewards. When a person lives, in this sense, he *lives on*. He becomes at least a ripple on the sea of human experience, spreading ever wider. He leaves a heritage. True, every person who merely exists *is*, but when such a person is gone, there is little trace of his ever having been.

FOUR KEYS TO GIVING

But if you have money, how can you give it away wisely and get maximum pleasure from it? Financial counselors recommend that people make provision for their necessities, obligations, and emergencies before making investments or gifts. Once one has arranged to take care of oneself, a whole range of possibilities for giving is open. One will probably treat most of these routinely, with small donations here and there. This is the point at which most people stop—and the pleasure is missed. To get the most out of your giving:

1. *Look around for a specific field or institution which interests you.*

Perhaps one of the many solicitations which comes across your desk has a special appeal for you. Or you might ask casually of professionals—social workers, physicians, educators—who is doing notable work in their fields, or what particular areas are not getting the support they should. Despite the availability of government funds, many deserving institutions and activities are poorly supported. The executives of business-sponsored charitable foundations are familiar with many different agencies. Ask their judgment. If you can do so, visit one or two projects or institutions.

As you try to select from among institutions and causes, the most important criteria from the point of view of your own satisfactions are your internal ones. Is the organization's ideal one which is really important to you—worth your long-time identification? Does it fight hard for solutions or against problems that you yourself would want to tackle if you could? Does it stand for you? In short, does this organization fit you and your need? Does it need *you*? Will it use what *you* have to offer?

2. *Evaluate the agencies or institutions to which you have narrowed your choices.*

Winthrop Rockefeller once remarked that it was a hard job to give away money wisely. It is. This part of the giving process, therefore, is most important. Talk with the people in whom you propose to invest your gift. What problems are they working on? Do they take a long-range or a short-range view of their work? Are they looking for simple answers or do they understand the complexity of the problems they propose to tackle? What do their professional peers think about their contributions? Be wary of people who have *the* answer or think there is *one*. Look at the results they have achieved. Is the project a one-person show, and will it survive that one person? If there is a strong leader, do people grow tall around that person or does he or she stunt them?

Is this a flexible organization, one so open to new knowledge and techniques that it can shift with them, or has it done much the same thing for years? Compare the proportion of funds which goes into administration and public relations with program expenditures. Is management an oligarchy, using the institution to serve its own personal ends? Is the board broadly representative and active? Is the institution living on its reputation? How are you treated when you walk in the door? Such questions are not new or strange to executives who must constantly make similar judgments about their own companies as well as other organizations.

3. *Take a hand in the project.*

Talk over their problems with the front-line workers when you can. Many organizations hold annual meetings of their donors for just such opportunities. Others provide for more flexible, more frequent contacts. Hold the hands of the staff, psychologically speaking. Watch the buildings grow. Let your faith bolster. But be extremely careful not to try to run the project. No gift entitles you to do that, and any efforts to do so will tear the organization apart. Intrusion into the work of the project by its financial supporters makes people feel subservient, dependent, and resentful. They rightfully feel they are being manipulated rather than supported.

4. *Invest in people and ideas.*

Look at the dreams of your prospective beneficiaries. Every imaginative person has a drawerful of dreams—things he or she would like to do if only he had the wherewithal. If there are no dreams, then the future is past. The dreams tell you where the organization or project will be tomorrow. If you like what you hear, particularly if what you hear is honestly self-critical, then, and only then, should you invest your gift. Your gift is a token of faith, and faith ultimately makes it possible to overcome the seemingly insurmountable.

Coda

"Becoming" middle-aged is the commonplace
but crisis event all executives must face sooner or
later. The key to the conflict is the word
"middle." Once a person reaches the middle, he
or she is inevitably on the descending path. The
period of adaptation to the shock of this sudden
realization usually lasts several years and varies
in its intensity and duration. The person who
fails to mature in this sense becomes a disease
that afflicts his or her organization; the one who
opts for wisdom becomes an organizational
resource.

24

AFTER THIRTY-FIVE

FOR MOST PEOPLE, attainment of executive rank coincides with the onset of middle age, that vast gulf which begins about thirty-five and endures until one has come to terms with oneself and one's human fate (for no one matures until he or she has done so). It is the peak time of personal expansion, when one lives most fully the combined multiple dimensions of his or her life. He has acquired the wisdom of experience and the perspective of maturity. One's activity and productivity are in full flower; one's career is well along toward its zenith. One is at the widest range of his travels and his contacts with others. One is firmly embedded in a context of family, society, career, and his own physical performance. One's successes are models for emulation, his or her failures the object lessons for others. One has become a link from the past to the future, from his family to the outside world, from those for whom he or she is organizationally responsible to those to whom he owes responsibility. In a word, one has it made.

Need it all come to a harsh and bitter end? No.

A person cannot alter his or her inevitable fate. But he can manage the way he comes to terms with it. If he does so, rather than simply letting events take their course, he can do much to prolong the richness of his life as well as his years.

Sophocles, who lived to be more than ninety, wrote *Oedipus Rex* at seventy-five and *Oedipus at Colonus* at eighty-nine. Titian completed his masterpiece, "The Battle of Lepanto," at ninety-five. He began work on one of the most famous paintings in the world, "The Descent from the Cross," when he was ninety-seven. Benjamin Franklin invented bifocals at seventy-eight. Benjamin Duggar, Pro-

276

fessor of Plant Physiology and Botanical Economics at the University of Wisconsin, was removed at age seventy by compulsory retirement. He then joined the research staff of Lederle Laboratories and several years later gave mankind Aureomycin. At ninety, Pablo Casals still played the cello as no other man ever had. Santayana, the philosopher, wrote his first novel, *The Last Puritan*, at seventy-two. Carl Sandburg wrote *Remembrance Rock* at seventy. Freud's activities continued into his eighties.

These men are the exceptions, of course. But the fact that many people can mature creatively indicates that there is indeed hope for all of us who are closer to thirty-five. In this chapter I propose to examine some of the experiences of middle age and suggest ways of maintaining creative potential.

First, however, permit me a brief qualification. I am not arbitrarily splitting executives into categories of under thirty-five and over thirty-five. That would be unrealistic. The figure thirty-five is not fixed. It will waver, because I am using it here in the sense of a stage of life, not a birth date.

INDEXES OF HEALTH

Behind the flowering of middle age, a critical physical and psychological turnaround process is occurring. This is reflected in indexes of health. Statistics from Life Extension Examiners indicate that specific symptoms—such as extreme fatigue, indigestion, and chest pains—rise sharply among young executives just moving into top management. Only one third of the symptoms found in the thirty-one- to forty-year-old management group can be traced to an organic cause, the examiners report. They suggest that these problems come about because of both the manner in which the executives live and the state of mind in which they work.

Psychological factors. While some explanations for this increase in symptoms are no doubt a product of the aging process itself, there are more pressing psychological forces. The British psychoanalyst, Elliott Jaques, contends that a peak in the death rate between thirty-five and forty is attributable to the shock which follows the realization that one is inevitably on a descending path. This produces what for most men is a transitory period of depression. Depression increases a person's vulnerability to illness. There is much medical evidence to indicate that physical illness is likely to occur more frequently and more severely in people who feel depressed.

Lee Stockford of the California Institute of Technology reports from his survey of 1,100 men that about five out of six men in professional and managerial positions undergo a period of frustration in their middle thirties and that one in six never fully recovers from it. Stockford attributes the crisis to a different kind of frustration: "This is the critical age—the mid-30's—when a man comes face to face with reality and finds that reality doesn't measure up to his dreams." I suspect the same forces are at work for women, but we do not yet have statistical evidence.

A number of factors in executive work life contribute to the intensification of these feelings and the symptoms which result:

Increasing contraction of the hard-work period. The average age at which people become company presidents is decreasing. As it does, the age span during which success can be achieved becomes narrower. The competitive pace therefore becomes more intense. It is further intensified by devices such as management by objectives and performance appraisals which give added impetus to the pressures for profit objectives.

Inseparability of life and career patterns. For managerial people in an intensely competitive career pattern, each year is a milepost. Time in job or level is a critical variable. If one does not move on time, one loses out on experience, position, and above all, the reputation for being a star. This means there necessarily must be repetitive subpeaks of anxiety around time dimensions.

Continuous threat of defeat. When both internal and external pressures for achievement are so high, the pain of defeat—always harsh—can be devastating, no matter how well a person seems to take it. Animal research indicates that when males are paired in combat, up to 80 percent of the defeated ones subsequently die although their physical wounds are rarely severe enough to cause death. We cannot generalize from animals to humans, but we can get some suggestion of the physical cost of the experience of personal defeat. When we turn back to the management pyramid and the choices that have to be made, obviously many people experience defeat, and all must live with the threat.

Increase in dependency. To cope with competition, the executive, despite his or her misgivings, must depend on specialists whose word he or she must accept because of lack of specialized knowledge. In fact, John Kenneth Galbraith advanced the thesis in *The New Industrial State* that the technical infrastructure of an organization really makes the decisions, leaving only pro forma approval for the executive. The specialists have their own concepts, jargon, and motivation, which often differ from those of the executive. Every executive wants to make good decisions. He or she is uneasy about decisions based on data he does not fully understand, gathered by people he does not fully understand, and presented in terms he does not fully understand. One is therefore often left to shudder at the specter of catastrophe beyond his control.

Denial of feelings. Commitment to executive career goals requires self-demand and self-sacrifice, and simultaneously inhibits close, affectionate relationships. One cannot allow oneself to get close to those with whom one competes or about whom one must make decisions, or who are likely to make decisions about one. Often one bears a burden of guilt for the decisions one must make about others' careers. No matter how strongly a person wants the achievement goals, he or she still has some feelings of anger, toward both himself and the organization which demands that sacrifice, for having to give up other desirable life goals. One must hold in tightly these feelings of anger, together with the feelings of affection and guilt, if they are unacceptable to one or in one's business culture. Repressed feelings must continuously be controlled, a process which requires hyper-alertness and therefore energy.

Constant state of defensiveness. The pursuit of executive success is like playing the children's game King of the Hill. In that game, each child is vying for the place at the top of the stump, fence, barrel, or even literally, the hill. All the others try to push the incumbent from the summit perch. Unlike the game, in executive life there is no respite. Given this state of affairs, together with the other conditions to which I have just referred, one must be always "at the ready," as the military put it. To be at the ready psychologically means that one's whole body is also in a continu-

ing emergency state, with resulting greater internal wear
and tear.

Shift in the prime-of-life concept. Western societies
value youth. It is painfully disappointing to have attained a
peak life stage at a time in history when that achievement
is partially vitiated by worship of youth, when there is no
longer as much respect for age or seniority. This is compounded by one's awareness of the decline of one's
physical capacities. Thus, at the height of an executive's
attainment, one is likely to feel also that one has only
partly made it, that one has already lost part of what one
sought to win. Since only rarely can one have youth and
achievement at the same time, there is something anti-
climactic about middle-age success.

SUBTLE CHANGES

The issues having to do with health are only one facet of
the middle-aging process. There are subtle, but highly significant, changes in (1) work style, (2) point of view, (3)
family relationships, and (4) personal goals. Let us look
more closely at each of these in turn.

Work style. Both the mode and the content of the work
of creative people differ in early adulthood, or the pre-
thirty-five stage, from that of mature adulthood, or the
post-thirty-five stage. Jaques pointed this out when he observed:

> The creativity of the 20's and early 30's tends to be
> a hot-from-the-fire creativity. It is intense and spontane-
> ous, and comes out ready-made. . . . Most of the work
> seems to go on unconsciously. The conscious production
> is rapid, the pace of creation often being dictated by the
> limits of the artist's capacity physically to record the
> words or music he is expressing. . . . By contrast,
> the creativity of the late 30's and after is sculptured
> creativity. The inspiration may be hot and intense. The
> unconscious work is no less than before. But there is a
> big step between the first effusion of inspiration and the
> finished creative product. The inspiration itself may come
> more slowly. Even if there are sudden bursts of inspira-
> tion they are only the beginning of the work process.

Jaques adds that the inspiration for the older person is followed by a period of forming and fashioning the external

product, working and reworking the material, and acting and reacting to what has been formed. This is an experience which may go on for a period of years. The content of work changes, too, from a lytical or descriptive content to one that is tragic and philosophical, followed by one that is serene. Jaques recalls that Shakespeare wrote his early historical plays and comedies before he was thirty-five, his tragedies afterward.

Contrary to popular misconception, creativity does not cease at an early age. It is true that creative people have made major contributions before forty, but it is equally true that those who demonstrated such creativity continued to produce for many years thereafter. In fact, in both the arts and sciences, the highest output is in the forties.

Executives have many of the same kinds of experiences as artists and scientists. Executives report the greatest self-confidence at forty. Though their instrumentality is the organization, younger and older people do different creative work with organizations. The younger person is more impulsive, flashy, and starlike with ideas; the older is more often concerned with building and forming an organization. A conspicuous example is the hard-hitting company founder who, to the surprise of his or her organization, becomes less concerned with making money and more preoccupied with leaving an enduring company. Suddenly, he or she is talking about management development!

Point of view. Concurrent with the shift in work style or orientation is a shift of view. This occurs in political and social thinking as well as in business. It is a commonplace that most people become more conservative as they grow older. It is an unspoken commonplace that they are more bored.

True, many activities are intrinsically boring and become more so with repetition, but others no longer hold interest when one's point of view has changed.

• *Disillusionment:* Some of the boredom results from disillusionment. Early idealism, the tendency toward action, and the conviction of the innate goodness in people are in part a denial of the inevitable. Young people in effect say, "The world can be rosy. I'll help make it that way. People can be good to each other if only someone will show them how or remove the conditions which cause their frustration."

But in mid-life, it becomes clear that people are not always good to each other; that removing the conditions of frustration does not always lead to good, friendly, loving behavior; and that people have a capacity for being ugly and self-destructive as well as good. One evidence for the denial of disillusionment is the effort in so many companies to keep things "nice and quiet." Such companies are characterized by the inability to accept conflict as given and conflict resolution as a major part of the executive's job.

• *Obsolescence:* Another factor in change in point of view has to do with the feeling of becoming increasingly obsolescent. The middle-ager feels himself or herself to be in a world apart from the young—emotionally, socially, and occupationally. This is covered today by the cliché "generation gap." But there is something real to the distance because there is a tendency to feel that one cannot keep up with the world no matter how fast one runs. Thus the sense of incompetence, even helplessness, is magnified. Some of this is reflected in an attitude that middle-aged executives often take.

For example, I once addressed the 125 members of the upper management group of a large company. When I finished, I asked them to consider three questions in the discussion groups into which they were going to divide themselves:

• Of what I had said, what was most relevant to their business?
• Of what was most relevant, what order of priority ought to be established?
• Once priority was established, who was to do what about the issues?

They handled the first question well when they reported back; none had difficulty specifying the relevant. They had a little more difficulty with the second. None touched the third; it was as if they felt they were not capable of taking the action with which they had been charged.

• *Vocational choice:* This incident might be excused on a number of bases if it were not for other unrelated or corroborative evidence that reflects a third dimension in our consideration of change in point of view. Dr. Anne Roe did a series of studies on vocational choice in the adult years while she was still a Harvard psychologist. In one study she was trying to find out how people made decisions about selecting jobs.

"The most impressive thing about these interviews," she reports, "was how few of our subjects thought of themselves as considering alternatives and making decisions based on thoughtful examination of the situation. . . . They seemed not to recognize their role as chooser or their responsibility for choices. It was, indeed, this last aspect we found most depressing. Even among the executives, we find stress on contingencies and external influences more often than not."

• *Pain of rivalry:* The sense of being more distant from the sources of change, from the more impulsive agents of change, and of not being a chooser of one's fate spawns feelings of helplessness and inadequacy. This sense of remoteness is further magnified, as I have already noted, by feelings of rivalry. For children, playing King of the Hill may be fun. For adults, the greater the stakes and the more intense the motivation to hold one's place, the more threatening the rivals become. Yet, in the midst of this competitive environment, one is required to prepare his rivals to succeed him and ultimately to give way. The very name of the game is "Prepare Your Successor."

I recall a particular corporate situation in which the president had to decide who was to be executive vice-president. When he made his choice, some of his subordinates were surprised because, they said, the man he picked was the hottest competitor for the president's job and usually such men were sabotaged. The surprising part of the event, as far as I was concerned, was not the choice, but the fact that the subordinates themselves had so clearly seen what tends to happen to rivals for the executive suite. It is indeed difficult to tolerate a subordinate when the executive senses himself to be, in any respect, on a downward trail while the subordinate is obviously still on his way up and just as obviously is demanding his place in the corporate sun.

This phenomenon is one of the great undiscussed dilemmas of the managerial role. Repeatedly, in seminars on psychological aspects of management, cases refer to executives who cannot develop others, particularly men who have nothing to fear, in the sense that their future security is assured and they still have upward avenues open to them. What is not seen, let alone understood, in such cases is the terrible pain of rivalry in middle age in a competitive business context that places a premium on youth. This paragraph from Budd Schulberg's *Life* review of *Thalberg* captures the rivalry issue in one pointed vignette:

> There was to be a dramatic coda to the Irving Thalberg Story: the inevitable power struggle between the benevolent but jealous L. B. Mayer and the protégé he "loved like a son." Bitter was the conflict between Father and Son fighting over the studio's Holy Ghost. They fought over artistic decisions. They fought over separation of authorities. They fought over their division of the spoils, merely a symbol of power, for by now both were multi-millionaires. It was as if the old, tough, crafty beachmaster L. B. was determined to drive off the young, frail but stubborn challenger who dared ask Mayer for an equal piece of the billion-dollar action.

In this case, the rivalry was evident in open conflict. It could be with men at that level and in that culture. However, in most cases, if the rivalry does not go on unconsciously, it is carefully disguised and rationalized. Executives are reluctant to admit such feelings even to themselves. Therefore much of the rivalry is unconscious. The parties are less aware of why they are quarreling or perhaps they are more aware of the fact that they never seem to settle their quarrels. Every executive can test such feelings in his own experience by reviewing how he or she felt when a successor took his place, even though he himself moved up, particularly when that successor changed some of his cherished innovations.

Thus it is difficult for each of us to see the unconscious battle he or she wages with subordinates, now wanting them to succeed, now damned if they will. Subordinates, however unable they are to see this phenomenon in themselves, can usually see it quite clearly in the behavior of the boss. But then there are few upward performance appraisals to help make such behavior conscious, and the behavior itself indicates to the subordinate that the rival would do well to keep his mouth shut.

• *Dose of anger:* The change in point of view which throws such problems into relief and intensifies fear (though rarely do executives speak of fear), is compounded further by a significant dose of anger. It is easy to observe the anger of the middle-aged executive toward today's youth—who have more money, more opportunity, and more sex than was available yesterday. There is anger, too, that the youngsters are free to "do their thing" while today's executives, pressed by the residuals of the Great Depression and the constraints of their positions, sometimes find it hard to do what they really want to do.

The anger with youth is most often expressed as resentment because "they want to start at the top" or "they aren't willing to wait their turn or get experience" or "they only want young ones around here now." It is further reflected in such simultaneously pejorative and admiring descriptive nouns as "whiz kids," "jets," and "stars." These mixed-feeling phrases bespeak self-criticism and betrayal. Every time the middle-aged executive uses such a phrase, he or she seems also to be saying that he has not done as well or that he has been undercut. One who had to learn how to size up the market from firsthand contact with customers finds that knowledge now useless, replaced by a computer model constructed by a person who never canvassed a customer. One who thought business to be "practical" and "hardheaded" now finds that he or she must go back to school, become more intellectual, and think ahead conceptually, or he is lost. The kids have outflanked him. They have it so good, handed to them on a platter, at his expense.

Older generations have always complained that the youth are not only unappreciative of their efforts, but take for granted what they have struggled so hard to achieve. Nevertheless, management has never taken seriously the impact of such feelings on executive behavior. The result is an expensive loss of talent as it becomes apparent to young people that managements promise them far more than companies deliver.

I am certain in my own mind that it is the combination of rivalry and anger which makes it so difficult to create challenging ways to use young people in management. (Certainly, it is not the dearth of problems to be tackled.) That, in turn, accounts for much of the astronomical turnover of young college graduates in their first company years and also for much of their subsequent disillusionment with managerial careers.

Family relationships. The same narrowing which occurs in the cycle of achievement in business has also been taking place within the family. As I noted in preceding chapters, children are becoming more independent earlier and therefore leaving their parents earlier. In turn, the parents live alone with each other longer (according to latest census figures, an average of sixteen years). This poses several problems which come to a head in middle life. By this point in time one usually has lost both his parents. Though he may have been independent for many years, for the first time he feels psychologically alone.

Because an executive can less readily establish close friendships at work, and his mobility makes it difficult for him to sustain them in his off-work relationships, he tends to have greater attachment to his children. He therefore suffers greater loss when they leave home, and he usually does not compensate for these losses any more than he actively compensates for the loss of old friendships through death and distance.

One's heavy commitment to one's own career and that of the spouse to his or her own interests tend to separate them from each other—a problem which is obscured while their joint focus is on the children. When the children leave home, one is left with the same conscious reasons for which one married the spouse as the basis for the marriage—intelligence, attractiveness, charm, liveliness—and often the same unconscious ones: a substitute for mother or father, anything but like mother or father, a guaranteed nonequal, and other reasons similarly unflattering.

But the spouse is no longer the young person one married. He or she has aged, too, and may no longer be the idealized self of twenty years before. If, in addition, the unconscious reasons for marrying are now no longer as important as they were earlier, there is little left for the marriage unless the couple has worked out another basis for mutual usefulness.

Meanwhile, for most couples there has been a general decrease in satisfaction with each other, less intimacy, decline in frequency of sexual intercourse, and fewer shared activities. Wives become more preoccupied with their husbands' health because age compels them to unconsciously rehearse for widowhood. Husbands sense this concern and the reasons (which sometimes include a wish for widowhood) for it, and withdraw even more. This is part of what increases the sense of loneliness mentioned earlier, in the context of the need for greater closeness. These factors contribute to the relatively new phenomenon of the "twenty-year" divorce peak.

Personal goals. Up to approximately age forty-five, creative executive effort is largely self-centered. That is, one is concerned with one's achievement and personal needs. One turns gradually to matters outside oneself. As psychologist Else Frenkl-Brunswick has shown, one becomes more concerned with ideals and causes, derived from religious or parental values. One also becomes more concerned with finding purpose in life.

For example, a young executive, a "jet" in his company, became a subsidiary president early. While in that role he became involved in resolving racial problems in his community. Though still president, and likely to be promoted to head the whole corporation, his heart is now in the resolution of community problems. Similarly, another executive has retired early to become involved in conservation. Still others leave business for politics, and not a few have become Episcopal priests. Some priests have become executives.

As part of this change (which goes on unconsciously), there are periods of restlessness and discomfort. There appears to be a peak in travel between the ages of forty-five and fifty, and also a transitory period of loneliness as one leaves old, long-standing moorings and seeks others.

The restlessness and discomfort have another source. When the middle-aged executive is shifting direction, he or she must necessarily use psychological energy for that task. As a consequence, it is more difficult to keep ancient, repressed conflicts under control. This is particularly true when the executive has managed to keep certain conflicts in check by promising himself or herself he would one day deal with them. As he begins to feel that time is running out and he has not delivered on his promises to himself, he begins to experience intense internal frustration and pressure. Sometimes he will try to hide such conflicts under a contemporary slogan like "identity crisis."

Not long ago, a forty-two-year-old executive told me that despite his age, his professional engineering training, and his good position he was still having an identity problem. He said he really did not know what he wanted to do or be. A few questions quickly revealed that he would prefer to be in his own business. However, the moment we touched that topic, he was full of excuses and wanted to turn away from it. He did indeed know what he wanted to do; he was simply afraid to face it. He wanted to be independent but he could not break away from the security of his company. He had maintained the fantasy that he might someday, but as the passing years made that less likely, his conflict increased in intensity.

Most people will come nowhere near doing all they want to do with their lives. All of us have some degree of difficulty and frustration as a result. We become even more angry with ourselves when the prospect arises that time will run out before we have sampled, let alone savored, much of what there is in the world. But most of us subtly turn our efforts to meeting those ideal requirements.

The important point in all this is that, as psychologist Charlotte Buhler points out, it relates directly to survival. The evidence indicates that a person's assessment as to whether he or she did or did not reach fulfillment has more to do with his old-age adjustment than literal loss of physical capacities and insecurity. Put another way, if a person has met his or her own standards and expectations reasonably well, he adapts more successfully to the aging process. If not, the converse holds: while experiencing the debilitation of aging, he is also simultaneously angry with himself for not having done what he should have. Anger with self is the feeling of depression. We have already noted the implications of depression for physical illness.

SIGNIFICANT IMPLICATIONS

Up to this point, we have been looking at the critical physical and psychological symptoms of the aging process. Now let us turn to the three personal and organizational implications in all this.

1. *Facing the crisis.* First, all of us must face up to the fact that there is such an event in people's lives as middle-age crisis. It is commonplace; it need not be hidden or apologized for. It frequently takes the form of depressive feelings and psychosomatic symptoms as well as increased irritability and discontent, followed by declining interest in and efforts toward mastering the world. For women it is also related to menopause and the loss of physical creativity.

There is a premature tendency to give in to fate, to feel that one can have no choice about what happens to one, and, in effect, to resign oneself to the vagaries of chance. This period is essentially a mourning experience: regret, sorrow, anger, disappointment for something which has been lost—one's precious youth—and with it the illusion of omnipotence and immortality. It is necessary to be free to talk about the loss, the pain, and the regret, and even to shed a tear, literally or figuratively. We do indeed die a bit each day; we have a right to be shaken by the realization when we can no longer deny it.

When a middle-aged executive begins to experience such feelings, and particularly if they begin to interfere with his or her work or enjoyment of life, he should talk to someone else about them, preferably a good counselor. This kind of mourning is far better than increasing the intense pace of running in an effort to escape reality. In the process of talking, the wise person reworks his or her life experiences and feelings until he is all mourned out and no longer afraid of being mortal.

When an executive can take his or her own life transitions and his feelings about them seriously, he has the makings of maturity. In the course of making wine, after the grapes are pressed, the resulting liquid is left to age. In a sense, it continues to work. In the process of aging, it acquires body, color, and bouquet—in short, its character.

Like wine, people who work over their feelings about their aging process acquire a certain character with age. They deepen their awareness of themselves and others. They see the world in sharper perspective and with greater tolerance. They acquire wisdom. They love more, exploit less. They accept their own imperfections and therefore their own contributions. As Jaques has put it, "The successful outcome of mature creative work lies thus in constructive resignation both to the imperfections of men and to shortcomings in one's own work. It is this constructive resignation which then imparts serenity to life and work."

The middle-aged executives who fail to take themselves, their crises, and their feelings seriously keep running, intensify their exploitation of others, or give up to exist on a plateau. Some executives bury themselves more deeply in their work, some run after their lost youth with vain cosmetic efforts, others by chasing prospective new partners, and still others by pursuing more power. A person's failure to mature in this sense then becomes a disease that afflicts his organization. He loses his people, his grasp of the realities of his life, and can only look back on the way it used to be as the ideal.

The executive who denies his age in these ways also denies himself or herself the opportunity to prepare for what is to come, following some of the suggestions I shall discuss in the next section. One who continues to deny and to run will ultimately have to face emptiness when he or she can no longer do either and must still live with himself. The wise person will come to terms with reality early: he or she will take seriously the fact that his time is limited.

2. *Taking constructive action*. Second, a person must act. Only one who acts on his or her own behalf is the master of himself and his environment. Too many people accept what is for what will be. They most often say, "I can't do anything about it." What they really mean is that they won't do anything. Check your own experience. How often do you mean "won't" when you say "can't"? Much of psychotherapeutic effort is directed to helping people see how they have trapped themselves this way. There are indeed alternatives in most situations. Our traps are largely self-made.

There are a number of fruitful avenues for action in both personal and business life. In personal terms the most important efforts are the renegotiation of the marriage and the negotiation of new friendships. Husband and wife might wisely talk out their accumulated differences, their disappointments and mutual frustrations as well as their wishes and aspirations. As they redefine their marriage contract, they clarify for themselves their interdependence or lack of it. If they remain silent with each other or attack in their frustration, they run the danger of falling apart in their anger at the expense of their need for each other.

In social terms, the executive must make a formal effort to find and cultivate new friends with a particular emphasis on developing companionship. We know from studies of concentration camp survivors and of the process of aging that those who have companions cope most effectively with the traumas of life. Those who do not almost literally die of their loneliness. As a person becomes less self-centered, he or she can devote more energy to cultivating others. When he individualizes and cultivates the next person, he creates the conditions for others' recognition of him as a person.

In public terms, the executive must become future-oriented, but this time in conceptions that go beyond himself and his job. One invests oneself in the future, when one actively involves oneself in some ongoing activity of social value which has enduring purpose. Hundreds of schools, colleges, hospitals, and community projects—most of them obscure—await the capable person who gives a damn and wants that damn to matter. Most executives need not look more than a few blocks beyond their offices for such opportunities.

In business terms, the executive should recognize that at this point in time he or she ideally should be exercising a different kind of leadership and be dealing with different organization problems. In middle age, the stage Erik Erikson has called "the period of generativity," if one opts for wisdom, one becomes an organizational resource for the development of others. One's wisdom and judgment give body to the creative efforts of younger people. They help turn impulse into reality, and then to shape it and reshape it into a thousand useful products and services. They offer those characteristics in an executive to be admired and emulated. One shifts from quarterback to coach, from day-to-day operations to long-range planning. One becomes more consciously concerned with what one is going to leave behind.

3. *Organizing for renaissance.* Third, organizations must take the middle-age period seriously in their thinking, planning, and programming. I know of no organization—business, university, church, or hospital—that does. No one knows how much effectiveness is lost.

If one of the needs for coping with middle-age stress is the opportunity to talk about it, then part of every supervisory and appraisal counseling should be devoted to some of the issues and concerns of this state. Company physicians or medical examining centers should provide time for the patient to talk with the doctor about the psychological aspects of his or her age and life. Sessions devoted to examining how groups are working together should, if they are middle-aged groups, have this topic on the agenda. Company educational programs should inform both executives and their spouses about this period and its unique pressures. Personnel counselors should give explicit attention to this issue in their discussions.

Obviously, executive or managerial training programs

for people over thirty-five should have a different slant from those for people under thirty-five. Pre-thirty-five programs should be geared to keeping the younger people "loose." They should be encouraged to bubble, to tackle old problems afresh. This is not the time to indoctrinate people with rules and procedures, but rather to stimulate them toward their own horizons. Training challenges should be around tasks requiring sparkle, flashes of insight, and impulsive action.

Development programs for people over thirty-five should be concentrated largely on refreshment, keeping up, and conceptualization of problems and the organization. Tasks and problems requiring reorganization, reformulation, refining, and restructuring are tasks for people whose psychological time it is to rework. Brilliant innovative departures are unlikely to come from such people, except as they are the fruition of a lifetime of ferment, as was the *aggiornamento* of Pope John XXIII.

For them, instead, more attention should be given to frequent respites from daily organizational chores to get new views, to examine and digest them in work groups, and to think of their application to organizational problems and issues. When they move toward the future, they are likely to go in protected steps, like the person crawling on ice who pushes a plank before him. Pushing them hard to be free of the plank will tend to paralyze them into inaction. Rather, training programs should specifically include small experimental attempts to apply new skills and views with minimum risk.

Much of managerial training for these people should be focused on how to rear younger people. This means not only emphasis on coaching, counseling, teaching, and supporting, but also time and opportunity to talk about their feelings of rivalry and disappointment, to ventilate their anger at the young people who have it so good—the whole world at their feet and no place to go but up. Finally, it should include the opportunity for them to recognize, understand, and accept their uniquely human role. Instead of rejecting the younger people, they can then more comfortably place their bets and cheer their favorites on. In the youngsters' winning, they, too, can win.

For the executive, his or her subordinates, and the company, middle age can truly be a renaissance.

Index

Index

295

More Titles from the MENTOR Executive Library

Other Titles from the MENTOR Executive Library